Best Dives'

SNORKELING
ADVENTURES

Joyce & Jon Huber

Starfish Ratings

Each snorkeling site has been given a rating of from one to five starfish by prominent guides of each area.

☆☆☆☆☆ Five Starfish

Best of the best for snorkeling - best visibility and water clarity, best marine life, best wreck or reef dive.

☆☆☆☆Four Starfish

Fantastic dive. Outstanding for marine life or visual interest.

☆☆☆ Three Starfish

Superb dive. Excellent visibility and marine life or wreck.

☆☆ Two Starfish

Good Dive. Interesting fish and plant life; good visibility.

☆ One Starfish

Pleasant dive.

Map Symbols

Snorkeling Area

Shipwreck

Airport

Critical Acclaim for the authors' previous work,

Best Dives of the Caribbean

" *Best Dives* is the bible of Caribbean dive-travel. . .I highly recommend it"
Christopher Lofting, The Travel Show, WOR Network Radio

". . .A terrific guide. . ."
John Clayton   The Travel Show, KABC Radio, Los Angeles

". . .a must have. . .for divers, snorkelers or those who just love to float in liquid turquoise"
Brenda Fine, Travel Editor, *The New York Law Journal*

"It's super! . . . a great reference and we love it."
Dive Travel Magazine

" a good travel planner . . ."
Jill Schensul, Travel Editor, *The Record*

". . .opens a new world of adventure to anyone with a mask and snorkel."
Pat Reilly, travel writer, *Commerce Magazine*

". . .the best coverage of the subject matter I've seen, and incredibly easy to read. . .essential for the serious or beginning diver."
Dr. Susan Cropper, DVM, Society of Aquatic Veterinarians

". . .details more than 200 of the finest dive sites in the Caribbean. . ."
Bill Smith, *Dive Travel News*, ICS Scuba

PhotoGraphics Publishing
c/o W.C. Books
100 Newfield Avenue
Edison, N.J. 08837
1-800-488-8040 or 732-225-2727, fax 732-225-1562
E-mail: wcbooks@aol.com

Editorial Address
PhotoGraphics Publishing
629 Edgewater Avenue
Ridgefield, N.J. 07657
E-mail: jonhuber@worldnet.att.net or bestdives@juno.com

ISBN 0-96438-441-8
1st edition © 1998 PhotoGraphics Publishing

Every effort has been made to ensure that information in this book is correct, but the publisher and authors do not assume, and hereby disclaim, any liability to any party for any loss or damage caused by errors, ommissions, misleading information or potential problems caused by information in this guide, even if these are a result of negligence, accident or any other cause.

Cover photo © Jon Huber
Key Largo, Florida

Maps and illustrations by Joyce Huber
Printed in the USA by Gilliland Printing

Acknowledgments

The authors wish to thank all of *Best Dives' Snorkeling Adventures'* contributors, correspondents, photographers and researchers for their effort and enthusiasm in preparing this guide.

Special thanks to Robin Bartlett, Barry Sheinkopf, Anita and Ken Liggett, Underwater Sports of NJ, Rick Ocklemann, Mina and Bill Heuslein, JoAnn and Jonathan Pannaman, Alvin Jackson, Joe Giacinto, Barbara Swab, Frank Holler, Mark Padover, Susan and Rick Sammon, Myra Bush, Dr. Susan Cropper, Karen and Dennis Sabo, Cathy Rothschild, Maria Shaw, Christopher Lofting, Mike Emmanuel, Lucy Portlock, Michael Young, Efra Figueroa, James Abbott, Jim Spencer, Joan Borque, Michelle Pugh, Myron Clement, Francois Fournier and Captain Diana Oestreich.

Authors' Note

Snorkelers of all ages, interests and athletic abilities helped create *Best Dives' Snorkeling Adventures*. With their help, this guide includes something for everyone, from protected lagoons with easy beach entry to open-water adventures and offbeat destinations.

Destination chapters cover the top snorkeling spots in the Bahamas, Caribbean, Florida, Hawaii and the Turks and Caicos Islands. If we missed your favorite spot and you wish to share it with others in the next edition, e-mail us at jonhuber@worldnet. att.com or bestdives@ juno.com.

Table of Contents

Snorkel Swimming and Free Diving

THE BASICS

Anyone in average health who can swim, don a mask and peer beneath the water's surface can easily master snorkeling. It's low-impact aerobic and a great way to keep fit. Once considered a macho endeavor, it has evolved into a family affair with fish-watching and photography the main focus.

Everyone finds his or her own skill level and degree of interest. Some relish floating on the surface (snorkel-swimming) while others work at being able to dive 30 feet or more below the surface (free diving or breath-hold diving). Some prefer beach locations, others enjoy exploring from a boat.

Like any sport, the more you do it, the better you get at it. One salty, Florida Keys dive boat captain, growing impatient with two scuba divers who were lingering over a wreck below, surprised the pair by snorkeling down 50 ft and tapping one on the shoulder—a reminder to surface.

Sightseeing Tours

A great variety of snorkeling trips and activities are offered throughout the tropics. Choices vary from sail-snorkel trips on shallow-draft catamarans or trimarans, glass-bottom-boat tours, snorkel-with-dolphins tours, snorkel-shelling tours, snorkel-picnic excursions, sunset-snorkel sails, snorkel-shipwreck-archaeological tours, snorkel-kayaking trips and learn-to-sail-and-snorkel vacations. One south Florida boat captain offers marriage

Portions of this chapter are excerpted with permission from Scubapro's *Snorkel Swimming and Breath Hold Diving* or *Snorkeling*.

ceremonies (with champagne and caviar included) while snorkeling with your choice of wild dolphins or reef fish. Variations on the sport such as snuba, offered on St. John, USVI and a few other spots, offers a cross between scuba and snorkeling; or helmet diving, popular in Bermuda and the Bahamas, with surface-supplied air that fills a helmet worn while you walk the ocean floor.

Marked underwater trails have been popping up in the USVI, Bahamas, Bermuda and Turks and Caicos. These are reef areas marked with signs identifying corals and other marine life.

Equipment

The best place to buy snorkeling equipment is at your local dive shop or specialty retailer. Many resorts and cruise ships will loan or rent you gear and very often it is of good quality. But rental rates can soar as high as $30 per hour for a mask and snorkel. Or, loan-out equipment may be worn or unavailable in your size. This is especially true for children. In comparison to the frustration you may encounter by renting, the cost of purchase is minimal. The basic equipment is a face mask and a snorkel. Fins and a safety vest are a good idea for all but ultra-shallow shoreline snorkeling.

Masks

Snorkelers who wear eyeglasses can select from masks that hold optically-corrected lenses or specially-ground face plates. Contacts may be worn with non-prescription masks although many have been lost to the sea. Goggles should *never* be used for breath-hold diving. Your nose must be included inside the air space for pressure equalization.

Ill-fitting, poor quality masks often leak or rip and can quickly sour you on the sport. You'll not regret buying a good quality mask. To check for a proper fit try holding the mask on your face just by inhaling—without using the strap. Be sure to first brush stray hair from your face. A mask that fits properly will not leak air or fall off. Most important, it should feel comfortable. Do not buy a mask that you cannot try on in the store. If you buy mail-order make sure you can return it, if desired.

If you wear a mustache, expect difficulty in getting a good seal. If shaving is out of the question, try a bit of Vaseline or suntan lotion on your face around the area where the mask seals. Some masks feature purge valves which allow you to easily clear them of water and others have nose-gripping devices to assist in equalizing pressure in your ears should you choose to dive down for a closer look. Whether to buy an oval or rectangular mask, one with three viewing ports or just a front plate is a matter of personal preference and comfort. Human faces come in a variety of shapes and sizes and, fortunately, so do masks. Be sure to try on several before you select.

Snorkels

Snorkels should be well fitting too. The mouthpiece should be easy to grip and fit comfortably. The size of the barrel should be commensurate with the size of the diver. Some top-of-the-line snorkels are equipped with a purge valve which is intended to help you clear water from the snorkel. These are more costly than the standard non-purge snorkels. To some divers these are considered a fad and to others a valued invention. Either will work. We prefer simple j-shaped snorkels because they are less fragile to transport. Oceanic's dry snorkels, available in dive shops, are terrific for beginners. They prevent you from getting a mouthful of seawater.

Masks and snorkels are made of rubber or silicone. It is important that you purchase both mask and snorkel of the same material or the rubber will discolor the silicone over time. Silicone has a softer feel and is more comfortable for prolonged use. The new colorful designer masks, fins and snorkels are a mix of thermoplastics and silicone. The choice is a matter of budget, comfort and personal preference. Rubber is less expensive and still the choice of many divers. Hypoallergenic silicone is available for sensitive gums. Mouthpieces can be molded to fit your teeth for ultimate fit and comfort. Average cost for a good quality mask is $70, a snorkel, $25. Decent fins range from $40 to more than $100. If you can't find a dive shop, mail-order companies such as Performance Diver or L. L. Bean sell masks, fins and snorkels. Most of the ultra-cheap masks and snorkels sold in pool-supply stores or beach shops are not suitable for extended use in the ocean.

Fins

Swim fins increase swimming efficiency so much that arm strokes can be completely eliminated. Like a good mask and snorkel, quality fins will last many years and are a worthwhile purchase in terms of comfort and usefulness. A proper fit is critical since poorly fitting fins will soon raise blisters and chafe your skin. Good dive retailers are trained to help you select the right sized fins. Flexible foot pocket fins which slip on like shoes are preferred for snorkeling. Those with very stiff, long blades will give you added speed and thrust and a good workout, but they require strong leg muscles. If you intend to snorkel in cold water consider open back fins which are worn with a wet suit boot.

Anti-Fog Solutions

We hear "I tried snorkeling on my vacation, but my mask fogged up and I couldn't see a thing" from many folks. In fact, unless you use an anti-fog compound, condensation of exhaled moisture from your nose or evaporation from the skin will fog your face mask and make snorkeling very unpleasant. To prevent this, first scour the inside of the glass plate with toothpaste(we

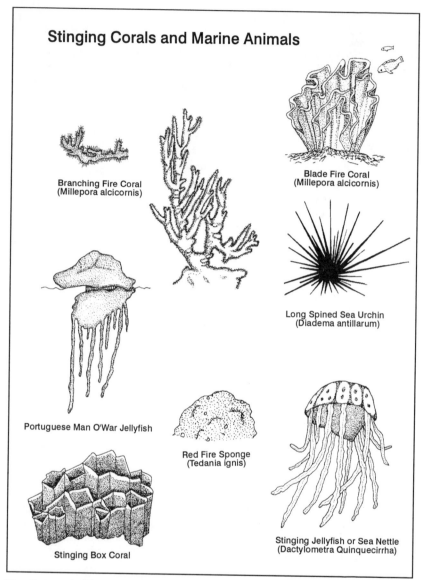

Stinging Corals and Marine Animals

Branching Fire Coral
(Millepora alcicornis)

Blade Fire Coral
(Millepora alcicornis)

Long Spined Sea Urchin
(Diadema antillarum)

Portuguese Man O'War Jellyfish

Red Fire Sponge
(Tedania ignis)

Stinging Box Coral

Stinging Jellyfish or Sea Nettle
(Dactylometra Quinquecirrha)

like Colgate). Then, before each dive moisten the face plate with anti-fog compounds. In a pinch you can rub a bit of saliva on the faceplace, but you'll find the commercial products, available in dive shops, far superior.

Snorkeling Lessons

An hour in a pool with a pro will teach you all you need to learn about snorkel swimming. You may also want to pick up a copy of Scubapro's

Snorkel Swimming and Breath Hold Diving or *Snorkeling*, available in dive shops, or *A complete Guide to the Underwater Experience* by John R. Clark or *Snorkeling for Kids of All Ages* which can be ordered from NAUI, P.O. Box 14650, Montclair, CA 91763.

Do's and Don'ts

This chapter cannot cover every possible risk, but you may be assured that few snorkel swimmers ever have serious problems. Common sense and the basic rule of "look but don't touch" will take care of most worries.

We recommend that first-time snorkelers sign up for a guided tour with a pro-dive instructor. In addition the following may be helpful. Never dive alone. Always dive with a buddy. Snorkel during daylight hours only. Check local water conditions—tides and current. Attempts to swim against currents that exceed one knot will produce severe fatigue. Most resort area dive tour operators are familiar with local sea conditions and can offer suggestions on favorable spots.

When anchored in open water, trail a buoyed safety line at least 100 ft long over the stern of the boat. Avoid snorkeling in shipping lanes or heavy traffic areas. Be sure to display a diver's flag to alert other boaters to stay clear of your area. Until you know what you're doing avoid handling marine life and corals. Coral skeletons are frequently razor sharp and can inflict deep painful wounds.

Touching or sitting on corals is outlawed in many marine sanctuaries. Fire coral will give you a painful sting, as will jellyfish or sea urchins, when touched. Never poke your hand into holes, caves or crevices; toothy moray eels and some poisonous fish camouflage themselves and hide in coral and holes. Some venomous creatures to watch out for are the stonefish, the lionfish, the cone shell (Pacific), the Portuguese Man-O-War and the fireworm.

Avoid snorkeling in shallow surges especially over coral or rocks, since you can easily be tossed onto them by an incoming wave. Avoid wearing shiny dangling jewelry. Although exploring a kelp garden, shipwreck or coral reef is fascinating, you can enlarge your underwater outlook by learning about marine life. Once you are able to distinguish the good guys from the no-touch-'ems you'll have fun handfeeding many species of fish. To get in the proper frame of mind pick up a waterproof pictorial fish guidebook. or a laminated fish I.D. card for use underwater. These are available dive shops.

Sunburn

Sunburn is often the biggest villain the snorkeler has to contend with. A thin layer of water covering your back will make you feel deceptively cool but offer no protection from the sun's harmful rays, you can be painfully burned on days when the sun is not visible. Snorkelers should wear long pants and a long-sleeved shirt or a long-sleeved lycra wetskin. At the very least wear a tee shirt. Seek out tour boats with canopies.

*Sea Feather Bay,
Cayman Brac*

Precautions: Avoid exposure when taking medicines that increase sunsensitivity. Use sunblock lotion with a protection factor of at least 15, wear sunglasses that block UV rays, select hats with a wide brim. If your activities require prolonged exposure wear protective clothing of fabrics made to block the sun's UV rays. The following manufacturers offer catalogues featuring protective clothing: **Sun Precautions Inc.**, Everett, WA ☎ 800-882-7860, **Solar Protective Factory**, Sacramento, CA ☎ 800-786-2562, and **Koala Konnection**, Mountain View, CA ☎ 888-465-6252.

Underwater Photos

Most dive shops rent submersible cameras, often with built-in flash. For simple still snapshots we tested the Minolta Weathermatic and found it to be a fabulous snorkeling camera. Nikonos cameras produce fine results. Housed, through-the-lens-viewing cameras are the choice of most professionals. If it's pure snapshots you're after, check out the housed "disposable" cameras by Kodak (these are actually recycled). The more comfortable and confident you become in the water the better your pictures will come out. For best results, shoot when the sun is high in the sky, with the hours between 10 am and 2 pm ideal. Try getting dramatic angles by diving down and angling the camera slightly up. We recommend keeping the camera attached to your wrist with a string or strap. Get in close (three ft.) for diver portraits. The more distance you allow between you and your subject the more free floating particles or "snow" is illuminated by your flash. Be careful not to stir up silty or sandy bottoms.

Getting cooperative fish to pose for your pictures is easy; just bring along some dried aquarium fish food or bread crumbs and sprinkle some where you want fish. We have seen long lines of grouper, grunts, hogfish and snapper waiting for scraps. In one instance, divers who were originally the

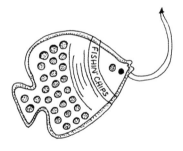

subject of the camera became lost behind a solid curtain of snack-loving fish. Be sure to feed fish only what fish would normally eat and that fish-feeding is allowed where you're diving. Marine parks often discourage or outlaw fish feeding because divers feed fish crazy things that hurt their digestive tracts such as aerosol cheese or pepperoni. Squid is usually a safe substitute or "Fishin Chips", a new, all-natural fish food that comes in fish-shaped cardboard dispensers holding 28 pop-out pills that dissolve in the water. For more information ☎ 800-522-2469. Avoid carrying bloody bait fish which might attract hungry sharks. Tapping on rocks attracts fish too.

Cruises and Package Tours

Oceanic Society Expeditions feature educational snorkeling vacations to Honduras Bay Islands; Silver Banks, a huge fish and mammal breeding ground off the Dominican Republic; Belize; Florida Springs; Midway, a remote coral atoll located 1,250 miles from Honolulu and the Bahamas. Tours and destinations may vary from year to year. For itineraries write to Ocean Society Expeditions, Fort Mason Center, Building E, San Francisco, CA 94123. ☎ 800-326-7491 or 415-441-1106, fax 415-474-3395.

Landfall Productions offers hassle-free, money-saving tours for groups and individuals to the Caribbean, Indonesia and South Pacific. Owners, Karen and Dennis Sabo, both avid divers and expert underwater photographers, personally check out each resort to insure quality service. ☎ 800-525-3833. E-mail: lndfall@aol.com. Website: http:ecotravel. com/landfall.

Dive Safaris, owned and operated by dive pro Cathy Rothschild, books deluxe vacations to Puerto Rico, most Caribbean destinations as well as the Pacific, Africa and Indonesia. This operator initiated shark-cage, scuba diving vacations. ☎ 800-359-0747, 212-662-4858. E-mail:rothschild@dive safaris. com. Website: http:www.divesafaris.com.

ICS Scuba books cruise-ship vacations aboard ships that make snorkeling and scuba stops (be sure to specify that's what you want), money-saving group and individual tours to all points in the Caribbean, Austrailia, New Zealand, Indian Ocean and most other exotic destinations. ☎ 800-722-0205 or 516-797-2132. E-mail: TheICS Gang@aol.com. Website: www.icstravel. com.

Aruba

If return visitors are the best testimony to an island's popularity, Aruba wins top prize. Each day the island's local paper fronts a group photo of ten-time returnees.

Lying well outside the hurricane belt, Aruba is a popular choice for snorkeling year round. Very low humidity and an average annual rainfall of only 20 inches eliminates freshwater runoff on the reefs, hence dependably good visibility. Easy to reach, this popular island sits just 18 miles from Venezuela's coast. And, at 20 miles long and six miles wide, it's easy to explore, both above and below the sea. Resorts and most tourist activity centers along its western (leeward) coast—minutes from popular reefs and wrecks. The shops and sights of the capital, Oranjestad, are nearby too.

Coral beds fringe the shore, many close enough to swim to, but attempting to find the channels and cuts through the extreme shallow reefs may be futile without a local guide, thus, access to Aruba's best snorkeling sites is easiest by joining a snorkeling cruise that may be booked through the hotel desks or dive shops listed in this chapter.

If you opt for beach snorkeling note that all of Aruba's beaches are open to the public except for a narrowstrip directly behind the private homes that is off limits. Homeowners have a sign marking where their back yard ends and the public beach begins.

Best Snorkeling Sites

The best beach snorkeling from the mainland is off **Malmok**. Get there by driving north from Palm Beach along L.G. Smith Boulevard, the main coast road. There is usually a snorkeling boat moored offshore which makes it easy to spot or if you look straight out to sea you'll spot the top of the Antilla. Park anywhere and walk down to the beach. Swim out from the shore about 10 ft to the rocks where you'll find hordes of small reef fish. Beware the spiny urchins hiding in the rocks. Always calm. Good for children.

☆☆ **Arashi**, a rocky reef offshore to the lighthouse at the northwest corner of the island, delights novice divers and snorkelers with throngs of juvenile fish, elkhorn and brain corals. Visibility is always 60 ft or better. Depths range from the shallows to 40 ft. Nice! Seas are calm with an occasional light surge. Boat access. Good for novice snorkelers.

☆ **Arashi Airplanes** denotes a twin-engine Beechcraft at 35 ft and a Lockheed Lodestar at 60 ft—both purposely scuttled to create an artificial reef. Visibility is good enough to see the Beechcraft from the surface. Both wrecks are broken up. Small fish inhabit the fuselages. Boat access.

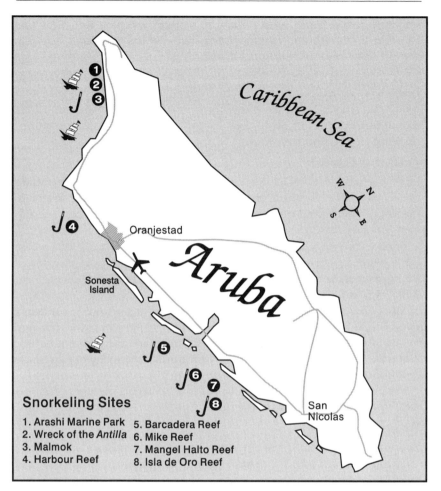

Snorkeling Sites

1. Arashi Marine Park
2. Wreck of the *Antilla*
3. Malmok
4. Harbour Reef
5. Barcadera Reef
6. Mike Reef
7. Mangel Halto Reef
8. Isla de Oro Reef

☆☆☆ Just south of Blue Reef sits one of Aruba's most unusual sights and most popular dives, the wreck of the 400-ft, German freighter, **Antilla**. The ship was scuttled when new in 1940, when Germany invaded Holland.

Locally referred to as the "ghost ship", it is covered by tube sponges and brilliant orange cup corals. Her twisted, rusting steelwork extends upward from the main section to above the surface. The remains of the hull are home to angelfish, moray eels and throngs of silversides. Schools of yellowtail and sergeant majors sway with the gentle current.

The wreck lies about a mile offshore, just north of Palm Beach in 60 ft of water. Visibility is between 50 and 70 ft.

☆☆ **Barcadera Reef,** four miles south of Oranjestad, ranges from 20 to 90 ft. Excellent for snorkelers, the reef supports dense stands of elkhorn and staghorn corals, finger corals, home to wrasses, scorpion fish, blue and stoplight parrot fish and French angels. The reef lies 600 yards from the shore at Barcadera Harbor (boat dive).

☆☆☆ **Mangel Halto** ("tall mangrove"), three-fourths of a mile south of Barcadera Harbor, can be reached by swimming out from the Mangel Halto Beach for 120 yards, but it's easier from a boat. The reef slopes from 15 ft to ledges and ridges at depth. Fish life includes copper sweepers, grunts, sergeant majors, and butterfly fish.

DePalm Island

First-time snorkelers (of all heights) will find waist-high snorkeling outside of DePalm Island, located one-quarter mile offshore from the Water & Electricity Plant—four miles south of Oranjestad along L.G. Smith Boulevard. A ferry ($5) to DePalm leaves the mainland every half-hour.

Snorkelers are immediately greeted by a dozen or more two-ft blue parrot fish looking for a handout. These fish meet you at the dock stairs and will leap up out of the water to eat offerings of bread or whatever munchies you tote. Feed with caution, they have sharp teeth!

More adventurous snorkelers swim out about 30 yards to find a dense coral reef, which gets more interesting the further out you swim. The reef supports an abundance of fish—blue tangs, blue and stoplight parrot fish, triggerfish, sergeant majors, yellowtail and grunts. Snorkeling depths range from four ft to 15 ft.

Facilities on DePalm include an open-air bar and grill, showers, changing facilities and an equipment rental shack. The bar sells fish food for $1.

Sonesta Island

Sonesta Island, a watersports outpost owned by Sonesta Resorts at Seaport Village, is reached by a short shuttle boat ride. Guests of the Sonesta may use the island for free. Others pay $25 for the day, which includes the shuttle to and from the resort, lunch and one cocktail.

Coupons for the island are sold in the Sonesta lobby. Snorkeling gear, rented on the island by Redsail Sports (☎ 861603) costs $10 for a day's use. Island facilities include a dive shop, beach restaurant, air-conditioned fitness center. Three separate beaches cater to families or adults (topless), with a special cove for honeymooners, divers and snorkelers.

☆☆☆ **South Airplanes**, just beyond the breakwater of the Sonesta Island main beach, is the site of two vintage twin-engine, aircraft wrecks—both unclaimed drug runners—a Beechcraft 18 and a Convair 400. Snorkelers can see the Beechcraft, which sits in 15 ft of water, from the surface. Normally calm with one to two foot swells and a mild current.

☆ **The Barge** in 12 ft of water lying about 100 yards off Sonesta Island's main beach, makes a fun snorkeling spot. Crowds of fish swarm the

Charlie's Bar, San Nicolas

wreckage. Usually calm with a one- to two-ft swell and light current. Check with the dive shop for current conditions. Swimming and snorkeling outside the protected lagoon is not recommended for small children, though swimming inside the lagoon is fine.

Snorkeling Tours & Rentals

Most Aruban dive shops offer snorkeling tours from $25. Mask, fins and snorkel rent for about $12 per day, but may be included at no extra charge on a sail tour.

Sail-snorkel cruises are offered by **DePalm Tours** (☎ 824400 or 837643), **Red Sail Sports** (☎ 861603) E-mail: info@redsail.com, **Pelican Watersports,** ☎ 831228/ fax 832655; **Mi Dushi** (snorkel/sail yacht), ☎ 826034 and **Wave Dancers**, ☎ 825520.

Red Sail and Pelican are full-service shops. Pelican is located on Palm Beach behind the Holiday Inn and offers gear rentals and sail-snorkeling tours.

Red Sail Sports 35-ft catamaran, *Balia*, sets sail for morning snorkeling tours as well as sunset and dinner cruises. Red Sail is on the beach between the Americana Aruba Beach Resort and the Hyatt. They are also on Sonesta Island and have a shop in Seaport Village. E-mail: info@redsail.com.

Where to Stay

Aruba's resorts fall into two main areas—high rise and low rise. The low rise hotels are near town and the Seaport Village, a mall packed wtih beautiful shops and trendy waterfront restaurants. The high rise resorts to the north are nearer to Malmok and the lighthouse. Most offer money-saving meal packages with vouchers that allow you to dine at other restaurants.

Best Western Bucuti Beach Resort, in the low rise section, features a beautiful beach, comfortable guest rooms, unique pirate-style restaurant, pool, on-site car rental and activity desk that will book snorkeling excursions. ☎ 800-344-1212. Website: www.olmco.com/aruba/bucuti.html.

Manchebo Beach Hotel, adjacent to the Bucuti Beach Resort, offers clean, modern rooms, a beautiful beach, restaurant, TV, phones, safes and in-room fridges. ☎ 800-223-1108, fax 310-440-4220.

Holiday Inn Aruba Beach Resort & Casino, in the high rise Palm Beach area, offers 600 guest rooms, palm-lined beach and all amenities. Adjacent Pelican Watersports has a huge catamaran that takes off for all the best snorkeling spots from the Holiday Inn docks. ☎ 800-HOLIDAY, fax 011-2978-65165.

Sonesta Beach Resort, a stunning 300-room hotel at Seaport village, sits amidst 120 shops, restaurants, casinos, cafés and entertainment facilities. A free-to-guests shuttle boat departs the hotel lobby for Sonesta Island Watersports Center. ☎ 800-SONESTA.

Travel Tips:

Helpful Phone Numbers: Police/ambulance, ☎ 824000, Airport, ☎ 824800, Hospital, ☎ 826034.

Getting There: American Airlines (☎ 800-433-7300) offers direct daily flights from New York, twice daily from Miami and San Juan, Puerto Rico with connections from Boston, Philadelphia, New Jersey, Baltimore, Miami, Raleigh, Washington, Hartford, Providence, Chicago, Dallas, Detroit, Pittsburgh and other major US cities.

Car Rentals: Hertz ☎824545, 824400, airport 824886; Dollar ☎ 822783, 831237, airport 825651, Budget ☎ 828600, airport 825423. AC&E Jeep ☎ 876373.

Language: English and Spanish are widely spoken.

Documents: Passport, official birth certificate, certificate of naturalization for US and Canadian citizens. Return or continuing ticket.

Currency: The Aruba florin = $1.77 US.

Credit Cards: Widely accepted.

Service Charges: There is a 12-15% service charge on room rates. The service charge on food and beverage is 12-15% which should not be considered a tip. Tips are extra.

Climate: Dry and sunny with a year-round average temperature of 82 degrees F.

Airport Departure Tax: $15 US.

Electricity: 110-120 volts AC, 60 cycles (same as in US).

Time: Atlantic Standard Time. Same as Eastern daylight saving time, all year round.

Religious Services: Roman Catholic; Protestant (Dutch Reformed, Anglican, Evangelican, Methodist, Seventh Day Adventist, Church of Christ, Baptist); Jewish; Baha'i Faith.

Additional Information: Aruba Tourism Authority, L.G. Smith Blvd. 172, Eagle, Aruba ☎ 2978, 23777, Fax 2978 34702. Aruba Tourism Authority, 1000 Harbor Boulevard, Weehawken, NJ 07047. Tel: 201-330-0800; Fax: 201-330-8757.

Website: http://www.interknowledge.com/aruba/.

Bahamas

Scattered across the Tropic of Cancer between Florida and Cuba—the Bahamas offer expert and novice snorkelers virtually every type of underwater adventure imaginable—from dives on finely structured coral reefs to sunken galleons, underwater movie sets, submerged freighters, trains, barges and some of the best shallow, snorkeling gardens in the world. Subsea walls and cuts between and around the islands form a bustling highway for turtles, dolphins, mantas and migrating whales.

The islands top two extensive barrier reefs—the Little and Great Bahama Banks. Nourished by the Gulf Stream to the west and the Antilles Current from the southeast, these extensive banks create a diverse marine habitat. Thriving coral communities, in turn, support every imaginable tropical fish and marine invertebrate including the largest population of spiny lobster in the world and the native "Nassau" grouper.

Three general vacation areas offer their own special delights—**New Providence Island** with submerged movie sets, and dazzling casinos; **Grand Bahama Island**, with Freeport, the second largest city, and the Under Water Explorer's Society (UNEXSO); and the **Family Islands,** also called the Out Islands, with tranquil settings, silky beaches, miles of unexplored reefs, Robinson-Crusoe-style hideaways and village-type resorts. The Out Islands also offer outstanding beach-entry snorkeling sites.

Traditionally the Bahamas high season, from mid December through mid April, offers the best weather and sea conditions for snorkeling. Its second season encompasses the rest of the year and is known as Goombay Summer, a period when hotel rates may drop as much as 50 percent.

May through October brings frequent showers and chance of a hurricane with heaviest rainfall during June, July and October, though showers are often brief. Some resorts close down from September till mid November.

NEW PROVIDENCE ISLAND

New Providence Island, home to Nassau, the Bahamas' capital is also the locale for two world-class resort areas—Cable Beach and Paradise Island. Reefs surrounding the island have been used as sub-sea settings for Disney's *20,000 Leagues Beneath the Sea, Splash, Cocoon,* and the James Bond thrillers, *Thunderball, Never Say Never, For Your Eyes Only,* and most recently *Jaws IV.* Shallow reefs and wrecks entertain thousands of snorkelers each year.

Best Snorkeling Sites of New Providence

All New Providence reefs and wrecks are boat access. Dive shops cater to scuba divers, but will take snorkelers along if space is available.

☆☆☆ **Thunderball Reef,** named for the James Bond film, is a beautiful shallow reef on the north coast of New Providence, a short boat ride from Athol Island. Visibility is exceptional and photo opportunities abound with surrounding clusters of pastel tube sponges, branching gorgonians, feather corals, pink-tipped anemones, staghorn, and elkhorn corals. Friendly grouper and French angels determined to find a handout will follow you around. Spiny lobsters and small critters hide in the crevices. Sea conditions are usually calm with little or no current. Depths range from 10 to 35 ft.

☆☆ **Southwest Reef**, a wall dive encompassing several other dives, has depths from 15 to 30 ft. Sunken aircraft, small wrecks, and a profuse fish population await. Gigantic southern stingrays bury themselves in the sandy plateaus.

☆☆ **Gouldings Cay,** a tiny island located off the west end of New Providence, shelters a very pretty coral reef which was used as the setting in the films, *Cocoon, Never Say Never, 20,000 Leagues Under the Sea* and *Splash.* The area encompasses several acres and offers shallow snorkeling sites. Eagle rays, turtles, old wreck sections, schools of tropicals, morays, and acres of elkhorn make this area a prime site.

BLUE LAGOON ISLAND

Fast ferry service to Blue Lagoon Island, a small watersports and picnic island located approximately one-half mile from Paradise Island in Nassau, is provided by Nassau Cruise and Ferry Service from Paradise Island. Watersports programs, (listed below) on the island are also offered by Nassau Cruise and Ferry ☎ 242-363-3577 or 242-363-1653.

☆☆ **Stingray City** on Blue Lagoon Island is surrounded by a three-acre marine park, home to grouper, moray eels, crawfish, barracuda and a group of affectionate southern stingrays who will eagerly rub up against you looking for a treat. Brutus, the largest female at Stingray City is the favorite. She stands out because she has no tail, a mishap she encountered in the wild. She arrived one day with an old rusty fish hook in her mouth which she allowed one of the staff members to remove and has been an endearing presence ever since.

☆☆☆ **Dolphin Encounters** at Blue Lagoon offers a Swim-With-The-Dolphins Program that includes a lengthy learn-about-dolphin session that allows you to get close up followed by a half-hour swim. The entire trip takes approximately 2 ½ hours including the boat ride to and from Blue Lagoon Island and educational lecture. ☎ 242-327-5066.

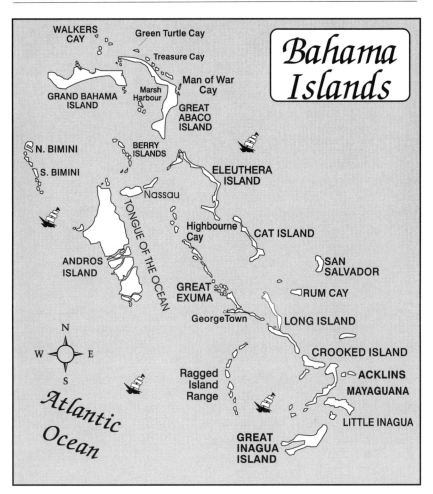

New Providence Snorkeling Tours & Rentals

Stuart Cove's Dive South Ocean, located at the South Ocean Resort offers group snorkeling trips, gear rentals and sales. If enough snorkelers sigh up they receive their own boat, otherwise they accompany the afternoon scuba dive boat. Snorkeling with the divers usually involves a wall dive with the top of the wall about 30 ft. down. The second site is always a shallow reef with depths between 15 and 40 ft. ☎ 800-879-9832 or 242-362-4171, fax 242-362-5227. Write to: P.O. Box CB11697, Nassau, Bahamas. Website: www.empg.com/stuart cove.

Nassau Scuba Centre caters primarily to scuba divers, but will take snorkelers along if space on the boat is available. Nearby Chub Cay is the

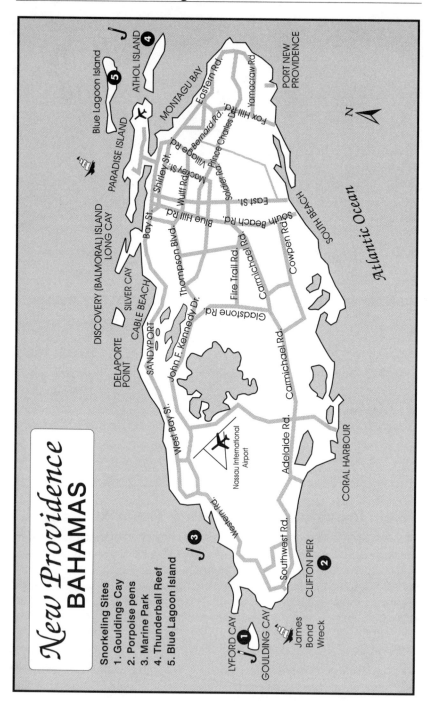

New Providence
BAHAMAS

Snorkeling Sites
1. Gouldings Cay
2. Porpoise pens
3. Marine Park
4. Thunderball Reef
5. Blue Lagoon Island

favorite shore-snorkeling spot. ☎ 800-327-8150 or 954-462-3400, fax 242-362-1964 or write P.O. Box 21766, Fort Lauderdale FL 33335. E-mail: nealwatson@aol.com.

Dive, Dive, Dive is a large, full-service dive center offering accommodation and travel packages. Snorkelers accompany scuba divers on the reef tours. ☎ 800-328-8029 or 954-943-5002, fax 242-362-1143 or write 11323 SE 17th St., #519, Ft. Lauderdale, FL33316. E-mail: info@ divedivedive.com.

Getting There
Nassau International Airport is served by Air Canada, Air Jamaica, American Eagle, BahamasAir, British Airways, Carnival Air Lines, Delta, Gulfstream/ United, Nassau Paradise Island Express, USAir and Continental.

Paradise Island Airport is served by Paradise Island Airline and Pan Am Air Bridge (seaplane) from Miami, Fort Lauderdale and West Palm Beach.

GRAND BAHAMA
Grand Bahama Island, the locale of Treasure Reef where over a million dollars worth of treasure was discovered in 1962, is home port to the Underwater Explorer's Society (UNEXSO) in Freeport/Lucaya. UNEXSO offers a variety of subsea programs and vacation packages to snorkelers.

UNEXSO, short for the Underwater Explorers Society, is world renowned for expert diver training and unusual underwater activities like the Dolphin Experience (see above) and Marine Identification Workshops, during which the resident naturalist will put you on a "first name basis" with dozens of marine creatures. Reliable gear rentals are available as are reef tours, video and still camera rentals. ☎ 800-992-DIVE or write UNEXSO, Box F-2433, Freeport, Bahamas. E-Mail: unexso@netrunner.net. Website: www. unexso com

The Dolphin Experience
One of Port Lucaya's more exciting attractions, The Underwater Explorers Society's Dolphin Experience, allows visitors—via headsets and underwater microphones—to learn about dolphins and listen to the variety of sounds they make as they "talk" and navigate. Participants sit on the dock around the dolphin enclosure with their feet in the water, which allows the dolphins to brush against them.

Guests signing up for the "Dolphin Assistant Trainer Program" can swim, snorkel and participate in feeding and training sessions with UNEXSO dolphins at Sanctuary Bay, a 20-minute ferry cruise from UNEXSO's dock. Assistant trainers must be at least 16 year old and speak English.

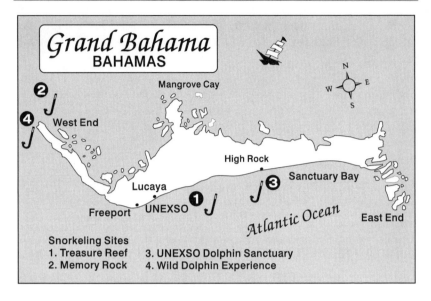

The Wild Dolphin Experience

For a truly wild experience, visitors will want to participate in the dolphin encounter at White Sand Ridge of the Bahama Bank, off the northwest point of the island. Here, a resident pod of Spotted Dolphins has long been accessible to humans. Often, when the dolphins meet the boat, they swim alongside and jump high out of the water. Snorkelers can join the dolphins for a fascinating experience that lasts as long as the dolphins want it to.

Best Snorkeling Sites of Grand Bahama

The Gulf Stream passes through many of the best snorkeling sites around the island, providing visibility that can exceed 200 ft at times. The sites, all boat access, are close (less than 15 minutes from shore). Depths range from 15 to 35 ft.

☆☆ **Treasure Reef**, the site where more than $2.4 million in Spanish Treasure was discovered in the 1960s, provides a habitat to thousands of reef fish, including large schools of grunts, snapper, goatfish, and sergeant majors. Depths range from four to 15 ft. Elkhorn and staghorn corals, gorgonians, and colorful seafans adorn the bottom.

☆☆ **Memory Rock** offers a look at spectacular brain, pillar and star coral formations. Friendly fish and usually calm seas make this a favorite snorkeling and photo spot.

Candy-striped lighthouse on Elbow Cay welcomes visitors to Abaco.

THE FAMILY ISLANDS

Twenty six out-island resorts offer a special program just for snorkelers. The Bahama Out Islands Snorkeling Adventures created by Jean-Michel Cousteau, combines guided reef excursions by professionally trained instructors. Participating resorts are listed under each island description.

ABACO

The Abaco Islands, the northernmost group in the Bahamas, stretch south 130 miles from Walker's Cay to Great Abaco. There are two main islands, Great Abaco and Little Abaco flanked by hundreds of smaller cays. Terrific snorkeling exists around Marsh Harbour, Walker's Cay, Great Guana Cay and Treasure Cay.

Best Snorkeling Sites of Abaco

☆**Charlies Canyons** —just 10 minutes from Walker's Cay by boat, is decked with ancient cannons, anchors and fish-filled crevices in 25ft of water. The reef is lush with hard and soft corals. Friendly Nassau grouped, wide-eyed squirrelfish, octopi and schools of French grunts reside in the canyons.

☆☆ To the west lies **Travel Agent Reef,** a perfect spot for new snorkelers, with a stunning coral gardens at depths from 5 to 10 feet.

☆ **Broad Bottom** off Walker's Cay's eastern tip starts just three feet below the surface, sloping down to a sandy bottom at 30 ft. The mini-wall reef is riddled with caverns and tunnels crawling with lobster.

☆☆☆ **North of Tom Brown's,** another Walker's Cay site, is a beautiful dive through shallow coral gardens colored with delicate vase sponges and a multitude of reef fish. Depths average 25 ft.

☆☆☆☆ Shallow reefs extend for a mile offshore at **Green Turtle Cay**.

☆☆☆ Prime shallow reefs off **Great Guana Cay** sit 50 ft from the white-sand beach at the Guana Beach Resort and Marina.

☆☆☆☆ Shallow reefs, populated by every imaginable fish and critter, sit 30 ft out from the shoreline at **Hopetown**.

☆☆☆☆☆ To the south lies **Pelican Cay National Park**, a 2,000-acre maze of coral tunnels, walls, pinnacles littered with the remains of modern and ancient wrecks. Shallow reef depths range from breaking the surface to about 30 ft. Spectacular marine life includes eagle rays, jacks, angels, huge groupers, and colorful sponges.

☆☆☆ The *USS Adirondack*, a Federal-era battleship, rests in 30 ft of water. Snork-elers exploring the twisted remains of its superstructure might catch a peek at the green moray that lives in one of the old cannons. Hordes of fish inhabit the wreck.

Abaco Snorkeling Tours & Rentals

Dive Abaco, at the Conch Inn Marina across from Abaco Towns, offers reef trips daily at 9:30 am returning at 2:00 pm. Accommodation packages with Pelican Beach Villas. ☎ 242-367-2787, VHF 16.

Brendal's Dive Shop at the Green Turtle Club has two trips daily, equipment rental, and certification courses. ☎ 242-359-6226.

Dive Odyssea in Marsh Harbour offers courses, trips, and equipment rental. ☎ 242-367-2736, VHF 16

Abaco Snorkeling Program Participating Hotels

Abaco Inn, Hope Town, Elbow Cay ☎ 800-468-8799 or 242-366-0133, fax 242-366-0113; **Bluff House Club**, Green Turtle Cay ☎ 800-688- 4752 or 242-365-4247, fax 242-365- 4248; **Great Abaco Beach Resort**, Marsh Harbour ☎ 800-468-4799 or 242-367-2158, fax 242-367-2819; **Green Turtle Club**, Green Turtle Cay, ☎ 800-688-4752 or 242-365-4271, fax 365-4272; **Pelican Beach Villas**, Marsh Harbour, ☎ 800-642-7268 or 242-367-3600, fax 912-437-6223; **Spanish Cay Inn** 800-688-4752 or 242-365-0083, fax 242-365-0466.

Guana Beach Resort, Guana Cay features seven miles of secluded ocean beach. A 50-ft swim from shore brings you over a barrier reef adorned by lavendar sea fans and soft corals. Lots of fish. ☎ 800-227-3366 or 954-423-9796, fax 242-366-0286.

Hope Town Harbour Lodge has a section of barrier reef 20 ft from their lovely, two-mile-long beach. With rare exception, it's calm and no currents. They also rent boats and book wild dolphin swims. ☎ 800-316-7844 or 242-366-0095, fax 242-366-0286.

Getting There

American Eagle, US Air, Airways International, Island Express and Pan Am serve the area from Florida. There are three airports in the Abacos, Walker's Cay in the north, Treasure Cay in the middle and the largest at Marsh Harbour to the south. Visitors to the Abacos may also take the mailboats, *M/V Deborah KII* and the *Champion II*, from Potter's Cay Dock in Nassau. Contact the dockmaster in Nassau at 242-362-4391 for departure times and itineraries. Schedules subject to weather conditions. Individual resorts may offer private charter flights from Miami or Fort Lauderdale.

Helpful Phone Numbers

Marsh Harbour Police: 919 or 367-2571; Marsh Harbour clinic ☎ 366-4010; Great Abaco Clinic, ☎ 365-2510; Treasure Cay Clinic, ☎ 367-2570. Green Turtle Cay Clinic, ☎ 365-4222.

ANDROS

Andros, the largest of the Bahama islands, stretches to more than 100 miles long and 40 miles wide. It boasts enormous bird and plant populations, including 48 species of wild orchids. Offshore lies the world's third largest barrier reef, famous for walls that drop 6,000 feet into the "Tongue of the Ocean" (TOTO). Between the awesome TOTO and the shore, the reef offers a peaceful haven for snorkelers with depths from nine to 15 ft.

Docking facilities for private boats are limited. At present, San Andros has eight slips with basic facilities, fuel, water, ice, accommodation and a restaurant.

Snorkeling from the beach and off shore is splendid with massive elkhorn and staghorn coral formations inhabited by a diverse fish and marine life population.

Best Snorkeling Sites of Andros

Small Hope Bay Lodge is the center of snorkeling tours and special programs on and around Andros.

☆☆☆ **The Wreck of the *Potomac*** is 350-ft, steel-hulled cargo ship resting in 25 ft of water. Her hull, split in two, is home to sweeping schools of sergeant majors, squirrel fish, copper sweepers, rays, barracuda and big parrotfish. Boat access.

☆☆☆☆ Excellent snorkeling at **Trumpet Reef**, (near Small Hope Bay Lodge) takes you through a beautiful forest of elkhorn, staghorn, brain and

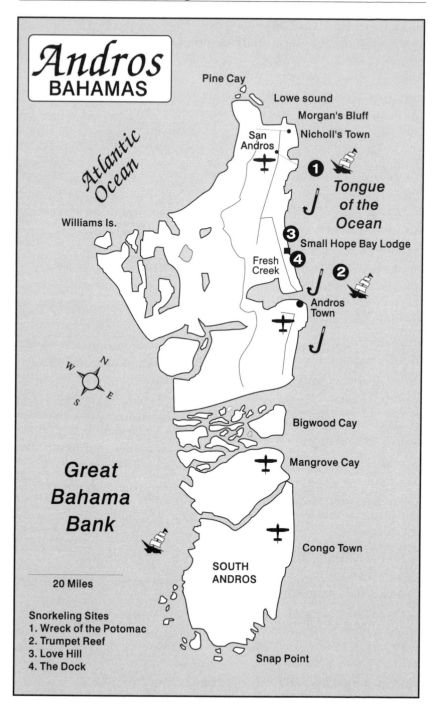

Andros
BAHAMAS

Pine Cay

Lowe sound

Morgan's Bluff

Nicholl's Town

San Andros

Atlantic Ocean

Williams Is.

①

Tongue of the Ocean

③

Small Hope Bay Lodge

Fresh Creek

④

②

Andros Town

Great Bahama Bank

Bigwood Cay

Mangrove Cay

Congo Town

SOUTH ANDROS

20 Miles

Snap Point

Snorkeling Sites
1. Wreck of the Potomac
2. Trumpet Reef
3. Love Hill
4. The Dock

soft corals. Hundreds of trumpet fish join striking queen and French angels, schools of grunts and yellowtail in depths from two to 15 ft.

☆☆☆ **Love Hill**, another super snorkeling site near Small Hope Bay Lodge, has a huge thickets of elkhorn and staghorn coral. Tropical fish and critters abound in depths from two to 15 ft.

☆☆☆ **"The Dock"** at Small Hope Bay Lodge is a great spot for a night snorkel. Fish are abundant and varied amidst 35 years of stuff that's fallen off the dock, including ruins of the previous dock.Sea life includes snappers, blue tangs, parrotfish, barracuda, angelfish, flounder, pufferfish, eagle rays, octopus and an occasional dolphin.

☆☆ **North Beach**, a line of patch shoals that make for pleasurable snorkeling, lies north of "The Dock," between two buoy markers. Look for ocotpus hiding in shells and a variety of starfish.

☆ **Davis Creek** (high tide only) is a sandy tidal flat north of the beach, past the point and the rocks. Small schools of baby barracuda, box fish and hundreds of other juveniles abound. Expect tidal currents.

☆☆☆☆ **Goat Cay**, the largest island visible from the Small Hope Bay Lodge dock, is flanked by sea grasses on one side—good hunting grounds for sea biscuits and sand dollars—and shallows of the barrier reef on the other side. Abundant coral and sea life.

Andros Snorkeling Program Participating Hotel

Small Hope Bay Lodge offers lodging in 20 lovely cottages, low-cost air service from Ft. Lauderdale, snorkeling and dive programs. Free snorkeling lesson around the dock. Besides beach snorkeling, the lodge offers daily excursions to the Andros Barrier Reef, a ten-minute boat ride. ☎ 800-223-6961, 242-368-2014, fax 242-368-2015. E-mail: shbinfo@small hope. com. Website: www. smallhope.com

Getting There

Andros has three airports, at centrally located San Andros, and Andros Town and Congo Town in the south. Air service is by Island Express from Fort Lauderdale, Bahamsair from Nassau, and several private charters—Small Hope Bay Charter, Southern Outbound Air, Miami Air Charter and Air Link.

Helpful Phone Numbers

Police: North Andros, ☎ 919; Central Andros, ☎ 368-2626; South Andros, ☎ 329-4620. Clinics at Mastic Point ☎ 329-3055, Lowe Sound Clinic, ☎ 329-2055. Fresh Creek Clinic, ☎ 368-2038.

THE BERRY ISLANDS

This chain of 30 small islands lies off the eastern edge of the Great Bahama Bank, 80 miles southeast of Bimini.

Chub Cay, a tiny, one-resort island just north of New Providence, features some of the best shore snorkeling and diving in the Bahamas. The waters around Great Harbour Cay provide fascinating coral formations and caverns packed with silversides and lobster. A few shipwrecks shelter nurse sharks and southern stingrays. Eagle rays circle the reefs.

Accommodations, snorkeling tours, boat rentals and yacht services are available at the **Chub Cay Club** ☎ 800-327-8150 or 242-322-5199 and the **Great Harbour Cay Resort** and adjacent yacht club ☎ 800-343-7256, 954-921-9084, fax 954-921-1044. Chub Cay offers boaters a 90-slip marina with all docking amenities.

Best Snorkeling Sites of the Berry Islands

☆☆☆☆ The reef at **Chub Cay** sits off the western shore about 15 ft from the shoreline with depths from three to 60 ft. Corals, abundant fish life, pretty sponges and gorgonians make this a terrific snorkeling spot. A more extensive reef sits about 150 yards offshore. Visibility averages about 100 ft, water temperature between 76°F in winter and 86°F in summer. Recently, Undersea Adventures installed a concrete pad and steps over the ironshore to allow snorkelers and divers easy entry and exit into the shallow elkhorn gardens. Beach dive.

☆☆☆ Red, pink and lavender sponges splash the shallow walls at **Mama Rhoda's Reef** where snorkelers explore coral crevices packed with schools of sergeant majors, eagle rays, grunts, hogfish, huge tiger groupers, jacks and yellowtail. Fantastic elkhorn and staghorn corals thrive at depths of 10 to 20 ft. Boat access.

Chub Cay Snorkeling Tours & Rentals

Chub Cay Undersea Adventures offers complete snorkeling and dive vacations including air transfers from Fort Lauderdale. Snorkelers join the dive boats on a space-available basis for $25. ☎ 800-327-8150 or 954-462-3400, fax 954-462-4100. E-mail: nealwatson @aol.com. Website: www.nealwatson.com/chub.htm.

Getting There

The Berry islands are reached by private charters. Island Express serves Great Harbour Cay from Fort Lauderdale. Southern Pride Aviation, ☎ 954-938-8991, provides transportation from Fort Lauderdale Executive Airport to Chub Cay for guests of the Chub Cay resort and snorkelers who book a package tour with Chub Cay Undersea Adventures ☎ 800-327-8150. Allow at least two-and-one-half hours between flights if you are arriving at Fort Lauderdale International. You'll need to take a taxi to Executive Airport at 1625 W. Commercial Blvd.

Helpful Phone Numbers

Police: On Great Harbour Cay, ☎322-2344; Medical Clinic, ☎ 322-2400.

BIMINI

Bimini, just a quick flight from Miami, offers snorkelers a huge fish population, some patch reefs and the half-submerged wreck of the *Sapona*, a large concrete ship. All sites are boat access, averaging 10 to 15 minutes. Bimini's commercial center is Alice Town.

Bimini Snorkeling

☆☆☆ **Rainbow Reef**, host to masses of butterfly fish, angels, parrotfish, lobsters, moray eels, grunts is a great spot for fish photos. Average depth: 15 ft. Boat access.

☆☆☆☆ **Wild Spotted Dolphin Pods** off Bimini make for an exciting encounter. Trips, which last three to four hours, are offered by Bimini Undersea Adventures. Time to the dolphin grounds runs about an hour. There is no guarantee that the dolphins will always be there, but they have been on four out of five trips and complimentary return tickets are given to passengers of no-see trips. Knowdla Keefe of Bimini Undersea Adventures has devised a program enabling visitors to interact with with these beautiful creatures.

☆☆ **Stones of Atlantis** resemble an undersea highway. Whether it's remnants of an ancient civilization or not is yet to be decided, but it's definitely a fun dive as you join scores of finned travelers.

Bimini Snorkeling Tours & Rentals

Bimini Undersea Adventures offers complete snorkeling vacations with a wide choice of resorts in every price range. All are within a five-minute walk of the dive shop. Vacations include use of a mask, fins and snorkel. The shop sells snorkeling gear and rents bikes, kayaks and windsurfers. Snorkelers join the dive boats on afternoon dives. There is also a swim-with-wild-dolphins program. 800-348-4644, 305-653-5572, fax 305-652-9148 E-mail: info@biminiunderseaadventures.com. Website: www.biminiunder sea.com.

Getting There

Air transportation to North Bimini is provided by The Pan Am Air Bridge (formerly CHALK'S International airlines). Pan Am flies 17-seat Grumman

Aerial view of Bimini

Mallard Sea Planes daily to Bimini from South Florida—Miami or Ft. Lauderdale, and Nassau. When you fly on a package with Bimini Undersea Adventures you automatically receive a 50 lb baggage allowance (normally 30 lbs) at no extra cost.

CAT ISLAND

Named for British sea Captain Catt, Cat Island will surprise you with its rolling hills and lush green forests spread over 50 tranquil miles. Located between Eleuthera and Long Island, it is home to the Bahamas' tallest summit—Mt. Alvernia, 206-ft high. Miles of deserted beaches, Arawak Indian caves, ruins of early plantations and excellent snorkeling off the beach make this island popular.

Cat Island Snorkeling Sites

Good shallow snorkeling exists off the beaches of the Greenwood Beach Resort and Fernandez Bay Village Resort with rocky outcroppings between 15 and 40 ft. At Port Howe, numerous coral reef sites start 10 feet from the shore.

Fernandez Bay Snorkeling Sites

☆ A five minute walk from the beach at Fernandez Bay village brings you to **Jumping Rocks Point** where you'll find hard and soft corals, purple sea fans, assorted reef fish, crabs and crawfish along an underwater ledge. Depths run from the surface to 12 ft. Good for beginners.

☆ **Big Lump of Limestone**, a five-minute swim from the Fernandez Bay Resort beach, brings you to hard and soft corals growing from 10 ft to the surface. Grouper and smaller fish inhabit the area. Good for beginners.

☆☆☆☆ **Dry Head Reef**, which sits 300 yards offshore, shelters vibrant sea fans, lettuce and brain corals, home to grunts, yellowtail, small barracudas and juvenile nurse sharks. The boat ride takes about 35 minutes.

☆☆ **Naked Point**, a maze of small coral heads, ledges and caves, sits two minutes by boat from Fernandez Bay's dock. Sergeant majors, grunts, yellow tail, stone crab, sting rays and spotted eagle rays zip by. Berginner to advanced.

☆☆ **Hazel's Hideaway**, a two-mile drive, walk or boat ride from Fernandez Bay offers nice beach-entry snorkeling over coral heads and rocks with plenty of fish. The best spots are in between the little islands scattered about. After your swim, stop in at Hazel's Hideaway Bar on the beach and meet Hazel.

Snorkeling Program Participating Hotels

Fernandez Bay Village features accommodations in spacious villas with patios and maid service. Besides the Snorkeling Adventures program, there is wonderful snorkeling off the resort beach in three to six ft of water. Good for children. Snorkeling trips are also offered by the resort. Gear rentals are available for adults, but it's best to bring gear for children. ☎ 800-940-1905, 954-474-4821, fax 954-474-4864; on Cat Island 242-342-3043, fax 242-342-3051. E-mail: fbv@batelnet.bs Website: www.fernandezbay village.com.

Greenwood Beach Resort, a 20-room beachfront inn sits on a lovely eight-mile pink beach. ☎ 800-272-9122 or 242-342-3053.

Getting There

Bahamasair connects from Nassau to Arthur's Town Airport. Fernandez Bay Village has private charters from Florida and Nassau.

CROOKED ISLAND

This remote islet, 380 nautical miles from Ft. Lauderdale, offers unexplored reefs and spectacular beaches, where you can walk for miles without seeing another soul. It is fabulous for snorkeling. The reef starts at the shoreline, slopes to 40 ft, then plunges steeply to 6000 ft in the Crooked Island Passage. The sole resort, Pittstown Point Landing (☎ 800-752-2322 or 242-344-2507) accommodates all watersports.

Getting There

Bahamasair (☎ 800-222-4262) flies into Colonel Hill twice weekly from Nassau. Private pilots can tie down at Colonel Hill Airport or Pittstown Point Landings airport. The 2400-ft airstrip (2000' blacktop, 400' crushed coral overrun) is just forty paces to the main building. Pittstown Point Landing the sole hotel, provides complimentary transportation. Phones are a rare find on Crooked Island. For medical assistance, clinics are at Arthur's Town, Smith Bay and Old Bight.

ELEUTHERA

Eleuthera is yet another unspoiled Bahamian paradise with endless pink-sand beaches, secluded snorkeling coves and impressive coral reefs. Shaped like a boomerang, the island is 100 miles long and, less than two miles wide with a population of 10,600—the largest of all the Family Islands. It lies 200 miles southeast of Florida and 60 miles west of Nassau.

Its neighboring out-islands include Spanish Wells, tiny Harbour Island, and a small cay called Current. Spanish Wells, one of the smallest but most progressive islands in the Bahamas, is known for its shallow wrecks.

Best Snorkeling Sites of Eleuthera

There are five beach-entry sites in the **Cove Eleuthera Hotel** area (Gregory Town) to explore. A four-ft deep artificial lagoon provides a safe spot for beginners to try out gear and meet local fish. More experienced snorkelers will find abundant coral heads surrounded by grunts, angelfish, yellow tail and stingrays in adjacent coves and peninsulas.

A pretty reef 20 yards off the beach at the **Governor's Harbour Hatchet Bay** shelters angelfish, yellowtail snappers, southern stingrays, anemones and parrotfish.

Additional beach-entry sites exist at **Rock Sound** where clear water and a throngs of parrotfish, triggerfish, blue tangs and other tropical fish reside.

☆☆ **Mystery Reef,** three miles outside of Current Cut, in the direction of Egg Island, encompasses six coral heads in 25 ft. of water. The heads, centered on a sprawling sand patch, are 10 to 20 ft. high and loaded with exquisite corals and fascinating marine life. Boat access.

☆☆☆☆ **Freighter Wreck.** Approximately five miles from Current Cut lies the rusting hull of a 250-ft Lebanese freighter which caught fire and was purposely run aground. The wreck sits perfectly upright in 20 ft. of water with most of her structure above the surface. Her keel is broke at mid-ship, making salvage out of the question. Although the propeller was removed by scrap metal salvors, furnishings and ship's parts are scattered around the hull. Large parrotfish, glasseye snappers, and angels hover the wreck.

☆☆☆☆ **Devil's Backbone,** north of Spanish Wells island is a long stretch of shallow coral reefs. Great clumps of razor-sharp elkhorn coral rise to the surface and are often awash at low tide. This treacherous barrier reef is a graveyard for ships, but a paradise for snorkelers. Boat access.

☆☆ Perhaps the most unusual shipwreck in all the Bahamas is **Train Wreck,** the remains of a steam locomotive, lying in 15 ft. of water. Still on the barge, which sank during a storm in 1865, it was part of a Union train believed captured by the Confederacy and sold to a Cuban sugar plantation. The wreck site also contains three sets of wheel trucks believed to be part of the same locomotive, and wood beams half buried in the sandy sea floor. The wreckage which is slowly settling in a garden of elkhorn and brain coral formations, offers some great angles for wide-angle photography. Boat access.

☆☆☆ Just a few hundred yards away from the Train Wreck lies the *Cienfuegos Wreck,*— the twisted remains of a passenger steamer that sank in 1895. Part of the Ward Line of New York, this 200-ft-long, steel-hulled ship crashed into the reef during a bad storm. All passengers on board survived and her cargo of rice was salvaged. The remaining wreckage lies in 35 ft. of water with some sections at 10 ft. Prominent features are two giant heat exchangers, a big boiler and the main drive shaft. The wreck, looking much like an undersea junk yard with jumbled steel plates, broken ribs and twisted steel beams, makes for a fascinating dive. Boat access.

☆☆ **Potato and Onion Wreck.** The *Vanaheim*, an 86-ft, coastal freighter carrying a cargo of potatoes and onions crashed into Devil's Backbone in February, 1969. The force of the heavy seas during the storm pushed her over the barrier reef into 15 ft. of water—an easy dive. Pretty reef surrounds the wreck. Boat access.

Eleuthera Snorkeling Tours & Rentals

Valentines Yacht Club and Dive Center, Harbour Island, offers free snorkel lessons every day that include a video show, booklet and pool practice. Snorkel trips come with a tour guide upon request. Sites include three ship wrecks and shallow reefs. They also carry "guppy gear" for tiny divers. Wet suits selections range from tiny tot to XXXL sizes.

The reef outside the dive shop breaks the surface in many spots with snorkeling depths starting at five feet. Advanced snorkelers can swim out to more lush growth at depths to 35 ft. ☎ 242-333-2309.

Snorkeling Program Participating Hotels

Terrific close-in snorkeling sites exist off the beaches surrounding the Cove Eleuthera Hotel and Rainbow Inn.

Cambridge Villas, located in Gregory Town, provide free transportation to and from the beach. ☎ 800-688-4752 242-335-5080, fax 242-335-5308.

The Cove-Eleuthera, a 24-room resort, sits on two beautiful snorkeling coves. ☎ 800-552-5960 or 242-335-5142, fax 242-335-5338.

Palmetto Shores Villas, ☎ 800-688-4752 or 242-332-1305.

Photo © Mina Heuslein

Sharks, photographed off Nassau, are seldom seen on shallow snorkeling reefs. They seem to prefer deeper, cooler water.

Rainbow Inn offers miles of deserted beaches, great snorkeling from the shore and friendly accommodations in studio apartments or villas. A five-minute walk from the resort brings you to additional shore-entry reef snorkeling spots. Free use of snorkeling equipment. ☎ 800 688-688-4752 or 242-335-0294.

EXUMA

The Exumas, a sandy chain of more than 350 mostly uninhabited islands and cays, extend more than 100 miles between New Providence and Long Island—35 miles southeast of Nassau. Offshore lie 200 miles of magnificent coral reefs.

Great Exuma, accessible by plane from Nassau and southern Florida, provides visitors with a selection of fine hotels, restaurants, shops and nightlife. In George Town, the capital city, waterside inns such as Peace and Plenty provide a modern base to venture into the uninhabited utopias of the neighboring cays where you can snorkel, beachcomb and birdwatch.

Snorkel trips to Pigeon Cay and Stocking Island—a sheller's haven—are readily available. The reefs lie about 100 yards from the beaches. Marinas rent small boats to those who wish to explore the offshore sites on their own.

Best Snorkeling Sites of Exuma

✰✰✰✰ Snorkelers can explore the **Exuma National Land and Sea Park,** a vast underwater preserve and the **Thunderball Grotto**, a super fish-feeding area near Staniel Cay, where the famous James Bond movie was filmed. Off the capital city, George Town, lies **Stocking Island,** where excellent snorkeling and shelling abound.

☆☆☆ **Stingray Reef**, adjacent to Uly Cay and north of Stocking Island has elkhorn stands and soft-coral patches that shelter trumpet fish, barracuda, big turtles, and large schools of grunts and yellowtail. Depths range from 15 to 40 ft.

☆☆☆☆ **Conch Cay**, a northern dive area, offers shallow walls and wide ledges for easy exploration. Marine life offers the big attraction—huge turtles, rays and occasional sharks. The reef ranges in depth from six to 20 ft.

LONG ISLAND

Long revered as a mecca for reef explorers, scenic Long Island, is the Bahamas' only island with significant high terrain. It's perimeter, blessed with sixty miles of snow white beaches, slopes down to magnificent shallow reefs, drop-offs, crystal-clear waters, and a profusion of marine life. Two resorts cater to visiting snorkelers.

Best Snorkeling Sites of Long Island

The best reefs lie offshore, but several terrific shore-entry sites exist off Cape Santa Maria and the area surrounding the Stella Maris Resort Community. Check with the dive shop at Stella Maris for wind and sea conditions before entering the water.

☆☆ **Coral Gardens** on the Atlantic side of the island, about three-fouths of a mile from the Stella Maris Resort, is an impressive dive when the seas and wind are calm. The reef sits on a shelf about 20 yards wide with depths from three to 20 ft. Massive, healthy stands of elkhorn and staghorn coral shelter a variety of angelfish, trumpet fish, small green and hawksbill turtles, barracuda, huge Nassau grouper and rockgrouper. The reef parallels the shore for about two miles. Get there by foot, bike or car. A road sign off Ocean View Drive points the way. Entry is over rock steps into a four-ft depth, then swim out about 20 yards to the reef. Beach entry.

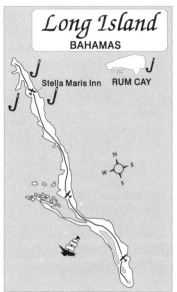

Long Island
BAHAMAS
Stella Maris Inn   RUM CAY

☆☆☆ **Poseidon's Point** starts at the shoreline with dramatic brain and elkhorn formations. You can jump in or climb down the rocks. Wildlife includes occasional

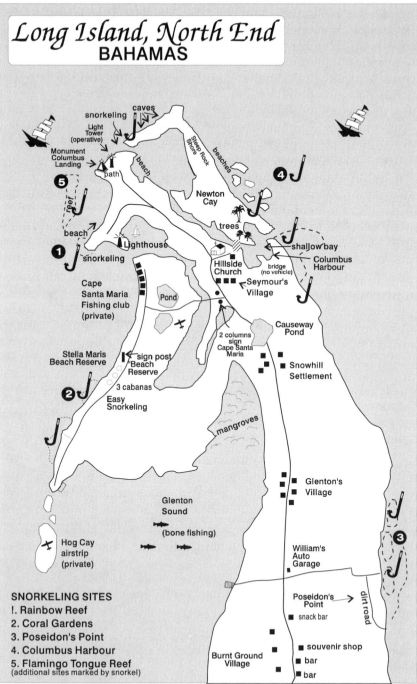

Long Island, North End
BAHAMAS

caves

snorkeling

Light Tower (operative)

Monument Columbus Landing

path

beach

Steep Rock Shore

beaches

5

reef

beach

1

snorkeling

Lighthouse

Cape Santa Maria Fishing club (private)

Pond

Newton Cay

trees

4

shallow bay

Columbus Harbour

Hillside Church

bridge (no vehicle)

Seymour's Village

2 columns sign Cape Santa Maria

Causeway Pond

Stella Maris Beach Reserve

sign post "Beach Reserve

3 cabanas

2

Easy Snorkeling

Snowhill Settlement

mangroves

Glenton's Village

Glenton Sound

(bone fishing)

Hog Cay airstrip (private)

William's Auto Garage

3

Poseidon's Point

dirt road

snack bar

SNORKELING SITES

!. Rainbow Reef
2. Coral Gardens
3. Poseidon's Point
4. Columbus Harbour
5. Flamingo Tongue Reef
(additional sites marked by snorkel)

Burnt Ground Village

souvenir shop

bar

bar

appearances by a mako, reef, bull or hammerhead shark. Residents include huge three- to five-ft tarpon, parrotfish, shrimp, crawfish, Nassau grouper, yellowtail, grunts and sergeant majors. Beach entry points are four miles from Stella Maris Resort. Seas are usually calm except during storms. Guided, night snorkeling tours are offered by the Stella Maris dive shop. Beach or boat entry.

☆☆ **Columbus Harbour**, where Columbus' fleet anchored on Oct 16th, 1492, features near-the-shore reef areas for novice snorkelers and deeper reef scenery further out for advanced snorkelers. To reach the site, head north on the main road till you see the Hillside Church. Turn right (or towards the sea) till you can't go any further. Park and walk about 300 yards across the walking bridge to the north end of the island. Following the shoreline to the left (north) brings you into shallow depths from 3 to 25 ft, and a variety of rocks and hard corals. Swim out from the shore for more interesting coral formations. Big parrotfish, Nassau grouper, rockfish, and crawfish hide in the caves and crevices. Good shelling exists along the outer beaches.

The eight-mile drive to Columbus Harbour takes about 10 minutes from Stella Maris Resort.

☆☆ **Rainbow Reef** has three easy entries from Cape Santa Maria Beach. It lies 20 yards from shore and is completely protected in most weather situations except northwest winds. Encrusting corals and sponges cover the rocky bottom, which is inhabited by a good mix of reef fish. Passing eagle rays are frequently sighted. Some large stingrays bury themselves in the sand. Beach or boat access.

☆☆☆ **Flamingo Tongue Reef** takes its name from the thousands of ruby-colored, Flamingo Tongue shells along its bottom. This spot is also noted for superb sea fans, gorgonia and pillar corals. Walls of schooling reef fish— squirrels, grunts, yellow tail —roam about. Beware the scorpion fish, stone fish and fire coral. The reef lies six miles from Stella Maris Marina within a half mile of the Cape Santa Maria shoreline. Depths average 25 ft. with shallower areas. Seas are usually calm. Boat access.

☆☆ **The West Bar** is a lovely, 600-ft long, 300-ft wide, bar-shaped shoal within a half-mile of two beautiful beaches. The reef consists of superb brain and staghorn corals, tube sponges, barrel sponges, feather corals, seafans and pillar corals. Depth is 15 ft. Waters are calm. Outstanding visibility. Boat access.

Angelfish Reef and Barakuda Heads are two massive, neighboring coral heads about six miles offshore. Tame groupers, rock fish, barracuda, large schools of jacks, crawfish, and small critters thrive at both sites. Depths vary to 40 ft with many shallow areas perfect for snorkeling.

San Salvador
BAHAMAS

Cut Cay

Boboys Reef

Atlantic Ocean

Bonefish Bay

Riding Rock Inn
Guanahani Dive

Cockburn Town

Reef

Reef

Submerged Caves

Watlings Castle

French Bay

Snow Bay

Atlantic Ocean

Snorkeling Sites
1. Snapshot Reef
2. Wreck of the Frescate

Reef

Snorkeling Program Participating Hotels

Stella Maris Resort offers two-, three- and four-bedroom villas and bungalows all situated high atop the hillcrest of the island's east shoreline and featuring breathtaking views of the ocean. The shoreline is rocky with several hiking paths which will bring you to secluded picnic and sunbathing areas. The operation is top-notch, offering guided reef tours and complimentary shuttle bus service to different shore-entry snorkeling spots. Superb beaches. Dive shop on premises. ☎ 800-426-0466, fax 954-359-8238 E-mail: smrc@stellamarisresort.com Website stellamaris resort.com.

You can wade out to a beautiful barrier reef from any point along the four-mile long beach at the **Cape Santa Maria Resort.** The resort has a catamaran for offshore snorkeling trips. ☎ 800-663-7090, 242-357-1006, fax 604-598-1361.

SAN SALVADOR

Miles of virgin shallow reefs, walls and new wrecks are yet to be explored in the waters around San Salvador, truly one of the diving jewels of the Bahamas. It is so remote the sole dive resort on the island, Riding Rock Inn, points out that it is NOT IN SOUTH AMERICA in their brochures. On the shore, visitors delight in miles of white-sand beaches including the site where Christopher Columbus first set foot in the New World.

Best Snorkeling Sites of San Salvador

San Salvador features shallow reefs heavily populated with Nassau grouper, rays, and walls of schooling fish. Most sites range in depth from 10 to 30 ft. Coral and fish can be seen off the Riding Rock Inn's beach, but the prettiest beach-entry sites lie about three miles south of the resort. You reach them by bicycle or rental car. There is also nice snorkeling off the end of the runway. Climb down a small slope to get there or swim north from the Riding Rock Inn beach.

Snapshot Reef packs in schools of angelfish, groupers, parrotfish, trumpetfish, damsels, blue chromis, tangs, tarpon, and invertebrates—all waiting for a handout. Boat access.

The wreck of the **Frescate**, a 261-ft freighter resting at twenty ft, hit the reefs in 1902 and has since attracted throngs of lobster, silversides, and barracuda. Outstanding visibility. Boat access.

Snorkeling Program Participating Hotel

Riding Rock Inn offers snorkelers all the comforts of home in a relaxed, casual atmosphere. This plush resort features 24 air-conditioned double rooms, conference center, pool, restaurant, and marina. Snorkelers join the dive boats for reef trips. Rental bicycles are available for island exploration and travel to beach snorkeling sites. Dive shop. ☎ 800-272-1492 or 305-359-8353, fax 359-8254.

Getting There

Bahamsair has scheduled flights from Nassau. Guests of the Riding Rock Inn are offered chartered flights from Ft. Lauderdale. The mail boat, *M/V Maxine* offers passenger service from Nassau.

BAHAMAS LIVE-ABOARDS

Note: passport needed

Nekton Diving Cruises caters to scuba divers and snorkelers. A special 17-ft tender on board the 78-ft yacht is dedicated to carrying snorkeling guests to the best shallow spots. A full-time snorkeling pro offers guided shallow reef or wreck tours daily.

The twin-hulled motor yacht carries 30 passengers and 10 staff members. Its unique design eliminates the rocking that causes most sea sickness. The ship features a spa, private baths and elevating dive platform. Rates range from $1400 per person for a week. ☎ 800-899-6753 or 954-463-9324, fax 954-463-8938. Website: www.nektoncruises.com.

Cruzan Yacht Charters, based in fort Lauderdale, offers a large selection of sail and power bare boats from 30 to 50 ft for weekend or weekly snorkeling cruises to the Bahamas or Florida Keys. Sample rate for a party of six aboard a 44-ft captained CSY sailboat would start at $2600 plus food, drinks and port taxes. The boat captains, all expert divers, will tailor guided dives for you. Be sure to specify snorkeling cruise when you call. Cruzan also offers a summer Seaquest Camp for 12- to 17-year olds that focuses on sailing and snorkeling. ☎ 800-628-0785 or 305-628-0785, fax 305-854-0887. E-mail: cruzanyc@aol.com. Website: www.cruzan.com. Write to P.O. Box 53, Coconut Grove, FL 33133.

Witt's End. Captains BJ and Greg Witt offer overnight "bunk & breakfast" outings and weekend or week-long cruises through the Florida Keys and Bahamas aboard Witt's End, a well-appointed 51-ft ketch docked at Land's End Marina, key West. Delightful customized, crewed charters include sumptuous breakfasts and candlelight dinners. Sails to prime snorkeling and diving spots. For reservations and prices, write to Captains Witt, P.O. Box 625 , Key Largo, FL 33037 ☎ 305-451-3354.

Travel Tips

Getting There: Daily flights service Nassau International Airport and Freeport from most US gateway cities. Freeport and the Family Islands are scheduled daily from South Florida by Bahamasair, ☎800-222-4262; American Eagle, ☎ 800-433-7300 and Pan Am Air Bridge ☎ 305-373-1120, which operates flights to Bimini, Paradise Island and Walker's Cay aboard a Grumman Mallard seaplane. Bahamasair flies from Nassau to Andros, Abacos, Eleuthera and Exuma daily.

Private Planes: Airstrips serving light planes are scattered throughout the Bahamas. Private aircraft pilots are required to obtain a cruising permit before entering Bahamas airspace and should contact the Bahamas Private Pilot Briefing Center, ☎ 800-32-SPORT-USA.

A 500-page, annually-updated book, *The Pilot's Bahamas and Caribbean Aviation Guide* published by Pilot Publications, PO Box 88, Pauma Valley, Ca. 92061 (☎ 800-521-2120) contains every airport in the Bahamas, Turks & Caicos, Hispaniola, Puerto Rico, USVI, Jamaica and the Eastern Caribbean islands plus Cancun and Cozumel, Belize and Roatan, Honduras. The flight guide also includes aerial photos, charts, maps, customs and other information on island flights. Cost $44.95 plus 6.00 shipping.

Pilots Publications also offers a Bahamas Travel Kit for pilots which contains all the papers for customs and immigration and VFR charts. Specify intended destination. (price subject to change)

Documents: United States law requires citizens to carry a current passport to re-enter the US. To enter the Bahamas US citizens and Canadians need a passport and a return ticket.

Currency: The Bahamian dollar is the monetary equivalent of the US dollar. The $3 Bahamian bill, square 15 cent pieces and fluted 10 cent pieces are popular among souvenir hunters.

Departure Tax: US $15.

Gratuities: The customary tip on the islands is 15%.

Climate: Average year round temperatures range from 70 to 85 ° F. The rainy season lasts from early June through late October. Islands toward the south end of the arc have warmer weather.

Clothing: Casual. A light jacket or sweater is needed in the evening, especially during winter months. You may want to dress up in the evening for some hotels, restaurants, and casinos in Nassau and Freeport. The Family Islands are very casual. Light wetsuits or wetskins are needed for snorkeling during winter months when water temperatures drop to 76 °F. Wetskins or long pants and long-sleeve shirts are a good idea anytime to prevent sunburn.

Religious Services: Houses of worship of many faiths minister to visitors in Nassau. Check with your hotel for individual island churches.

Additional Information: For Nassau and Paradise Island ☎ 800-327-9019 or 305-931-1555, fax 305-931-3005. Write to The Bahamas Tourist Office, 19495 Biscayne Blvd., Suite 804, Aventura, FL 33180.

For Grand Bahama Island ☎ 242-352-8356 or fax 242-352-2714.

More about the Bahamas Out Islands resorts may be available through the Family Islands Promotion Board ☎ 800-OUT-ISLANDS (688-4752) or 954-359-8099, fax 954-359-8098. Website: www.bahama-out-islands.com

Barbados

Barbados, a tiny island just 21 miles long and 14 miles wide, sits 300 miles from Venezuela—the farthest east and the most isolated of the West Indian Islands.

Lush and beautiful, Barbados touts first-rate resorts, vibrant nightlife, duty free shopping and a well-rounded selection of water sports.

The best time to snorkel Barbados is between April and November when fabulous visibility on the barrier reef and calm seas exist. This changes during December through March when a "North Swell" decreases visibility near shore and on the outer reefs.

During spring, summer and fall, the island's shallow shipwrecks offer a variety of dive experiences. The best wrecks rest on the offshore barrier reef that extends along Barbado's western coast. Camouflaged by soft corals, sea fans, and sponges, the wrecks shelter thriving communities of fish and other marine animals.

Best Snorkeling Sites

☆☆☆ Wreck of the 150-ft **Pamir** was intentionally sunk in 30 ft of water to form an artificial reef. Its superstructure breaks the surface, making it perfect for snorkelers and snorkel-swimmers. Swarms of sergeant majors and butterfly fish inhabit the wreck.

If you don't mind a 200-yard swim, you can reach it from the beach. Although visibility varies, seas are usually calm. Dive operators request no spearfishing or collecting. Beach or boat access.

☆☆☆ **Folkestone Park,** the favorite beach-snorkeling site in Barbados, features an underwater trail around its inshore reef. The park, also a favorite area for boaters and jet skiers, has been roped off near the shore for swimmers to insure safety. Snorkel with or near a group and if you venture out be sure to tote a floating dive flag.

A 200-yd swim from the beach will take you to a raft anchored over the wreckage of a small barge sitting in 20 ft of water.

During winter when the North Swell rises, visibility can drop drastically for as long as two days. During the rest of the year, Folkestone is the number one snorkeling choice.

☆☆ The **Wreck of the Berwyn,** a 45-ft long, French tugboat that sunk in the early 1900s, sits at the bottom of Carlisle Bay, 200 yards off the island's southwest shore at 25 ft. Encrusted with plate corals, the wreck hosts sea horses, frogfish, wrasses, arrow crabs and other small creatures. It is a favored photo site with calm sea conditions.

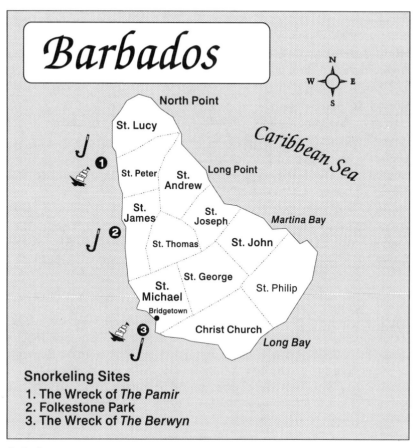

Barbados

North Point

St. Lucy

Caribbean Sea

St. Peter
St. Andrew
Long Point

St. James
St. Joseph
Martina Bay

St. Thomas
St. John

St. George

St. Michael
St. Philip

Bridgetown

Christ Church

Long Bay

Snorkeling Sites
1. The Wreck of *The Pamir*
2. Folkestone Park
3. The Wreck of *The Berwyn*

☆☆☆ **The Ce-Trek**, an old cement-constructed boat at a depth of 40 ft, has attracted hordes of fish and invertebrates since its sinking in 1986. She sits 300 yards off shore near the *Berwyn*.

Two nice spots for beginning snorkelers are **Mullins Beach** and **Paynes Bay**. Both offer calm waters and ample parking.

Snorkeling Tours & Rentals

Dive shops are located along the southwest shores.

Bubbles Galore Barbados Dive Shop at the Sandy Beach Island Resort, Worthing, Christ Church, offers snorkeling trips to Carlisle Bay. Friendly service. ☎ 246- 430-0354, fax 246-430-8806. E-mail: bubbles @caribsurf. com.

Underwater Barbados, a PADI five-star dive shop in Carlisle Bay Centre, visits all the best sites aboard a 31 ft pirogue boat. ☎ 246-426-0655, fax 246-426-0655. Write to: Michael Young, Underwater Barbados, Carlisle

Bay Centre, St. Michael, Barbados, W.I. Website: www.ndl.net/~uwb/. E-mail: myoung@ndl.net.

Hightide Watersports fields a new custom built, 30-ft dive boat, *Flyin' High*. This PADI shop offers snorkeling trips, equipment sales and rentals, video camera. Gear storage. ☎ 246-432-0931.

WestSide Scuba Centre, next door to The Sunset Crest Beach Club, Holetown, St. James, offers snorkeling tours. Free transportation to and from your hotel. ☎ and fax 246-432-2558.

Hazell's Water World Inc. in the Sandy Bank complex, Hastings, Christ Church sells a wide range of scuba and snorkeling equipment. ☎ 246-426-4043.

Reserve Sail-Snorkeling, sunset, lunch and dinner tours through **Jolly Roger Cruises**, Bridgetown. ☎ 436-6424, fax 429-8500, **Tiami Catamaran Sailing Cruises**, Bridgetown, ☎ 427-7245, fax 431-0538, **Secret Love**, ☎ 432-1972 or **Irish Mist** ☎ 436-9201. Mask and snorkel included.

Where to Stay

Most hotels and nightlife exist on the south and central western coast of the island. There are none with good snorkeling off the beach, but all will arrange for offshore tours. Several guest houses, cottages and apartments may be rented for $30 per night and up. A current list is available from the Barbados Board of Tourism. In the US ☎ 800-221-9831; In Canada ☎ 800-268-9122 or 416-512-6569, fax 416-512-6581. In Barbados ☎ 246-427-2623/4; fax 246-426-4080. Website: www. barbados.org

To book on the internet, go to the website, then hotels. Click on E-mail to book reservations with the hotel of your choice.

Almond Beach Club features 131 air conditioned guestrooms and suites with ocean or pool views. All inclusive rates include meals, drinks, snorkeling, fishing, windsurfing, kayaking. ☎ 800-4-ALMOND.

Grand Barbados Beach Resort is a luxury, beachfront resort with a dive shop on the premises. Located in Carlisle Bay, one mile from Bridgetown, the resort is just minutes from reef and wreck dives. ☎ 246-426-4000, fax 246-429-2400.

Coral Reef Club, a posh, beachfront resort with its own dive shop (Les Wooten's Watersports) sits on 12 acres of gardens adjacent to a superb, white sand beach. Guest activities include cruises on the club's 30-ft catamaran. ☎ 246-422-2372, fax 246-422-1776

Alleyne, Aguilar and Altman Ltd., St. James, offer crewed, luxury yacht charters. ☎ 246-432-0840, fax 246-432-2147.

Travel Tips:

Helpful Phone Numbers: Police ☎ 112; ambulance, ☎ 115.

Getting There: British West Indies Airlines (BWIA), ☎ 800-327-7401, offers regular service from London, Frankfurt, Stockholm, Zurich, New York, Miami, and Toronto. American Airlines, ☎ 800-433-7300, from New York. Air Jamaica from US. Air Canada and American airlines from Canada. Inter-island service: BWIA, LIAT, Carib Express and Air Martinique. Barbados' Grantley Adams International Airport is modern and well kept.

Island Transportation: Taxi service is available throughout the island. (Note: cab fares should be negotiated before accepting service) Local auto-rental companies are at the airport. **National** ☎ 246-426-0603, **P&S** ☎ 424-2907; **Corbins** ☎ 427-9531; **Drive-A-Matic** ☎ 422-3000; **Courtesy Rent A Car** ☎ 431-4160.

Driving: Traffic keeps to the left in Barbados.

Documents: Canadian and US citizens require a birth certificate with a current photo I.D. or passport and return ticket in order to enter Barbados. Entry documentation is good for three months.

Customs: Personal effects of visitors, including cameras and sports equipment, enter duty free. Returning US citizens may take back free of duty articles costing a total of US$600 providing the stay has exceeded 48 hours in length and that the exemption has not been used within the preceding 30 days. One quart of liquor per person (over 21 years) may be carried out duty free. Not more than 100 cigars and 200 cigarettes may be included.

Note: Cameras and dive equipment should be registered with Customs BEFORE you leave the US.

Currency: Barbados dollar (BD)= US$2.00.

Climate: Temperatures vary between 75 and 85 degrees F. Average rainfall is 59 inches.

Clothing Lightweight casual clothing is recommended. A jacket for men may be desirable for visiting nightclubs or dressy resort restaurants. Swim suits, bikinis and short shorts are not welcome in Bridgetown shops or banks.

Electricity: 110 AC, 50 cycles.

Time: Atlantic Standard (EST + 1 hr.)

Language: English with a local dialect.

Taxes: A 10% service charge is added to the bill at most hotels. A sales tax of 5% is also added to hotel and restaurant bills.

Religious Services: Anglican, Baptist, Catholic, Methodist, Moravian, Seventh Day Adventist, Jehovah's Witnesses.

For Additional Information: Barbados Board Of Tourism, 800 Second Ave.,NY, NY 10017, ☎ (800)-221-9831; in NY (212)-986-6510. In Florida, 150 Alhambra Circle, Suite 1270, Coral Gables, FL 33134. 305-442-7471, fax 305-567-2844. In Barbados: Harbour Road, Bridgetown, W.I. ☎ 246-427-2623/2624 or 800-744-6244, fax, 246-426-4080. Website: Http://barbados.org.

$\mathcal{B}$elize

Belize offers snorkelers access to the largest barrier reef in the western hemisphere and three beautiful atolls—Lighthouse Reef, the Turneffe Islands and Glovers Reef. Within the reef system are hundreds of uncharted islands.

Just 750 miles from Miami, Belize lies on the Caribbean coast of Central America between Guatemala and Mexico. Its 185-mile-long barrier reef parallels the shore from 10 to 30 miles out, with prime diving locations around the out islands.

Most snorkeling vacations center on Ambergris Caye, a bustling resort and fishing community and the largest of the out islands or "cayes." Its main town, San Pedro, lies a few hundred yards from the Hol Chan Marine Preserve, the northernmost point of the Barrier Reef and the jump-off point to Belize's smaller cayes and atolls. Ambergris can be reached in 20 minutes by air from Belize City or one hour, fifteen minutes by ferry (see end of chapter for transportation details). The northern portion of Ambergris is accessible by boat only, but plans for a road are under consideration.

An intriguing new place for snorkeling excursions is Placencia, a small fishing village 100 miles south of Belize City. There are some coral heads off the beaches, but a half-hour boat ride will bring you to Laughing Bird Caye, a small island surrounded by pristine reefs, and the remains of old wrecks. Several Spanish galleons went down in this area over the years and occasionally a gold piece washes up on the beach.

Visit Belize during the dry season, from February to May. Annual rainfall ranges from 170 inches in the south to 50 inches in the north. Heaviest rainfall is from September to January.

The climate is sub-tropical with constant, brisk winds from the Caribbean Sea. Summer highs are rarely above 95° F, winter lows seldom below 60° F. Bug repellent is always needed as mosquitoes and sand flies are a constant annoyance.

Note: Crocodiles are occassionally sighted off the atolls and inland swamps. Avoid swimming or snorkeling in areas where sightings are reported.

Best Snorkeling Sites of Belize

THE BARRIER REEF

☆☆☆ **Hol Chan Marine Preserve**, a five-square-mile reef area off the southern tip of Ambergris Caye, is characterized by a natural channel that attracts and shelters huge communities of marine animals. Maximum depth inside the reef is 30 ft with many shallower areas. Schools of tropicals line the walls with occasional glimpses of big turtles, green and spotted morays, six-ft stingrays, eagle rays, spotted dolphins and nurse sharks.

A constant flow of sea water through the cut promotes the growth of large barrel and basket sponges, sea fans, and beautiful outcroppings of staghorn and brain corals. Check tide charts before diving on your own, currents can be very strong in the channel at outgoing tides.

The inner reef, that area facing land, is shallow, with coral slopes that bottom out between 20 and 40 feet. Throngs of juvenile fish, barracuda, invertebrates, grouper, stingrays, conch, nurse shark and small critters ramble about its staghorn and elkhorn coral thickets.

The Atolls

Atolls are ring-shaped coral islands or island groups surrounding a lagoon. Belize's three—Lighthouse Reef, Glovers Reef and the Turneffe Islands are surrounded by miles of shallow reefs. The sheltered lagoons are dotted with pretty coral heads and are great for snorkeling. Visibility is excellent. Generally, the islands are primitive, remote and largely uninhabited, with the bulk of the population made up of free-roaming chickens, though each location has at least one dive resort.

☆☆☆☆ **The Turneffe Islands**, 35 miles from Belize City and beyond the barrier reef, encompass 32 low islands bordered with thick growths of mangroves. The lower portion of the chain forms a deep V shape with Cay Bokel at the southernmost point. Cay Bokel is where you'll find the Turneffe Island Lodge, a quaint resort offering dive and snorkeling services. West of the southern point are sheltered reefs at 15 to 30 ft depths with shallower areas. Along the reef are some old anchors overgrown with coral, a small, wooden wreck, the *Sayonara,* and a healthy fish population. Passing dolphins and rays are the big attraction as they upstage the reef's "blue collar workers"—cleaner shrimp, sea cucumbers, patrolling barracuda, defensive damsel fish, schooling yellowtail, grunts and coral crabs. Snorkeling is excellent, with outstanding water clarity, protected areas, and diverse marine life.

☆☆☆☆ **Lighthouse Reef**, 40 miles from Belize City, is the outermost of the offshore islands within the Belize cruising area. Its circular reef system features several islands and small cayes. Located on its southeast boundaries is a beautiful old lighthouse and Half Moon Caye Natural Monument, the first marine conservation area in Belize and a bird sanctuary for colonies of the red-footed boobie, frigate birds, ospreys, mangrove warblers and white-crowned pigeons.

Turtles frequent Belize reefs

Half Moon Caye Natural Monument features white-sand beaches with a dropoff on the north side and a shallow lagoon on the south end. A dock with a pierhead depth about six ft and an area for amphibious aircraft are on the north side of the island. Dive boats are required to anchor in designated areas to prevent reef damage. All boaters must register with the lighthouse keeper upon arrival. Co-ordinates of an approved anchorage for craft with a length less than 120 ft are 17° 12' 25" N 87° 33'11"W

The solar-powered lighthouse, situated on the tapering eastern side of Half Moon Caye, was first built in 1820. It was replaced in 1848 and reinforced by a steel-framed tower in 1931. A climb to the top offers a spectacular view.

Endangered loggerhead turtles and hawksbill turtles come ashore to lay their eggs on the sandy southern beaches.

To the north is the Lighthouse Reef Resort, an air-conditioned colony of English villas catering to divers and fishermen.

☆☆☆☆ South of the Turneffe Islands and Lighthouse Reef is the third and most remote atoll, **Glover's Reef**. It is a reef system formed by coral growing around the edges of a steep, limestone plateau. An almost continuous barrier reef encloses an 80-square-mile lagoon, an outstanding snorkeling spot, with over 700 coral heads. Visibility exceeds 100 ft. Grouper, queen trigger fish and parrot fish are in abundance. Spotted eagle rays and sea turtles are occasionally spotted on the reefs. It is a spectacular spot with more than 25 coral species to be explored and thousands of sheltered spots. Two resorts, Glovers Reef Resort and Manta Reef Resort, offer guides.

Where to Stay

Note: Direct dial service is available between Belize and the US and Canada. To call Belize, dial 011-501, drop the first zero from the local number, then dial the remaining numbers. E-mail may be used to book direct.

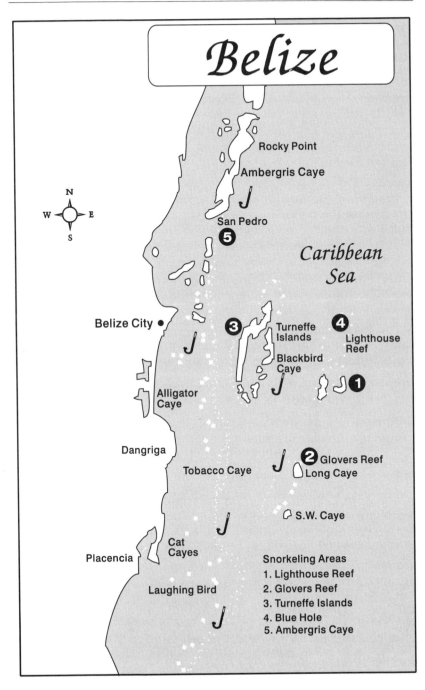

Belize

Rocky Point

Ambergris Caye

San Pedro

5

*Caribbean
Sea*

Belize City ●

3   Turneffe
Islands

4

Lighthouse
Reef

Blackbird
Caye

1

Alligator
Caye

Dangriga

Tobacco Caye

2 Glovers Reef
Long Caye

S.W. Caye

Cat
Cayes

Placencia

Laughing Bird

Snorkeling Areas
1. Lighthouse Reef
2. Glovers Reef
3. Turneffe Islands
4. Blue Hole
5. Ambergris Caye

N
W E
S

Ambergris Caye

There are flights between Belize City and San Pedro, the main town on Ambergris Cay, every 30 minutes from sunrise to sunset.

Ramon's Village in San Pedro offers 20 lovely, air-conditioned, thatched-roof bungalows with double beds and full baths. The resort has a nice poolside bar, saltwater pool, restaurant, and fully-equipped dive shop offering reef trips and basic rentals. ☎ 800-MAGIC 15 or 601-649-1990; fax (601) 425-2411; or write P.O. Drawer 4407, Laurel MS 39441. Website: www.ramons.com.

Vacation packages with air from the US also offered. Website: http://ecotravel.com/landfall; E-mail: lndfall@ aol. com.

Victoria House, on its own nine-acre beach, features 31 casually elegant rooms, suites, apartments and villas. An on-site PADI dive shop, restaurant and tour desk make this deluxe resort a popular spot coupled with the fact that the barrier reef lies ¾ of a mile directly in front of the hotel. ☎ 800-247-5159 or 504- 865-0717, fax 504-865-0718. Local 026-2067; fax 026-2429. Website: www.belize.com/victoria house.html. E-mail: victoria @bze.com or victoria@communique.net

Belize Yacht Club, within easy walking distance of San Pedro Town and restaurants, features modern, one- and two-bedroom suites with fully-equipped kitchens. Amenities include a freshwater pool, marina, bar, dive shop, fishing, snorkeling excursions. Book through Belize International Expeditions: ☎ 800-633-4734.

Caribbean Villas Hotel, ¾ mile from San Pedro, features 10 air conditioned, beachfront rooms. Nice pier and beach. Hot tubs, elevated perch for bird watching. ☎ 800-633-4734 or direct 011-501- 26-2715, fax 011-501-26-2885. E-mail: c-v-hotel@btl.net

Captain Morgan's Retreat, a thatched-hut village on the beach, features roomy cabanas with ceiling fans and solid mahogany floors. Modern baths. The resort, 3.5 miles north of San Pedro, is reached by water taxi. Snorkeling excursions. ☎ 800-447-2931 or 218-847-3012, fax 218-847-0334. E-mail: information@captainmorgans.com

Journey's End, an outstanding, beachfront hotel, sits just 500 yards from the Barrier Reef. This 50-acre resort is accessible by water taxi—10 minutes from the airstrip. Pampered guests stay in luxurious, beach cabanas, poolside villas, or waterfront rooms. All watersports are offered. ☎ 800-447-0474, 800-365-6232 or 281-996-7800, fax 281-996-1556.

Rocks Inn, on the beach in walking distance of San Pedro, offers attractive, air-conditioned suites. ☎501-26-2326, 501-26-2358. E-mail: rocks@ btl.net

Sunbreeze Beach Hotel, a 39-room, air-conditioned, beachfront hotel, teams up with Belize Undersea Adventures to offer accommodations and boat tours. Rooms have private bath, oceanviews, balconies, phone, color cable TV. ☎ 800-327-8150 or (954) 462-3400, fax (954) 462-4100. E-mail: nealwatson@aol.com or sunbreeze @btl.net. Website: www.twofin. com/twofin/belize.htm.

South Water Caye

Escape the masses on this private 18-acre island off Dangriga, 35 miles south of Belize City. Transfers from the mainland are by The Blue Marlin Lodge launch or by charter flight. By boat, the trip takes about 90 minutes. Driving from Belize City to Dangriga takes about 2 ½ hours, by air about 20 minutes.

The big plus for this pristine spot is easy beach snorkeling on the barrier reef that sits 120 feet offshore. Sounds like a short swim, but actually the water is so shallow between the shore and the drop off, that it's a short walk. Despite Belize's current trend towards marine conservation, spearfishing is allowed here.

The Blue Marlin Lodge, South Water Caye's sole resort, spreads over six acres. Catering primarily to divers and fisherman, the all-inclusive, rustic lodge features nine clean, modern rooms (each with two double beds) cooled by ceiling fans and three air-conditioned cottages on the water's edge. All rooms have a private bath with hot and cold running water. No phones and no TV in the rooms or cottages, but there is a phone in the office that guests may use, and the bar has one satellite TV and a VCR. Bring your own snorkeling gear.

Snorkel trips are aboard a fast Pro 42 dive boat or one of two 26-ft power boats. ☎ 800-798-1558, 011-501-52-2243 or 011-501-52-2296. E-mail for reservations: blue marlin @netrunner.net. E-mail to resort: marlin@btl.net. Website: www. belize net. com/marlin.html.

The Turneffe Islands

Turneffe Island Lodge accommodates guests in 12 air-conditioned, beachfront cottage rooms with private bath or in the main lodge. Cellular and fax service (No phones). American owned and operated, this delightful outpost lies approximately 30 miles from Belize City— a two-hour boat trip supplied by the lodge.

Outstanding snorkeling reefs lie about 350 yards off the resort beach. Get there by either paddling one of the resort's four sea kayaks, sailing a Sunfish or taking the skiff. Bring your own snorkeling gear. ☎ 800-874-0118, fax (770) 534-8290 Write to P.O. Box 2974, Gainesville, GA 30503. E-mail: info@turneffelodge.com. Website: www.turneffelodge.com.

Hotel/airfare packages from the US are offered through Landfall Productions ☎ 800-525-3833. E-mail lndfall@aol.com.

Blackbird Caye Resort, located 35 miles from Belize City within the Turneffe Reef Atoll on Blackbird Cay defines "ecotourist paradise." Unique and exciting with miles of deserted beaches and jungle trails, the island sits close to 70 impressive dive sites with depths from 10 ft. Reefs are spectacular with huge tube and barrel sponges, dramatic overhangs, large loggerhead turtles, dolphins, perfect coral formations. Lots of grouper and reef fish. Manatee sightings. Great snorkeling lies just 400 yards off the shore, a two-minute boat ride. Calm waters inside the reef make it a safe spot for novices. Morning and afternoon snorkeling excursions. Boat to the island departs from Ramada docks in Belize City. Travel time is four to five hours. Accommodations are in thatch-roofed cabanas with ceiling fans and private baths. ☎ 888-271-DIVE (3483) or 310-937-6470, fax 310-937-6473. E-mail: dive@blackbirdresort.com. Website: http://dive.blackbird resort. com

Lighthouse Reef

Lighthouse Reef Resort on Northern Cay, a private island at the northern end of the Lighthouse Reef Reserve, boasts a protected lagoon perfect for snorkelers of all ages.

The resort offers luxury air-conditioned rooms and villas. Tropic Air meets incoming flights at Belize International Airport to deliver guests to the resort's private airstrip. Flight time is 20 minutes. ☎ 800-423-3114. Write: P.O. Box 26, Belize City, C.A.

Glovers Reef

Manta Reef Resort, a 2½ hour boat trip from Belize City, sits on 12 palm-studded acres at the southern tip of Glovers Reef Atoll, conveniently perched over a deep coral wall with easy beach entry. Guests unwind in modern, though simple, mahogany cabanas with private baths and showers. A spacious waterside restaurant and bar decorated with hand-rubbed native woods, fast dive boats, an E6 photo lab and gift shop fill most snorkelers' vacation wishes. ☎ 800-326-1724; local, 011-501-232767, fax 011-501-234449. E-mail: dive@blackbirdresort.com. Website: http://dive.blackbird resort.com

Placencia

Placencia, a great spot for off-the-beaten-track adventures and for those on a low budget, offers pristine snorkeling around forty cayes between the mainland and the barrier reef. Placencia Village has guest rooms for as low as $20 per night. Affordable open air bars serve pizza, chili and Creole fish dishes. Camping is available at the Bonaventure Resort in Seine Bight Village. For complete listings contact the Belize Tourist Board ☎ 800-844-3688.

Rum Point Inn, three miles from Placencia Village comprises ten, seaside cabanas, a main house and a small sandy swimming beach. E-6 processing. Pro-42 "Auriga" dive boat. ☎ 800-747-1381 or 011-501-6-23239, fax 011-501-6-23240,Or book through International Expeditions ☎ 800-633-4734 or 205-428-1700. E-mail: 76735@ compuserve.com.

Turtle Inn, a mile north of Placencia Village, offers six thatch-roofed cabanas along 500 feet of Caribbean beach front. Cabanas have private baths, solar generated lighting and kerosene lanterns. Guests are offered a number of snorkeling and jungle trips. Book through International Expeditions ☎800-633-4734 or 205-428-1700. E-mail: 76735@compuserve.com.

Nautical Inn, the newest resort on the Placencia peninsula in Sein Bight Village, features beachfront rooms with private baths, the Oar House Restaurant, transfers from Placencia airstrip, a gift shop, salon, scooter rentals, canoeing, scuba, snorkeling and jungle tours. ☎ 800-225-6732 or 011-501-6-22310. E-mail: seaexplore-belize@worldnet.att.net.

Singing Sands Inn, features private, individual, thatch-roofed cabanas, modern on the inside with private bathrooms. Excursions for diving, snorkeling and day-trip visits to Maya ruins and the Cockscomb Jaguar Preserve are offered. Book through International Expeditions ☎800-633-4734 or 205-428-1700. E-mail: 76735@compuserve.com.

Soulshine Resort tours take off to Laughing Bird Caye, Ranguana Caye and Little Caye. This small dive resort offers clean accommodations and low rates. ☎ 800-890-767-7914. Website: www. soul shine.com.

The Placencia Dive Shop, offers friendly service and interesting snorkeling trips such as their Creole-seafood-feast-and-snorkel-trip to nearby French Louis Cay. ☎ 501-62-3313 or 501-62-3227, fax 501-62-3226.

Tours

The following tour companies offer expeditions to Belize. There are pre-planned packages for groups and individuals or design your own and they will make all the arrangements. Most Belize tours from the US depart Houston or Miami. Package rates for week- long trips are usually much lower than buying air, accommodations, diving, meals and transfers separately.

American Canadian Caribbean Line Inc. features luxurious, small ship cruises from Ambergris Cay, Belize to the Rio Dulce, Guatemala and cays between. They stop for snorkeling at the best spots. ☎ 800-556-7450.

Landfall Productions, a dive-travel specialist, features well-planned, money-saving vacations from the US, including transfers, and accommodations. Call for group rates. ☎ 800-525-3833, fax 510-794-1617. E-mail: lndfall@ aol.com.

ICS Travel books cruise-ship vacations to various Caribbean and exotic locations, including ships that offer snorkeling and diving. 800-722-0205 or 516-797-2132. E-mail: The ICSGang@aol.com.

International Expeditions Inc. has custom-guided trips for the naturalist. Tours are well organized to consider both skilled diver and novice snorkeler. ☎ 800-633-4734 or 205-428-1700; write to Number One Environs Park, Helena AL 35080.

Oceanic Society Expeditions offers guided, small-yacht tours to Belize that combine a mainland tour of the Mayan ruins. ☎ 800-326-7491 or 415-441-1106.

CEDAM (Conservation, Ecology, Diving, Archaeology, Museums) is a non-profit organization that offers scientific expeditions. ☎ 914-271-5365 or fax 914-271-4723. Write to 1 Fox Road, Croton, NY 10520.

Ocean Connection offers snorkeling, fishing and diving trips with a choice of islands and hotels. Beach & jungle treks, Mayan ruins & Belize national park tours are their specialty. Budget rates. Combination tours with Mexico are possible. ☎ 800-934-6232 or 713-996-7800; fax 713-996-1556; or write 211 E. Parkwood #108, Friendswood, TX 77546.

Magnum's Belize features packages to Ambergris Caye, Placencia, Corozal, Caye Caulker and Lighthouse Reef. ☎ 800-447-2931; write to 718 Washington Ave., Detroit Lakes, MN 56502. Website: www. magnum belize.com/Dive.html.

Travel Tips

Helpful Phone Numbers: Police and ambulance, *Belize City:* ☎ 90; *San Pedro:* ☎ 02-82095; *Placencia:* ☎ 06-23129. 911 works in some several areas. Hospital, *Belize City:* ☎ 02-77251 or 90. Tourist board: ☎ 800-422-3435 or (501) 26-2012, fax 011-501-26-2338. Coast Guard: ☎ 02-35312. Philip S.W. Goldson International Airport ☎ 02-52014. Maya Airways: ☎ 2-44032/45968/44234 Service throughout Belize.

Health: Anti-malaria tablets are recommended for stays in the jungle.

Airlines: Scheduled commercial service from the US and Canada is by American Airlines (☎ 800-433-7300), Continental, and TACA. Tropic Air flies from Cancun, Mexico. ☎ 800-422-3435 or (501) 26-2012, fax 011-501-26-2338. In Belize, Tropic Air (☎ 2302, In San Pedro 2012 or 2439) services major cities Ambergris Caye and the out-islands. Additional Belize cities are served by Island Air (☎ 2219 or 2435) or Maya Airways (☎ 2336 In San Pedro 2515).

Private Aircraft may enter Belize only through the Phillip Goldson International Airport in Belize City. Belizean airspace is open during daylight hours. Pilots are required to file a flight plan and will be briefed on local conditions. Landing fee for all aircraft.

By Car: Belize can reached from the US and Canada via Mexico though reports of hold-ups on the roads deter most motorists. You must possess a valid drivers license and registration papers for the vehicle. A temporary permit will enable use of your vehicle without payment of customs. A temporary insurance policy must be purchased at the frontier to cover the length of stay in Belize. After three days, visitors must obtain a Belize driving permit; for which they need to complete a medical form, provide two recent photos and pay $20.

Private Boats must report to the police or immigration immediately. No permits are required. Boaters need documents of the vessel, clearance from last port of call, four copies of the crew and passenger manifest and list of stores and cargo.

Documents: Visitors are permitted to stay up to one month, provided they have a valid passport and have a ticket to their onward destination. For stays longer than 30 days, an extension must be obtained from the Immigration Office, 115 Barrack Road, Belize City.

Transportation: Bus service around Belize City is readily available via Batty Brothers ☎ 02-72025; or Z-Line ☎ 02-73937/06-22211. Since few cars are available on the islands, transportation is usually arranged by the resort. On the mainland reservations can be made through National (☎ 800 CAR-RENT, In Belize: 2-31650 or Budget ☎ 800-927-0700, In Belize: ☎ 2-32435 or 33986). Reserve prior to trip. Jeeps and four wheel drive vehicles are mandatory on back roads. Avoid local car rental companies or carefully check vehicles for scratches or dents and have them documented by the renter beforehand.

Ferries: Ambergris Caye can be reached by ferry boat from Belize City. The **Andrea I and Andrea II** operate from Belize City to San Pedro leaving the docks of the Bellevue Hotel at 4 pm from Mon to Fri and 1 pm on Sat, returning to Belize at 7 am. Also available to San Pedro is the **Miss Belize** which runs daily. Tickets may be purchased from the Universal Travel Agency in Belize City. *Miss Belize* departs from the docks behind the Supreme Court building. Travel time to San Pedro is one hour and 15 minutes. US$10 one way.

Departure Tax: US$10.

Customs: Personal effects can be brought in without difficulty, but it is best to register cameras, videos and electronic gear with customs before leaving home. American citizens can bring home $400 worth of duty-free goods after a 48-hour visit. Over that purchases are dutied at 10%. Import allowances include 200 cigarettes or ½lb. tobacco; 20 fluid oz alcoholic beverage and one bottle of perfume for personal use. Note: removing and exporting coral or archaeological artifacts is prohibited. Picking orchids in forest reserves is illegal.

Currency: Belize dollar = US50¢.

Climate: Belize has a sub-tropical, humid climate. Average temperature 79 deg F. The rainy season is from April to December. Hurricanes form during late summer. Best time to visit is February through May though summer diving when weather permits (mid-August) often brings calm seas and excellent visibility.

Clothing: Lightweight clothing with long sleeves to protect against sunburn and a light sweater for evening wear. The dive resorts are extremely casual. Leave dress wear at home. Those who want to combine an expedition into the jungle with their diving vacation should check with the tour company. Bring mosquito repellent.

Gear: Divers' rental equipment is limited in Belize so be sure to bring all of your own personal equipment. The resorts do supply weights and tanks, but little else.

Electricity: 110/220V 60 cycles. Most island resorts run on generators, which are out of service for at least part of the day. Air conditioning is limited on the out islands.

Time: Central Standard Time.

Language: English

Additional Information: Belize Tourist Board, 421 Seventh Ave, New York, NY 10001; ☎ 800-624-0686/ 800-563-6011, fax: 800-563-6033. In Belize, 83 North Front St, P.O. Box 325, Belize City, Belize, C.A. Website: www.belize.com.

$\mathcal{B}ermuda$

Lying hundreds of miles from anywhere, or more precisely 650 miles off the coast of North Carolina, Bermuda is noted for its delightful powder-soft beaches, secluded coves and lush vegetation. Considered one island, it is actually more than 150 islands surrounded by one of the largest fringing reef systems in the world where three centuries of shipwrecks lie at rest.

The best time to visit Bermuda is from June through October. During this period the Gulf Stream moves close to shore and air and water temperatures reach as high as 85°. During the winter the main flow of this warm water moves away from Bermuda, causing local air temperatures to drop as low as 55°.

Shipwrecks

The Government officially acknowledges the existence of as many as 400 shipwrecks, though local historian and author Robert Marx notes that there are at least 1500 shipwrecks and possibly 2000 in Bermuda waters based on original photographs of ships that sank in the past 100 years or so and drawings of older ships or their sister ships. Local divers agree that figure may not be an exaggeration. Some of the older and more historically important wrecks are protected sites, off limits to snorkeling or scuba-equipped explorers.

Best Snorkeling Sites

Beach-Entry Sites

☆☆ **The Snorkel Park** at The Royal Naval Dockyard (fort) is adjacent to the Maritime Museum, a short walk from the cruise ship dock, ferry and bus stops. It open daily from 10:30am to 6pm.

The park, a protected coral reef preserve, has well marked reef trails, floating rest stations and a helpful staff, including experienced life guards. Depths are shallow and the seas calm. Bottom terrain consists of plate corals and gorgonians. Schools of grunts, doctor fish and parrot fish roam about. Several historic cannons dating back to the 1500s are marked off. Look along the base of the fort for ceramic shards, musket miniballs and insulators dating from the fort's use as a radio station in WWII.

Rental equipment is available on site, including flotation vests, masks and snorkels. ☎ 234-1006, fax 441-292-5193. E-mail: bic@ibl.bm

☆☆☆ The reef at **Elbow Beach** starts 10 yards from the shoreline then stretches seaward for a mile. If you are not staying at the Elbow Beach Hotel, be sure to enter the water from the public beach to the west of the resort and swim east towards the restaurant. Marine life is quite good with swarms of squirrelfish, parrotfish, grunts and critters. Further out, tarpon and horse-eyed jacks roam the cuts and ledges in the reef. A rocky bottom terrain supports encrusting corals and sponges. Visibility averages 60 ft.

A 300-yard swim from Elbow Beach seaward takes you over the wreck of the **Pollockshields**, a 323-ft German built steamer, originally called the *Herodot* that was captured by the English in World War I. While carrying ammunition and provisions for WWI, the ship hit heavy fog and ran aground during a hurricane on September 7, 1915. Many of the ship's shell casings are embedded in the reef. Some are considered unstable and are best left untouched.

The easiest route to the wreck runs along a break in the reef line that starts directly in front of the Surf Club Restaurant. The swim out takes about 10 to 15 minutes. A strong surge makes this a bad choice on windy or choppy days. For advanced snorkelers only.

☆☆☆ **Church Bay**, a terrific spot when seas are calm, may be entered anywhere along the beach. A shallow reef that parallels the shoreline acts as a barrier to most wind- and storm-driven waves. Armies of fish and invertebrates inhabit the reef's nooks and crannies. Soft and hard corals abound. Park along the road above the beach and climb down the steep stairway.

☆☆☆ **John Smith's Bay**, on the beautiful south shore, is handicapped accessible and has a lifeguard from April through October. A 50-yard swim brings you over a shallow reef, alive with midnight parrotfish, grunts, goatfish, squirrelfish, rock beauties, surgeonfish and lobster. The reef's caves and tunnels, easily seen from the surface, shelter small fish, crabs and shrimp. Usually calm with exceptional visibility.

Small caves at one end of the beach provide shelter for people who enjoy the view but not the sun. A mobile vendor offering food and drink frequents the picnic area.

☆☆ **Tobacco Bay's** grassy subsea terrain shelters soft corals, eels, sea horses, crabs, octopi, and schools of juvenile fish. A rocky breakwater separating the bay from the ocean keeps this area calm. Depths run from 3 to 10 ft. Most interest is along the shoreline. Beach access.

In season, the beach shack rents snorkeling gear and sells snacks and beverages . To reach this site take Duke of Kent Street from St. Georges till you reach the sea.

☆☆ Rocky outcrops and ledges make **Warwick Long Bay** tricky to enter and tricky to snorkel without getting scraped by the rocks, but visibility and fish life are excellent and make it worth a try for advanced snorkelers. Neighboring **Jobson's Cove** is an easier, though narrow, entrance. Expect some wave action. Beach access.

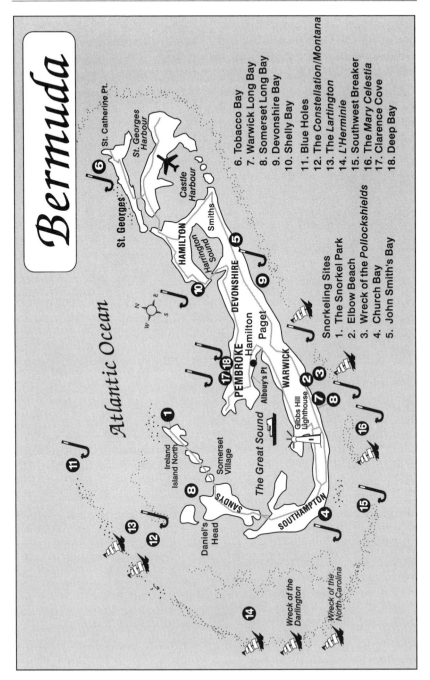

Bermuda

Atlantic Ocean

St. Georges

St. Catherine Pt.

St. Georges Harbour

Castle Harbour

HAMILTON

Harrington Sound

Smiths

DEVONSHIRE

Hamilton

Paget

PEMBROKE

Albouy's Pt.

WARWICK

Gibbs Hill Lighthouse

The Great Sound

Ireland Island North

Somerset Village

SANDYS

Daniel's Head

SOUTHAMPTON

Wreck of the Darlington

Wreck of the North Carolina

6. Tobacco Bay
7. Warwick Long Bay
8. Somerset Long Bay
9. Devonshire Bay
10. Shelly Bay
11. Blue Holes
12. The Constellation/Montana
13. The Lartington
14. L'Herminie
15. Southwest Breaker
16. The Mary Celestia
17. Clarence Cove
18. Deep Bay

Snorkeling Sites

1. The Snorkel Park
2. Elbow Beach
3. Wreck of the Pollockshields
4. Church Bay
5. John Smith's Bay

☆**Somerset Long Bay** on Bermuda's southwest end, appeals to first time snorkelers with calm, shallow water and a wealth of marine life. Expect rocks, grass and good visibility. Nice spot for a picnic.

The rocks encircling **Devonshire Bay**, on the south shore, harbor a wealth of fish and invertebrates. Bigger fish hang out in the rocks along mouth of the bay.

☆ On a calm day, **Shelly Bay**, on the north shore, features easy access and impressive marine life. Swim out 50 yards to the reef where you'll find a good variety of fish, including peacock flounder, octopi, and parrotfish. Avoid this spot on windy day unless you want to go board sailing. The long beach, shallow water and recently renovated park—complete with jungle gym, slides and swings make it a good choice for children. The parking lot and surrounding area are accessible to people with disabilities.

Offshore Snorkeling Sites

More dramatic reef structures and shipwrecks lie offshore. Several tour companies offer boat trips and instruction on ocean snorkeling.

☆☆☆ **The Blue Holes**, seven miles offshore north of Somerset, are deep sand pockets that drop straight down into an iridescent teal blue, reaching a maximum depth of nearly 60 ft. The surrounding shallow reef, between three and six ft depths, displays vibrant sea fans, soft corals and black coral bushes. An occasional enormous (150-200 lb.) black grouper storms by. Prolific fish life, lobsters and invertebrates.

☆☆☆☆ *The Constellation/Montana*. Located a few miles off the northwestern coast of Bermuda, these two ships sank on exactly the same site, although 80 years apart. The *Montana,* also known as the *Nola, Gloria* and *Paramount*, was an English paddle wheel steamer that was on her maiden voyage as a Confederate Blockade runner during the American Civil War. She was a sleek vessel, 236 ft. in length, with a beam of 25 ft. Her steam engines and twin paddle wheels were capable of turning 260 hp. She ground to a halt in shallow reefs some five and one-half miles from the west end of Bermuda on December 30, 1863. As she was an iron-hulled ship, a great deal of her hull and boilers are remarkably intact and make for an excellent dive. Numerous reef fish and some rather large barracuda make the *Montana* their home.

Literally overlapping the *Montana* are the remains of the *Constellation*. This four-masted, 192-ft., wooden-hulled schooner sank on the Bermuda reefs enroute from New York to Venezuela on July 31, 1943. Hers was a general 2,000 ton cargo, but on her deck she carried 700 cases of Scotch whiskey, an assortment of drugs and hundreds of bags of cement which, when washed with seawater, solidified into concrete and so remains.

Used as a cargo vessel during World War II, the wreck is often referred to as the "Woolworth" or "Dime Store Wreck" because of the wide variety of artifacts that have been recovered, including red glass, cut glass, china, glasses, tea and coffee cups and saucers, tickets to Coney Island (in Spanish), Yo Yo's, 78 rpm records by RCA (with labels in Spanish), cases of pistachio nuts, parts for radios, radios, religious artifacts, devotion altars of pewter, crucifixes, cosmetic supplies by Mennen and Elizabeth Arden, cold cream, Vaseline, pharmaceutical products, including at least eight different types of drug ampules, which provided Peter Benchley with the premise for the movie, *The Deep.* When seas are calm, this is a very enjoyable snorkeling spot. The site lies about five miles offshore and is recommended for ocean-experienced snorkelers. Areas of the reef are as shallow as eight ft. Sea conditions vary with the wind direction and speed.

☆☆☆☆ *The Lartington,* listed on the Bermuda wreck chart as an unidentified 19th-century wreck, was often referred to as the *Nola,* until one of Blue Water Divers' guides discovered her name under the port side of the partially intact bow. After writing to Harland & Wolf, a builder of this type of vessel during the 1800's, we learned that this sort of ship, a sailing steamer, was very common in the late 1800's. She gave rise to the expression, "tramp steamer," because every time the coal burning engines were fired up, she belched out a cloud of coal dust, liberally coating everything and everyone aboard with black soot. Then everyone resembled railroad hoboes, or tramps, and the name stuck.

When visibility is good, the *Lartington's* saturation steam boilers are visible amidships and, at the stern, the drive shaft and propeller. The steering controls located on the fantail are now well encrusted with over 100 years of coral growth. The bow, partially destroyed, lies a few feet above the 30-ft.-deep sand bottom. The surrounding reef is honeycombed with small caves and some tunnels. Many places come to within 10 ft. of the surface. The entire length of the wreck is visible from the surface, although it's too long to explore in its entirety on one snorkeling trip. Sea conditions vary with the wind.

☆☆☆ **L'Herminie** sank on a flat calm day in 1838. This huge French ship was lumbering along in the doldrums with her crew of 495 returning to France after seeing action against Maxmillian in Mexico. She ground to a halt on the very shallow flats of Bermuda's western ledge. The reef in this area is bland, visibility is rarely in excess of 60 to 80 ft., and the water has a greenish tone, but it is an exciting dive with 40 cannons, easily visible from the surface. The wreck rests at 30 ft.

☆☆☆ **Southwest Breaker,** a massive breaking reef, has caused at least one wreck along Bermuda's south shore. The reef rises from a 30-ft. bottom and actually protrudes through the surface, casting up considerable white water even on the calmest days. Through the center of the breaker is a massive tunnel, actually large enough to drive a boat through. The tunnel is often occupied by one or two black grouper and a resident barracuda who is none too shy of photographers. In early summer, clouds of fry or glass eye minnow now feed in the nutrient rich and oxygenated waters here. They draw others and then more still until the breaker is home to more fish than you can count. The surrounding reef is very colorful and appears quite lush with many smaller non-breaking heads known locally as "blindbreakers". These are carved with numerous ledges and caves. This area is excellent for experienced ocean snorkelers and is particularly interesting to photograph. Expect to encounter surface swells.

☆☆☆ The **Mary Celestia**, after making at least five round trips to Wilmington, NC, successfully running the Northern blockade of Confederate ports, ran aground on the "Blind Breakers" and sank on September 13, 1846, only nine months after her sister ship, the *Montana* was wrecked on the northern reefs. The story, as reported in the *Royal Gazette* a week later, states that her captain, knowing the waters of Bermuda, warned the navigator of the breakers. The navigator remarked with a certain surety, "I know these waters like I know my own house!" He apparently hadn't spent much time at home, for within minutes the *Mary Celestia* struck bottom. She was towed off the reef the next morning and reportedly sank within ten minutes, the seas rushing in through a great hole torn in her underside.

Today, the *Mary* sits quietly in just shy of 60 ft. of water as if she were still steaming along. More than 120 years' accumulation of sand covers most of her hull, but her two rectangular steam boilers and engine machinery are visible from the surface. One of her paddle wheels stands upright, with the other lying on its back next to the boilers. The entire wreck is surrounded by a high reef, honeycombed with caverns, canyons and cuts that open onto the sand bottom. Her anchor lies in 30 ft. of water. Schools of very large parrotfish are common. The reef surrounding the wreck starts at 15 ft. and drops off to 60 ft. Expect surface swells.

Snorkeling Tours & Rentals

Snorkeling cruises cost from $25 for a short tour to $45 for a half day.

Blue Water Divers and Watersports offers a Guided Snorkel Cerfificate Program for all ages and abilities. They teach mask defogging, clearing and adjustment, removing and replacing the mask on the surface. swimming in waves and surf, surface exit and entry techniques, surface breathing, basic knowledge of marine life, clearing the snorkel, submerging, exploring, resurfacing and regaining position, use of a snorkel vest, first aid, clearing the snorkel, free dive techniques, use of weight belt, fish and coral identifying. ☎441-234-1034, fax 234-3561. E-mail: bwdivers@ibl.bm Website: www. divebermuda.com

Bermuda Barefoot Cruises Ltd. departs Darrell's Wharf, Devonshire for snorkeling and sightseeing aboard the 32-ft *Minnow*. Equipment and instruction provided. Complimentary refreshment on return trip. ☎ 441-236-3498.

M.V. Bermuda Longtail Party Boat operates a 65-ft motor catamaran that carries 200 people. Tours depart Flag Pole, Front Street, Hamilton. Snacks and drinks sold on board. ☎ 292-0282, fax 441-295-6459.

Bermuda Water Tours offers both glass-bottom and snorkeling cruises aboard the 50-ft, 75-passenger *Bottom Peeper*. Tours depart near the Ferry Terminal, Hamilton. Gear provided. Full bar and changing facilities on board. Refreshments on return trip. Operates from the end of April 1 to November 30. ☎ 236-1500, fax 441-292-0801.

Bermuda Water Sports, departs St. Georges for half-day snorkel cruises aboard the 100-passenger, glass-bottom boat, *Sun Deck Too*. Anchors in shallow, waist high water on an island beach. Guides feed and identify fish and corals. Instruction and equipment provided. Full bar and snack bar on board. May to November. ☎ 293-2640 or 441-293-8333 ext. 1938.

Fantasea Diving and Snorkeling, on Darrell's Wharf on the Warwick Ferry Route, takes snorkelers with scuba divers to the favorite wrecks and reefs. ☎ 236-6339, fax 441-236-8926, 888-DO-A-DIVE. E-mail: fantasea @ibl.bm Website: www.bermuda.com/scuba

Hayward's Cruises' 54-ft, 35-passenger, snorkeling and glass-bottom boat, *Explorer* departs next to the Ferry Terminal in Hamilton. Bring swim suit and towels. Snorkeling gear provided. Instruction. Changing facilities on board. Cameras available for rent. Complimentary swizzle on return trip. May to November. ☎ 292-8652.

Jessie James Cruises aboard the 57 ft., 40-passenger *Rambler* and 48-ft, 75-passenger *Consort* depart Albouy's Point, Hamilton. Pick-ups at Darrell's and Belmont wharves. ☎ 441-236-4804, fax 236-9208.

Pitman Boat Tours' snorkeling and glass-bottom boat trip departs Somerset Bridge Hotel dock and cruises five miles northwest to the perimeter reef. Snorkeling instruction on ancient shipwrecks and coral reefs. Gear supplied. Changing facilities on board. No children under 5 years. ☎ 441-234-0700.

Salt Kettle Boat Rentals Ltd., Salt Kettle, Paget, offers snorkeling cruises to the western barrier reef and shipwrecks. Refreshments. ☎ 441-236-4863 or 441-236-3612, fax 441-236-2427.

Sand Dollar Cruises are aboard the 40-ft, 189-passenger, Bristol Sloop *Sand Dollar*, departing Marriott's Castle Harbour dock, Hamilton. Gear provided. This boat may be chartered. ☎ 236-1967 or 234-8218.

Daniels Head, off Bermuda's northwest coast.

Nautilus Diving Ltd., at the Southampton Princess Hotel, offers morning and afternoon reef and wreck tours. All equipment provided. Snorkeling is from a 40-ft. boat to reefs within 10 minutes of shore. Group charters available. ☎ 441-238-2332 or 441-238-8000 ext. 6073.

Tobacco Bay Beach House on Tobacco Bay, St. George's. Snorkeling and underwater cameras for rent. Ideal for beginners. ☎ 441-293-9711.

Helmet Diving is fun for all ages. No lessons needed. Depth 10 to 14 ft.. Does not get your hair wet. Available at **Hartley's Helmet**, Flatt's Village Smith's, ☎ 441-292-4434, or **Greg Hartley's Under Sea Adventure**, Village Inn dock, Somerset. ☎ 234-2861.

Sailing Yachts

The following may also be chartered for private groups. Most require reservations. Three-hour cruises rates start at about $38 per person. All offer complimentary snorkeling gear.

Allegro Charters 32-ft , eight-passenger *Allegro* departs Barr's Bay Park ☎ 441-295-4074, fax 441-295-1314.

Bermuda Caribbean Yacht Charter's 52-ft ketch, *Night Wind* carries 25 people. Departs Waterlot Inn. ☎ 441-238-8578.

Golden Rule Cruise Charters's 60-ft, 35 passenger schooner, *Golden Rule*, departs King's Steps, Dockyard and Darrell's Wharf. ☎ 441-238-1962.

Harbour Island Cruises" 50-ft ketch *Sundancer* carries 24 passengers. Departs Albuoy's Point.

Longtail Cruises offers snorkeling tours aboard the *Longtail of Hinson's*, a 40-ft, 10-passenger Cheoy Lee ketch. Departs Darrell's Wharf or hotel docks in Hamilton harbour. ☎ 441-236-4482, fax 236-7393.

Sail Bermuda Yacht Charters carries 15 people on their 40-ft ketch *Alibi*. Departs Albouy Point and the hotel docks in Hamilton Harbour. ☎ 441-234-9279, fax 441-232-2644.

Where to Stay

Accommodations range from ultra-luxurious resorts to inexpensive housekeeping cottages. A complete list is available by calling 800-223-6106 (US), 416-923-9600 (Canada) or 071-734-8813 (England). Following is a sampling of hotels popular with snorkelers.

Southampton Princess Hotel features a three-acre lagoon in East Whale Bay that houses several friendly dolphins. The lagoon opens to the sea and has an underwater fence. Marine mammal specialists offer several interactive "Dolphin quest" programs for children and adults. Southampton guests get priority bookings, but non-guests may sign up on a space available basis.

The resort sits on one of the highest points in Bermuda with panoramic views from all rooms. Air conditioned. Nautilus Diving on premises. ☎ 800-223-1818 (US) or 441-238-8000, 800-268-7176 (CDA), fax 441-238-8968. Write to P.O. Box HM 1379, Hamilton HM FX, Bermuda.

The Reefs sits on a cliff overlooking Christian Bay, Southampton. This hotel features snorkeling off the adjacent sand beach. ☎ 800-742-2008, fax 441-238-8372. Write, South Road, Southampton SN 02, Bermuda. E-mail: reefbda@ibl.bn

Sonesta Beach Hotel & Spa is a modern luxury resort hotel with 25 acres of picturesque grounds. Dive shop on premises. ☎ 441-238-8122 or 800-SONESTA (US), fax 441-238-8463. Write to P.O. Box HM 1070, Hamilton HM EX, Bermuda.

Grotto Bay Beach Hotel & Tennis Club sits on 21 acres of beachfront gardens in Hamilton Parish. Dive shop on premises. A private beach features two small coves in an enclosed bay. Deep water dock. All rooms have private balconies and panoramic sea views. Air conditioned. ☎ 800-582-3190 (US) or 441-293-8333, fax 441-293-2306. Write to 11 Blue Hole Hill, Hamilton Parish CR 04, Bermuda.

Travel Tips

Getting There. Daily direct flights leave from most US east coast gateway cities aboard American (800-433-7300), Continental, USAir, Air Canada, or British Airways.

Island Transportation. There are no rental cars available to visitors. Taxis, pink buses, ferries, bicycles or mopeds offer a variety of transportation methods. Traffic is on the left side of the roads at a speed limit of only 20 mph. Moped drivers must be

Bermuda shipwreck

at least 16 years of age and wear safety helmets. **Documents.** Passport are the preferred document to enter Bermuda. Visitors from the United States are required to have one of the following: a passport, or a birth certificate with a raised seal and photo ID. Canadians need either a valid Canadian passport, a Canadian certificate of citizenship, proof of their landed immigrant status or a birth certificate with photo ID.

Currency. Legal tender is the Bermuda dollar which is equal to $1 US. Travelers' checks and major credit cards accepted in most establishments.

Climate. Bermuda is a semi-tropical island. Rainfall is distributed evenly throughout the year. Average temperature during the period April to November is in the mid 70's to mid 80's. Cool months: December-March, 65-70° F.

Clothing. Conservative. Bathing suits, abbreviated tops and short shorts are not acceptable except at beaches and pools. In public, beach wear must be covered. Casual sportswear is acceptable in restaurants at lunch time but many restaurants require gentlemen to wear a jacket and tie in the evenings. **Electricity.** 110 volts, 60 cycles A.C. throughout the island.

Time. Atlantic Standard (Eastern standard + 1 hr.)

Tax. A 7.25% hotel occupancy tax is payable upon checkout. Airport departure tax, $20.

For Additional Information. *US*, Suite 201, 310 Madison Avenue, New York, NY 10017, ☎ 800-223-6106. ☎ 416-923-9600. *United Kingdom,* Bermuda Tourism, BCB Ltd., 1 Battersea Church Road, London SW11 3LY, England. ☎ 071-734- 8813.

Bonaire

Bonaire, located 50 miles off the northern coast of Venezuela, is a mountain in the sea surrounded by dense coral reefs that grow to its shoreline. With only 22 inches of rain annually, there is no freshwater run-off, which insures good visibility, often exceeding 70 feet. Excellent snorkeling exists off all the south coast beaches, which are sheltered from high winds and waves.

Dependably dry weather and calm seas prevail most of the year, though changing global weather patterns bring an occasional storm, windshift and water temperature drop during mid winter.

Bright yellow painted rocks along the coast road mark the dive sites, most of which can be explored from the beach.

Bonaire Marine Park

In 1979, the Netherlands Antilles National Parks Foundation (STINAPA) received a grant from the World Wildlife Fund for the creation of the Bonaire Marine Park. The park was created to maintain the coral reef ecosystem and ensure continuing returns from diving, fishing and other recreational activities.

The park incorporates the entire coastline of Bonaire and neighboring Klein Bonaire. It is defined as the "sea bottom and the overlying waters from the high-water tidemark down to 200 ft (60 m)."

All visitors are asked to respect the marine park rules—no sitting on corals; no fishing or collecting of fish while scuba diving; no collecting of shells or corals, dead or alive. Spearfishing is forbidden. Anchoring is not permitted except in the harbor area off town (from the yacht club to the new pier). All craft must use permanent moorings, except for emergency anchoring. Boats of less than 12 ft may use a stone anchor.

Popular dive sites are periodically shut down to rejuvenate the corals. Moorings are removed and placed on different sites.

Bonaire's Best Snorkeling Sites

Hotels and dive shops offer daily trips to nearby offshore sites. Most are less than a 10-minute boat ride, but you don't need a boat or even a mask to see Bonaire's reefs. They grow to the surface in many areas and are visible from the shore. Excellent beach dives exist along the shores on the leeward side where channels have been cut allowing access to deeper water. These reefs slope down to a narrow ledge at 30 ft. then drop off to great depth.

Expect to pay a $10 "annual" fee for using the marine park. Most of the resorts and dive shops offer guided snorkeling trips.

☆☆☆☆ To reach **Red Slave** drive south from Kralendijk, past the Solar Salt Works beyond the second set of slave huts. Strong currents and surf limit this site to experienced open-water divers.

The size and number of fish at Red Slave is spectacular. It is not unusual to spot four-foot tiger, yellowfin, or Nassau groupers. Gorgonians, orange crinoids, and black corals are found on the southern slope. Artifacts from pre-lighthouse wrecks rest on the slope, such as anchors and ballast stones from the 1829 shipwreck *H.M.S. Barham.*

☆☆☆☆ **Salt City** is a boat or shore dive located at the southern end of the island where you'll spot mountains of glistening white salt. To reach it, drive south from Kralendijk past the salt loading pier (very visible). You'll spot a large buoy south of the pier. Enter along the left "bank" formed by the large "sand river," a wide, sand stretch which eventually drops off the shallow terrace into a short, reef slope "island."

The terrace is landscaped with star, fire, elkhorn and staghorn corals. Sea life is superb, featuring scad, palometa, big groupers, snappers, garden eels, tilefish and French angelfish. Check currents with one of the local dive shops before entering the water.

☆☆☆ **Windsock Steep** is known for great snorkeling. This dive is off the small sand beach opposite the airport runway. Check local dive shops for currents before entering the water. Watch out for fire coral as you explore the shallow terrace. The bottom is sandy, but stacked up with sergeant majors, angelfish, snappers, trumpetfish and barracuda.

☆☆ **Calabas Reef**, just off the beach in front of the Divi Flamingo Resort, is reached by swimming over a sand shelf. Giant brain and star corals grow from the slope. Old anchors are scattered about. To the north is a small sailboat wreck.

Reef inhabitants are parrotfish, French angels, damsels, Spanish hogfish and yellow snappers. Spotted, goldentail and chain morays peek out from the crevices.

☆☆☆ **La Machaca** lies off the main road in front of the Habitat Resort and dive shop. Named after a small, wrecked fishing boat, La Machaca is noted for its huge and varied fish population. Mr. Roger, a huge green moray, an old tiger grouper, friendly rock beauties, and two black margate inhabit the area.

☆☆☆ **Petries Pillar** derives its name from the colony of pillar coral that grows on the reef face. To reach this site travel north toward Gotomeer, turn left about 4/10 of a mile after the last house onto an unpaved road. Follow that road down to the sea. Fine for boat or shore entry.

Boca Slagbaai, a perfect picnicking spot within Washington/Slagbaai National Park, is one of Bonaire's most picturesque beaches

☆☆☆☆ **1000 Steps (Piedra Haltu)** may be either a boat or a shore dive, though a boat dive may be easier and will definitely save you carrying your gear down the (actual count, 67) steps. To reach 1000 Steps, drive north from town along the scenic road towards Gotomeer until you reach the entrance of the Radio Nederland transmitting station. On your left are steep concrete steps leading down the mountainside to a sandy beach and the dive site.

Swim through the marked channel to a sandy shallow terrace. Gorgonians and flower corals are abundant. Lavender shrimp, barracuda, black durgons, yellowtail snappers, horse-eye jacks and schoolmasters populate the reef.

☆☆☆☆ **Ol' Blue**, a favorite with snorkelers for its walls of reef fish, cleaning stations and calm waters, may get choppy when the wind kicks up. Get there by driving north along the scenic road to Gotomeer past the transmitting station to the white coral-rubble beach. The dive site is at the point where the road descends to the ocean and the cliff bends away from the road.

☆☆☆☆☆ **Nukove** lies off a little road between Boca Dreifi and Playa Frans. It is a particularly nice shore dive with a channel cut through the jungle of elkhorn coral which grows to the surface.

Numerous juveniles, shrimp and anemones may be seen in the cut. Scrawled filefish, black durgons, grouper, wrasses and barracuda are in residence.

☆☆☆☆ **Boca Slagbaai** provides opportunity to see the best examples of buttress formations in Bonaire water. In addition, green morays, white spotted filefish, tarpon and barracuda are in abundance. Slagbaai boasts six concrete cannon replicas, halved and buried for the 1974 film, *Shark Treasure.*

To reach this dive site, drive through the village of Rincon, into Washington/ Slagbaai National Park where you will follow the green arrows to Slagbaai. Excellent snorkeling is to the south where two real cannons may be viewed at the southernmost point of the bay.

☆☆☆☆ **Playa Funchi**, located in Washington/Slagbaai National Park, is another popular snorkeling area. From Rincon follow the green or yellow signs. Enter next to the man-made pier and swim north for the best snorkeling. Rays, parrotfish, rock hinds, jacks, groupers and angels swim through fields of staghorn coral. On shore, picnickers are greeted by hoards of fearless lizards in search of scraps.

KLEIN BONAIRE

The dive sites surrounding Klein Bonaire offer terrific snorkeling. Some may be closed down for rejuvenation.

☆☆☆ **Leonora's Reef**, on the north side, is a snorkeler's paradise heavily covered with yellow pencil coral, fire coral, star coral and elkhorn stands on a narrow shallow terrace. West of the mooring are pillar coral formations. Expect to be greeted by masses of fish. "Attack" yellowtail snappers and tiny, royal blue fish are joined at cleaning stations by tiger, yellowmount and rare yellowfin groupers.

☆☆☆☆ The at **Forest**, another fabulous snorkeling spot, starts at 15 ft, then drops off to great depths. Two-foot-long queen triggerfish, morays, black durgons, puffers and an abundance of small critters roam the "forest."

☆☆☆☆ **Twixt**, just north of Forest, around the southwest bend of Klein Bonaire, provides excellent opportunities for wide-angle photography with huge basket sponges, sea whips, black coral, huge pastel fans, tube sponges and star corals. Depths range from 15 feet. The coral wall slopes down to a sandy bottom. Seas are almost always calm and flat here.

Large groupers frequent the pillar coral cleaning station at the upper edge of ☆☆☆☆☆ **Carl's Hill**. Named after photographer Carl Roessler, this delightful spot tops at 15 ft and drops sharply. An occasional strong current cleanses the huge purple finger sponges on the slope. West of the mooring, keep an eye out for cleaning stations—areas where fish line up to have "barber" or "cleaner" shrimp pick parasites from their mouths.

☆☆☆☆ **Ebo's Reef** (aka Jerry's Jam) provides superb video and still photography opportunities. Dramatic overhangs of black coral grow in less

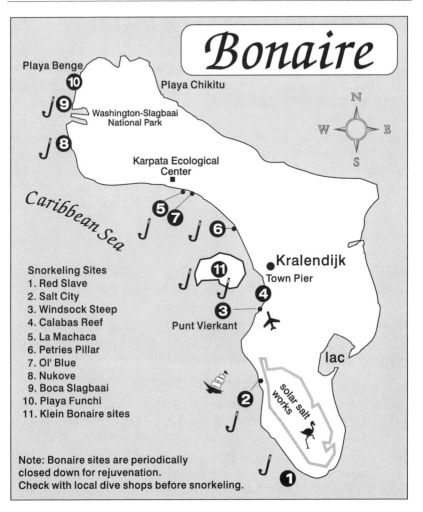

Bonaire

Playa Benge
Playa Chikitu
Washington-Slagbaai
National Park
Karpata Ecological
Center
Caribbean Sea
Kralendijk
Town Piel
Punt Vierkant
lac
solar salt works

Snorkeling Sites
1. Red Slave
2. Salt City
3. Windsock Steep
4. Calabas Reef
5. La Machaca
6. Petries Pillar
7. Ol' Blue
8. Nukove
9. Boca Slagbaai
10. Playa Funchi
11. Klein Bonaire sites

Note: Bonaire sites are periodically closed down for rejuvenation. Check with local dive shops before snorkeling.

than 30 ft of water. Masses of grunts, Spanish hogfish, groupers, sergeant majors, parrotfish and yellowtail swarm the shelf. The drop-off starts at 15 ft and slopes off to a sandy bottom.

☆☆☆☆ At **Knife Reef**, a shallow, half-circle of elkhorn coral creates a mini "lagoon" protecting star coral heads, gorgonians, and a multitude of fish. Bermuda chubs, peacock flounders, lizardfish and yellowhead jawfish rove the terrace.

☆☆☆☆ **Sampler** shelters spotted eels and hordes of tamed, friendly fish that will charm you as you investigate the lovely pillar and staghorn corals.

Snorkeling Tours & Rentals

Snorkelers join scuba divers on the dive shop boats.

Peter Hughes Dive Bonaire, at the Divi Beach Resort & Casino, specializes in reef trips, underwater photo and video courses. Daily E-6 and color print processing. Equipment sales, rental, and repair. ☎ 800-367-3484, in Bonaire 8285.

Sand Dollar Dive and Photo, within the Sand Dollar Condominium Resort complex, offers guided snorkeling tours and courses. Reef trips, park trips, underwater photo and video courses. Same day E-6 and print processing. Equipment sales, rental and repair. Fishing, sailing, snorkeling, water skiing . ☎ 800-345-0805 or (011) 599-7-5252, fax (011) 599-7-8760 or write: P.O. Box 175, Bonaire, NA.

Sunset Beach Dive Center, at the Sunset Beach Hotel, offers boat trips and equipment rentals. E-mail: sundive@caribbeans.com.

Peter Hughes Dive Bonaire, on the beach at the Divi Flamingo Beach Resort, features comfortable dive boats, snorkeling tours, equipment rentals, courses. ☎(011) 599-7-8285, fax (011) 599-7-8238.

Habitat Dive Center at Captain Don's Habitat offers reef trips. ☎ (800) 327-6709; (011) 599-7-8290, fax (011) 599-7-8240 or write P.O. Box 88, Bonaire, NA. E-mail: maduro@netpoint.net.

Where to Stay

Bonaire's entire tourist trade revolves around its beautiful reefs. All but three of the island's hotels were built in the last 20 years and especially to accommodate divers. All have dive shops attached or nearby.

Buddy Beach & Dive Resort sits just north of Kralendijk, offering 40 luxury oceanfront apartments. ☎ 800-359-0747 for Rothschild Dive/Travel packages, 800-786-3483 for Caribbean Dive Tours, direct (011) 599- 7- 5080, fax (011) 599-7-8647.

Bruce Bowker's Carib Inn is one of Bonaire's most intimate dive resorts. Oceanfront accommodations are air conditioned and have cable TV. Maid service, pool. Full service dive shop. ☎(011) 599-7-8819 or write P.O. Box 68, Bonaire NA. E-mail: carib inn@bonairenet.com.

Divi Flamingo Resort & Casino on the beach overlooking Calabas Reef features deluxe rooms. A few have balconies directly over the water where you can view the reef and fish swimming by. ☎ 800-367-3484 or write Divi Hotels, 6340 Quadrangle Drive, Suite 300 Chapel, NC 27514.

Lions Dive Hotel Bonaire features 31 apartments with patio or balcony, each with a fully-equipped kitchen. ☎ 888-546-6734 or (011) 599-7-5580, fax (011) 599-7-5680.

Flamingo salt flats

Plaza Resort Bonaire, a 224-unit luxury hotel, offers snorkeling, water-skiing, banana boating, knee boarding, tube rides, windsurfing, kayaking, tennis, beach volleyball, aqua jogging, water-polo, body-fit training and has Boston Whalers and catamarans for rent. ☎ 800-766-6016 or 800-786-DIVE.

Sunset Beach Hotel, located on Playa Lechi Beach (one of Bonaire's loveliest), features recently renovated rooms, all air-conditioned with cable TV, and telephone. Reef snorkeling off the hotel beach. ☎ 800-344-4439 or (011) 599-7-8291, fax 305-225-0572, or (011) 599-7-4870. **Captain Don's Habitat** offers deluxe, oceanfront cottages, cabanas, villas, studios. Good snorkeling off the beach. ☎ 800-327-6709 or (011) 599-7-8290; fax 305-438-4220 or (011) 599-7-8240 or write P.O. Box 115, Bonaire NA. Website: www.bonaire.org/habitat

Sand Dollar Condominium Resort features deluxe oceanfront condos and an excellent roped-off snorkeling area off the sundeck (no beach). Adjacent dive shop offers boat trips. Casual restaurant overlooks the sea. ☎ 800-288-4773, 407-774-9322 or (011) 599-7-8738; fax (011) 599-7-8760 or write P.O. Box 3253 Longwood FL 32779.

Travel Tips
Helpful Phone Numbers: Police, ☎ 8000; Taxi, ☎ 8100; Airport, ☎ 8500; Medical Facility, ☎ 8900 (San Francisco Hospital) ☎ 8000.

Getting There: ALM Antillean Airlines offers regularly scheduled service to Bonaire's Flamingo International Airport from Miami and Atlanta. Air Aruba offers direct service out of Newark, Baltimore and Tampa. American Airlines offers regularly scheduled service to Curacao with connections via ALM to Bonaire. Guyana Airways from La Guardia connects with ALM in Curacao.

Driving: Foreign and international licenses accepted. Traffic to the right.

Language: The official language for Bonaire is Dutch, but residents speak Papiamento—a blend of Dutch, African and English. English and Spanish are widely spoken.

Snorkeling over elkhorn corals, Klein Bonaire

Documents: US and Canadian citizens may stay up to three months providing they prove citizenship with a passport, birth certificate or a voter's registration card accompanied by a photo identification.

All visitors must have a confirmed room reservation before arriving and a return ticket. A visa is required for visits over 90 days.

Customs: US citizens may bring home $400 worth of articles including one quart of liquor and 200 cigarettes. Canadian citizens may bring in C$300 of goods once each calendar year.

Currency: Netherlands Antilles florin or guilder, but US dollars are widely accepted. US $1.00 = NA fl 1.77.

Credit Cards: Widely accepted.

Climate: Mean temperature 82° F year-round; 22 inches rainfall annually.

Clothing: Casual lightweight. A wet suit is not necessary most of the year, but water temperatures occasionally drop down in mid-winter, especially late January and February.

Electricity: 127 volts, 50 cycles. Adapters are necessary.

Time: Atlantic (EST + 1 hr).

Tax: Airport departure tax $15.

Religious Services: Roman Catholic, Seventh Day Adventist, Jehovah's Witnesses.

Additional Information: Tourism Corporation Bonaire, 10 Rockefeller Plaza, Suite 900, New York, NY 10020. ☎ (800) U-BONAIR (826-6247). **E-mail:** 102372. 3337@compuserve.com. **Website:** www.interknowledge.com/bonaire.

British Virgin Islands

The British Virgin Islands encompass more than 60 islands with most tourist activity around the four largest—Tortola, Anegada, Virgin Gorda and Jost Van Dyke. Except for Anegada, a flat coral slab surrounded by shallow reefs, the islands are mountainous and of volcanic origin.

Clustered around the Sir Francis Drake Channel and protected from high wind and waves, the BVI rate particularly high with sailors. In fact, half the tourist "beds" are aboard the hundreds of yachts in Tortola's marinas.

Snorkeling is superb amidst towering coral pinnacles, canyons, massive boulders, lava chutes and almost 200 different shipwrecks. Most areas have little or no surge and only gentle currents. Visibility may reach anywhere from 50 to over 100 ft.

The best time to visit the BVI is between October and June, with warmest water temperatures between mid-March and early December. Reduced rates at hotels and for charter boats exist during hurricane season, July through October. Air temperature ranges between 80 and 90° F year-round with an occasional drop in February.

Best Snorkeling Sites

Snorkeling gear may be rented or borrowed from most hotels and charter boats. Be sure to bring your camera. Reef and wreck dives are easily arranged through the dive shops. Many offer "rendezvous" service which means they will pick you up from your charter boat or arrange a meeting place convenient to all.

A wetsuit top, shortie, or wetskin is recommended for winter snorkeling. The BVI reefs are protected by law, and no living thing may be taken. "Take only pictures, leave only bubbles."

Beach Entry Sites

☆☆☆☆ **The Baths**, at the southern tip of Virgin Gorda, encompasses the islands' most famous beaches. The area, a natural landscape of partially submerged grottoes and caves formed by a jumble of enormous granite boulders, is a favorite beach-access snorkeling area and one of the biggest tourist attractions in the BVI. The caves shelter a variety of tropical fish. Find this area by taking the trail which starts at the end of the Baths Road. A small bar just off the beach rents snorkel equipment. Beware of dinghies! The Baths is a favorite of cruise ship visitors.

☆☆ **Spring Bay**, neighboring the Baths, has a gorgeous sandy beach and good snorkeling amidst the rocks.

☆☆ **Crawl National Park**, a great spot for beginning snorkelers, also on Virgin Gorda, is reached via a palm-lined trail from Tower Road, just north of the Baths. A natural pond created by a boulder formation is ideal for children.

☆☆☆ **Smugglers Cove,** off the beaten path on the northwest end of Tortola, may be tough to find but, well worth the effort. The last mile leading to this spot is rough driving. There are two lovely reefs, about 100 ft out, with crowds of grunts, squirrel fish, parrot fish and some good-sized trunk fish to keep you company. Depths are shallow and seas usually calm. Good for children. The beach is shaded by palms and sea grape trees. No rest rooms or changing facilities, but there is an honor bar with sodas, beer and some snacks and a phone with a couple of taxi numbers.

Guests of the neighboring **Long Bay Beach Resort** are shuttled to Smugglers Cove twice a day.

☆☆ **Brewers Bay**, on Tortola's north coast road, has two good snorkeling sites, one to the left along the cliffs with depths from eight to 10 ft , the other in the center of the beach opposite the rock wall edging the road. The reef starts close to shore and stretches out in shallow depths for a long way. Schools of trumpet fish, barracuda, octopus, stingrays and sergeant majors inhabit the area.

☆☆☆☆☆ **Loblolly Beach,** on Anegada's northern shore, is one of the best shore-entry snorkeling spots in the Caribbean when winds are calm. Coral heads teaming with fish and invertebrates are close to shore. Visibility can exceed 100 ft. There is usually some surf, but it breaks on the front of the reef which is quite a distance from shore. The Big Bamboo bar and restaurant on the beach is worth the trip. Owner Aubrey Levons welcomes everyone with island stories and hospitality. Loblolly Beach may be reached by taxi, bike or jeep from the Anegada Reef Resort docks.

Avoid this area during strong winds. The sea gets stirred up and visibility drops from super to silty, the beach becomes a sand blast area. Spring and summer are usually the best times to dive and snorkel Anegada.

Anchoring on Anegada Reef is prohibited. Dive and snorkeling day trips can be arranged through the dive operators. Dive BVI offers a particularly nice snorkeling trip aboard their fast 45-ft *Sea Lion* to Anegada which also includes beachcombing and a local lobster lunch at the Anegada Reef Hotel.

Additional excellent snorkeling sites are found on the northeast corner of **Benures Bay**, Norman Island; the **Bight** and **Little Bight** also off Norman Island. At Peter Island, try the south shore at **Little Harbor** and the western shore at **Great Harbor**. **Diamond Reef** on the southeast side of Great Camanoe can be reached by dinghy fom Marina Cay. The shallow reef sits straight out from the utility pole on the shore.

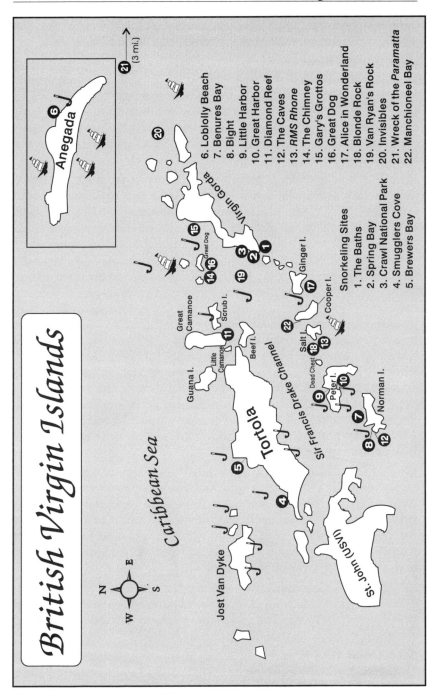

British Virgin Islands

Caribbean Sea

N
W ● E
S

Jost Van Dyke

Tortola

Sir Francis Drake Channel

Guana I.

Little Camanoe

Great Camanoe

Beef I.

Scrub I.

Virgin Gorda

Great Dog

Anegada

(3 mi.)

St. John (USVI)

Norman I.

Peter I.

Dead Chest

Salt I.

Cooper I.

Ginger I.

Snorkeling Sites

1. The Baths
2. Spring Bay
3. Crawl National Park
4. Smugglers Cove
5. Brewers Bay

6. Loblolly Beach
7. Benures Bay
8. Bight
9. Little Harbor
10. Great Harbor
11. Diamond Reef
12. The Caves
13. *RMS Rhone*
14. The Chimney
15. Gary's Grottos
16. Great Dog
17. Alice in Wonderland
18. Blonde Rock
19. Van Ryan's Rock
20. Invisibles
21. Wreck of the *Paramatta*
22. Manchioneel Bay

Long Bay, near Smugglers Cove, Tortola, has pretty corals and the biggest fish, but water entry is difficult as the coral grows to the surface.

Boat Access Sites

☆☆☆☆ **The Caves** at Norman Island are accessible by boat. It is a favorite snorkeling-photo site, bright with sponges, corals and schools of small fish. The reef slopes down to 40 ft. Norman Island is rumored to have inspired Robert Louis Stevenson's *Treasure Island* and the Caves are reputed to be old hiding places for pirate treasure. Moorings are maintained by the National Park Trust.

☆☆☆☆☆ Wreck of the **R.M.S. Rhone**, featured in the movie *The Deep*, is by far the most popular dive in the BVI. Struck by a ferocious hurricane in October, 1867, the Royal Mail Steamer, *Rhone* was hurled onto the rocks at Salt Island as its captain, Robert F. Wooley, struggled desparately to reach open sea.

The force with which the 310-ft vessel crashed upon the rocks broke the hull in two leaving a great snorkeling area at the stern, which lies in 30 ft of water amid rocks and boulders. The top of the rudder sits just 15 ft below the surface. Its superstructure, encrusted with corals, sponges, and sea fans, provides a dramatic setting for underwater photography.

Fish greet snorkelers upon entering the water. Living among the wreckage are a 300-pound jew fish, a very curious 4½ ft barracuda named Fang, schools of snappers, grunts, jacks, arrow crabs, squirrel fish, and yellow tail.

Usually calm sea conditions make this a good spot for surface snorkeling or free diving. Excellent visibility runs between 50 to over 100 ft. Also, the *Rhone* is a national park and off limits to coral collecting and spear fishing. The wreck sits off Black Rock Point on the southwest tip of Salt Island. Boat-access.

☆☆☆ **The Chimney**, located at Great Dog Island off the west end of Virgin Gorda, is a spectacular coral archway and canyon covered with a wide variety of soft corals, sponges and rare white coral. Hundreds of fish follow snorkelers along the archway to a coral-wrapped, tube-like formation resembling a huge chimney. The many shallow areas and protected-cove location make this a terrific snorkeling spot. Boat access only. Some surge and currents when wind is out of the north.

☆☆☆ **Gary's Grottos** lies near the shoreline, four miles north of Spanish Town on Virgin Gorda. It is a shallow reef characterized by three huge arches which resemble a tunnel. This rocky area is teeming with shrimp, squid and sponges. Depths average 30 ft.

☆☆ **Great Dog Island's** south side drops off to a shallow reef with 10-to-60 ft depths. Nice elkhorn stands hide spotted and golden moray eels, spiny lobster and barber shrimp. Good for snorkeling when seas are calm.

☆☆☆☆☆ **Alice in Wonderland**, a coral wall at South Bay off Ginger Island, slopes from 15 ft. Named for its huge mushroom corals, villainous overhangs, and gallant brain corals, this ornate reef shelters longnose butterfly fish, rays, conch and garden eels. Visibility is good and seas are usually calm. Boat dive, good for photography, and free diving.

Private yachts should choose the eastern mooring which is closer to the larger coral ridges.

☆☆☆ **Blonde Rock**, a pinnacle between Dead Chest and Salt Island, starts at 15 ft below the surface. Coral encrusted tunnels, caves and overhangs support a wealth of crabs, lobsters and reef fish. Good for snorkeling when seas are calm. Boat access.

☆☆ **Van Ryan's Rock**, a seamount in Drake's Channel, sits between Beef Island and Virgin Gorda. The top is at 16 ft with boulders and coral leading down to a sandy plain. Nurse sharks, eels, huge turtles, lobster, jacks, spade fish, and barracuda circle. Snorkelers should take care to avoid the huge clumps of fire coral. A light current is occasionally encountered.

☆☆☆ **Invisibles** , a sea mount off Tortola's northeast tip, is a haven for nurse shark, eels, turtles and all types of reef fish from the smallest to the largest. Diver, Gayla Kilbride describes this area as a "Symphony of Fish." Depths go from three ft to 65 ft.

☆☆☆☆ **Wreck of the *Paramatta***, which ran aground on her maiden voyage in 1853, rests at 30 ft off the southeast end of Anegada. The ship sits on a dense coral reef—perfect for snorkelers. If you stand on the ship's engine, you'll be shoulder deep. Enormous reef fish swim around the wreck, including a 200-pound jew fish, 30-pound groupers, butterfly fish, turtles, and rays. Still remaining are the stern and bow sections, long chain, port holes, and cleats of the wreck, all sitting amid beautiful elkhorn and staghorn coral formations, large sea fans, brain corals and red and orange sponges. This is a great spot for underwater portraits.

☆☆ **Manchioneel Bay,** Cooper Island, has a beautiful shallow reef with packs of fish around the moorings.

Snorkeling Tours & Rentals

Dive BVI Ltd., a PADI five-star shop, operates out of Leverick Bay, Virgin Gorda Yacht Harbour, Peter Island and Marina Cay. Owner Joe Giacinto has been diving and snorkeling the BVI for 29 years and knows all the best spots. Snorkeling trips are offered to Anegada and other spots aboard the *Sealion*, a fast 45-ft wave-piercing catamaran. Write: P.O. Box 1040, Virgin Gorda, BVI ☎ 800-848-7078/284-495-5513, fax 284-495-5347. E-mail: dbvi@caribsurf.com.

Underwater Safaris, at the Moorings Mariner Inn on Tortola and Cooper Island, offers fast 42- and 30-ft dive boats. The Tortola shop is the BVI's largest retail dive shop. Write: P.O. Box 139, Road Town, Tortola. ☎ 800-537-7032 or 284-494-3235, fax 284-494-5322.

Baskin in the Sun at the Prospect Reef Resort Marina offers reef and wreck trips. Package tours can be booked through Baskin in the Sun, P.O. Box 8309, Cruz Bay, St. John, USVI 00831. ☎ 800-650-2084 or 284-494-2858/9, fax 284-494-4303. E-mail: baskin@usmall.com.

Island Diver Ltd at Village Cay Marina, Road Town offers reef and wreck tours, resort courses and snorkeling. ☎ 284-494-3878/52367.

Kilbride's Underwater Tours, now owned by Sunchaser Scuba Ltd., located at the famous Bitter End Yacht Club on Virgin Gorda, features a variety of services and tours to 50 different dive locations. Snorkelers join the scuba divers on reef and wreck tours. ☎ 800-932-4286 or 284-495-9638; fax 284-495-7549. E-mail: sunscuba@caribsurf.com. Or write to Sunchaser Scuba, Box 46, Virgin Gorda, BVI. Most sites are near islands with superb snorkeling.

Rainbow Visions Photography at Prospect Reef offers underwater, still and video camera rentals. Processing. Custom videos and portraits. ☎ 284-494-2749. Write: P.O. Box 139, Road Town, Tortola, BVI.

Live-Aboards Vacations

Sail-dive vacations are an easy way to enjoy a variety of snorkeling sites and destinations. Live-aboard yachts are chartered with captain, captain and crew, or "bare" to qualified sailors. Navigation is uncomplicated, you can tour most of the area without ever leaving sight of land.

With sailing almost a religion in the BVI, it is easy to customize a live-aboard snorkeling vacation. If you are an experienced sailor you can charter a bareboat and see the sights on your own. If you've never sailed before, you can "captain" a crewed yacht to find the best snorkeling spots. Or book a week-long cruise on a commercial live-aboard where you'll meet other avid snorkelers. Prices on private charters vary with the number of people in your party. With four to six people, a crewed yacht will average about the same cost as a stay at a resort. Be sure to specify that you are a snorkeler.

CUAN LAW

One of the world's largest trimarans (105 ft), *Cuan Law* was specifically designed with divers and snorkelers in mind. As with most live-aboards, you are offered "all the diving you can stand." *Cuan Law* accommodates 18 passengers in 10 large, airy double cabins, each with private head and shower.

Cruises are booked up from three months to a year in advance. ☎ 800-648-3393 or write Trimarine Boat Company, P.O. 4065, St. Thomas, USVI 00803.

Yacht Promenade, a sleek, 65-ft tri-hull sailing yacht for couples or groups of six to 12 features spacious air-conditioned cabins, full breakfasts, lunches, cocktails, hors d'oeuvres and three-course gourmet dinners. There are five guest staterooms, one in each outer hull and three at the rear of the center hull, three queen-sized berths and two that are larger than king and can be converted into four single berths. A 20-ft Wellcraft launch whisks snorkelers off to all the best spots. Vacations include use of 11-ft kayaks, a sailing dinghy, and a windsurfer. Pick up at Village Cay Marina, Road Town, Tortola. ☎ (US) 800-526-5503 or 284-494-3853, fax 284-494-5577. E-mail: promcruz@caribsurf.com.

The Moorings Ltd. offers "Cabin 'N Cruise" tours for those wishing to enjoy a fully crewed sailing vacation without having to charter an entire yacht. ☎ 800-535-7289. See listing below.

Bareboating

Private sailing yachts with diving guides and instructors are available from most of the charter operators listed below. You can arrange for your own personal live-aboard snorkeling vacation. Be sure to specify your needs before going.

Bareboating can be surprisingly affordable for groups of four or more. Boats must be reserved six to nine months in advance for winter vacations and at least three months in advance for summer vacations.

Experience cruising on a similar yacht is required and you will be asked to fill out a questionnaire or produce a sailing resume. Instructor-skippers are available for refresher sailing. A cruising permit, available from the Customs Department, is required. For a complete list of charter companies contact the BVI Tourist Board at ☎ 800-835-8530 or write 370 Lexington Ave. Suite 1605, New York, NY 10017.

The Moorings Ltd., Tortola, has been operating for 18 years. Their charter boats include Moorings 35, 38, 51, 50, 432 (43 ft), and 433 plus 39- and 42-ft catamarans. A Moorings 51, Morgan 60 or Gulfstar 60 may be chartered, but with crew only. The Moorings' book *Virgin Anchorages* shows through aerial photographs the best anchorages in the British Virgin Islands.

A three-day sailing vacation can be combined with a four day resort vacation at the Moorings Mariner Inn. Write to The Moorings, Ltd., 19345 US Hwy 19 N, Clearwater, FL. 34624. ☎ 800- 535-7289 or 813- 535-1446.

A Fast Track to Cruising course, offered by Offshore Sailing School, includes the complete Learn to Sail course and Moorings/Offshore Live Aboard Cruising course on consecutive weeks. Available starting Sundays year-round (two person minimum for Live Aboard cruising), the package includes 10 days/nine nights accommodations ashore, six days/five nights aboard a Moorings yacht, Learn to Sail and Live Aboard Cruising courses, textbooks, certificates, wallet cards, logbook, full day practice sail, split yacht provisioning during onboard portion of Live Aboard Cruising course (five breakfasts, five lunches, three dinners) graduation dinners ashore, airport or ferry transfers in Tortola. ☎ 800- 221-4326 or 941-454-1700, fax 941-454-1191. Write to: Offshore Sailing School, 16731 McGregor Blvd., Ft. Myers, FL 33908.

Where to Stay

Web site: www.britishvirginislands.com/divebvi.

Tortola

Every type of accommodation is available in the BVI from tents to cottages, guesthouses, condos, luxury resorts to live aboard sailboats and motor yachts. Reservations can be made through your travel agent or the BVI Tourist Board at ☎ 800- 835-8530 or in New York, 212-696-0400. For a copy of the Intimate Inns brochure ☎ (US) 800-835-8530. Website: www.carib.com/carib/bvi.

Island Hideaways rents upscale private homes and villas. ☎ 800-784-2690 or 202-232-6137, fax 202-667-3392.

Long Bay Beach Resort on Tortola's north shore has 82 deluxe hillside and beachfront accommodations. Dive with Baskin' in the Sun. ☎ 800-729-9599. Write: P.O. Box 433, Road Town Tortola, BVI.

The Moorings-Mariner Inn, Tortola, is home port to The Moorings charter boat operation. No beach. The poolside bar and restaurant are just a few steps from Underwater Safaris, the largest retail shop in the BVI.

The resort offers a new Shore 'N Sail vacation with three nights aboard a luxurious sailing yacht (snorkeling included) with your own skipper and provisions and four nights at the resort. ☎ 800- 535- 7289, 284- 494-2332, fax 813-530-9747, or write The Moorings Mariner Inn, 1305 US 19 S., Suite 402, Clearwater, FL 34624. E-mail: yacht@moorings. Website: www. moorings.com

Nanny Cay Resort & Marina, two miles southwest of Road Town, has 41 air-conditioned rooms, TV, phones, pool, restaurant, bar, tennis, Windsurf school and on-site, Blue Water Divers. ☎ 800-74CHARMS or 800-742-4276 or 284-494-4895, fax 914- 424-3283. Write: P.O. Box 281, Road Town, Tortola, BVI.

Prospect Reef Resort is a sprawling 10-acre resort located on the west end of Road Town, Tortola, facing Sir Francis Drake Channel. The resort has over 130 rooms ranging from studios to standard rooms, full apartments, and luxury villas. Amenities include six tennis courts, miniature golf, two restaurants for casual food and drinks, and three pools. Rooms are cooled by ceiling fans and a breeze from the sea. Snorkeling trips are with Baskin' in the Sun. ☎ 800-356-8937 or, 284-494-3311. Write Box 104, Road Town, Tortola, BVI.

Sugarmill, on the northwest shore of Tortola, is a village of hillside cottages built around the remains of a 360-year-old sugar mill. Its proprietors, Jeff and Jinx Morgan, are famous for their gourmet meals (they write for *Bon Apetit*). Snorkeling tours with Baskin' in the Sun. ☎ 800-462-8834 or 284-495-4355, fax 284-495-4696. Write P.O. Box 425, Tortola, BVI.

Treasure Isle Hotel, Roadtown, has 40 air-conditioned rooms, pool, restaurant, bar. ☎ 284- 494-2501. Write: P.O. Box 68, Road Town, Tortola, BVI. Snorkeling trips with Underwater Safaris. ☎ 800-437-7880.

MARINA CAY
Marina Cay, a six-acre island off the northeast tip of Tortola, features Dive BVI's newest dive and water sports center offering daily snorkeling trips, ocean kayaks, two new Hobe catamarans, Pusser's Fine Dining and a large Company Store.

Marina Cay Resort offers four one-bedroom units and two two-bedroom villas that accommodate up to 16 guests. All have been recently refurbished. ☎ 284-494-2174 or fax 284-494-4775. Packages may be reserved through Dive BVI. ☎ 800-848-7078.

VIRGIN GORDA
The Bitter End Yacht Club on Virgin Gorda's North Sound offers guest rooms in luxury villas along the shore and hillside or on a Freedom 30 live-aboard yacht. The club bar is *the* favorite story-swapping place for sailing and diving folk. Daily snorkeling trips, arranged through Kilbrides Underwater Tours, leave from the Bitter End Docks every morning. ☎ 800-872-2392, or 284-494-2746 or write P.O. Box 46, Virgin Gorda, BVI.

Drake's Anchorage on Mosquito Island, just north of North Sound off Virgin Gorda, is a hideaway with 10 beachfront units and two deluxe villas. The island has four lovely beaches, with snorkeling offshore and moorings for cruising sailboats. Diving is arranged with Kilbride Underwater Tours or Dive BVI. The dive shops pick you up at the dock. Mosquito Island can be reached by flying into Virgin Gorda and taking a cab to Leverick Bay where a Drake's boat will pick you up. ☎ 800- 624-6651 or write Drake's Anchorage Resort Inn, P.O. Box 2510 Virgin Gorda, BVI.

Biras Creek Estate, located on a 140-acre peninsula, can be reached by scheduled ferry from Tortola. The resort has 34 luxury villas with garden and ocean views overlooking North Sound. Recently refurbished, the resort provides complimentary use of Boston Whalers, windsurfers and 25-ft sailboats. ☎ 800-608-9661 or 284-494-3555, fax 284-494-3557. In the US ☎ 800-223-1108; from the UK 0-800-894. 057 Write: P.O. Box 54, Virgin Gorda, BVI.

Little Dix Bay features 90 luxury suites and guest rooms on a half-mile of pristine beach surrounded by tropical gardens. Paradise Watersports on premises offers snorkeling tours. ☎ 800-928-3000 or book through your travel agent.

Peter Island Resort & Yacht Harbour offers luxurious beachfront rooms overlooking Sprat Bay and the Sir Francis Drake Channel. Excellent snorkeling off the beach. Dive BVI facility on site. ☎ 284-495-2000, fax 284-495-2500.

ANEGADA

Tiny Anegada, 12 miles northwest of Virgin Gorda, covers just 15 square miles. This off-the-beaten-track coral atoll, surrounded by uninterrupted beaches and gorgeous reefs, is home to 250 residents and a huge community of exotic Caribbean birds including a flamingo colony, herons, terns and ospreys. Shipwrecks and coral heads abound, a delight for snorkelers, but sailors beware—approaching the island by boat can be treacherous without local knowledge and eyeball navigation. Snorkeling, diving and fly fishing, done from shore, is outstanding

Much of the island's interior is a preserve for 2,000 wild goats, donkeys and cattle. Not for the average tourist, but a great spot if you want to get away from it all. Expect encounters with a ferocious mosquito population—carry as much repellent as you can. Fly in from Beef Island, Tortola or go by boat from any of the marinas.

Anegada Reef Hotel, on Setting Point, offers great beaches, snorkeling and fly fishing, 16 air-conditioned rooms, tackle shop, tank fills. Informal restaurant. Jeep and bicycle rentals. ☎ 284-495-8002, fax 284-495-9362.

Anegada Beach Campground offers 8 x 10' tents, a restaurant and snorkeling tours. ☎ 284-495-9466 or write to Box 2710, Anegada, BVI.

Travel Tips

Getting There: San Juan, Puerto is the airline hub for the Caribbean, with frequent service to all parts of the United States, Canada and Europe. Beef Island is the major airport of Tortola and the BVI. Flights to San Juan with connections to the BVI from the United States on American, Delta and Continental Airlines. Atlantic Air BVI, Sunaire Express or American Eagle fly from San Juan to Beef Island. Gorda Aero Services (☎ 5-2271) flies to Anegada from Tortola on Mon., Wed., and Fri. Inter-island ferry service is also available from St. Thomas to St. John and Tortola. Ferries run from Tortola to Virgin Gorda, Peter Island, Jost Van Dyke. Note, Baggage can sometimes be delayed by a day on the small airlines.

Car rentals: *Tortola*: Hertz ☎ 54405; Avis, ☎ 4-3322; Budget, ☎ 4-2639; International, ☎ 4-2516. *Virgin Gorda*: Speedy's, ☎ 4-5240.

Driving: Valid BVI driving license required. A temporary license may be obtained from the car rental agencies. Driving is on the left-hand side of the road. Maximum speed is 30 mph. Bicycles must be registered at the Traffic Licensing Office in Road Town. License plate MUST be fixed to the bicycle.

Fishing: The removal of any marine organism from BVI waters is illegal for non-residents without a recreational fishing permit. ☎ 4-3429.

Documents: A valid passport is required to enter the BVI. For US and Canadian citizens an authenticated birth certificate or voter registration card with photo identification will suffice. Visitors may stay up to six months, provided they possess ongoing tickests, evidence of adequate means of support and pre-arranged accommodations. Visitors from some countries may need a visa. ☎ (284) 494-3701.

Currency: US Dollar. Personal checks not accepted.

Clothing: Casual, light clothing; some of the resorts require a jacket for dinner. Nudity is punishable by law. A wetsuit top, shortie, or wetskin is recommended for winter diving. Snorkelers should also have protection from sunburn.

Time: Atlantic Standard (EST + 1 hr).

Language: English.

Climate: The BVI are in the tradewind belt and have a subtropical climate. Average temperatures are 75º to 85º F in winter and 80 to 90Æ F in summer. Nights are cooler. The hurricane season extends from July through September.

Religious Services: Methodist, Anglican, Roman Catholic, Seventh Day Adventist, Baptist, Jehovah's Witness, Pentecostal and Church of Christ.

For Additional Information and a list of all guesthouses, apartments, hotels, campgrounds, charter operators, and restaurants contact the British Virgin Islands Tourist Board. *In Tortola:* P.O. Box 134, Road Town, Road Town, Tortola, British Virgin Islands, ☎ (284) 494-3134. *In New York:*—BVI Tourist Board, 370 Lexington Avenue, Suite 1605, New York, N.Y. 10017. ☎ (800) 835- 8530, or 212-696-0400. *United Kingdom:* BVI Information Office, FCB Travel Marketing, 110 St. Martin's Lane, London WC2N 4DY, England, ☎ 44-171-240-4259. Website: www.british virginislands.com/divebvi.

Cayman Islands

The Cayman Islands—Grand Cayman, Cayman Brac and Little Cayman—host more than 200,000 watersports enthusiasts each year. Located 480 miles south of Miami, a two-hour flight, the islands boast some of the most exciting snorkeling spots in the world with outstanding visibility, diverse marine life and robust coral communities—many a short swim from shore.

Physically beautiful, both above and beneath the sea, each island is blessed with an extraordinary fringing reef, superb marine life and long stretches of sparkling, palm-lined beaches.

Underwater Cayman is a submerged mountain range complete with cliffs, drop-offs, gullies, caverns, sink holes and forests of coral. The islands are the visible above-the-sea portions of the mountains. At depth, the Cayman Trench drops off to more than 23,000 ft.

Grand Cayman, the largest and the most developed of the three, has several snorkeling boat operators and a wide choice of beachfront resorts. Cayman Brac and Little Cayman lie 89 miles northeast of the big island and are separated by a seven-mile-wide channel. Both wildly beautiful, each has its own special personality.

With daily direct flights from North America and easy access from many other parts of the globe, most vacationers head first for Grand Cayman. Its famed Seven Mile Beach is headquarters for snorkeling activity with several teriffic beach-entry sites.

When To Go

Late summer and fall bring chance of a hurricane, but snorkeling is possible year round. Conditions are generally mild, although steady winds can kick up some chop. When this happens dive boats simply move to the leeward side of the island and calmer waters. Air temperature averages 77°F. Water temperature averages 80°F.

Marine Park Regulations

With a dramatic growth in tourism and an increase in cruise ship arrivals, the islands have enacted comprehensive legislation to protect the fragile marine environment. Marine areas are divided into three types: Marine Park Zone, Replenishment Zone and Environmental Zone.

The Marine Park Zones outlaw the taking of any marine life, living or dead, and only line fishing from shore and beyond the dropoff is permitted. Anchoring is allowed only at fixed moorings. (There are more than 200 permanent moorings around the islands.)

It is an offense for any vessel to cause reef damage with anchors or chains anywhere in Cayman waters.

In a Replenishment Zone, the taking of conch or lobster is prohibited, and spear guns, pole spears, fish traps and nets are prohibited. Line fishing and anchoring (at fixed moorings) are permitted. (Spearguns and Hawaiian slings may not be brought into the country.)

Environmental Zones are the most strictly regulated. There is an absolute ban on the taking of any kind of marine life, alive or dead; anchoring is prohibited and no in-water activities of any kind are tolerated. These areas are a breeding ground and nursery for the fish and other creatures which will later populate the reef and other waters.

The Marine Conservation Board employs full-time officers who may search any vessel or vehicle thought to contain marine life taken illegally. Penalties may include a maximum fine of CI$5,000 or imprisonment, or both.

Best Snorkeling Sites of Grand Cayman

BEACH SITES

Patch reefs and coral heads teeming with reef fish lie just a few yards off several of the island's swimming beaches. The best shore spots exist off West Bay Cemetery, Seven Mile Beach, the Eden Rock Dive Center in Georgetown, Smith Cove, The Treasure Island Resort beach, Rum Point Club, Parrots Landing, Seaview Hotel, Coconut Harbour, Sunset House, Pirates Inn, Frank Sound, Half Moon Bay, East End Diving Lodge and Morritt's Tortuga Club. Depths range from three to 20 ft. Clearer water and more dramatic coral formations are found farther offshore and may be reached by boat. Snorkeling cruises, some with dinner or lunch, are offered by the hotels and dive shops. Snorkelers are urged to inquire about currents and local conditions in unfamiliar areas before attempting to explore on their own.

Swimmers off the Rum Point Club beach should stay clear of the channels, which have rip tides. Grand Cayman's Southwest Point shows a good variety of juvenile reef fish and invertebrates on a rocky bottom close to shore. Currents beyond 100 yards are dangerous.

A trail marked by a round blue and white sign with a swimmer outline denotes access through private property to the beach. All Cayman beaches are free for public use.

☆☆ **Smiths Cove,** south of George Town, shelters a shallow reef whiskered with pastel sea fans and plumes. Trumpet fish, squirrel fish, schools of grunts, sergeant majors, butterfly fish, parrot fish and angels offer constant entertainment. The reef sits 150 ft from the beach at Southwest Point. Depths are from 15ft.

☆☆ **Eden Rocks,** favored by cruise ship groups, lies less than 200 yds offshore from the Eden Rock Diving Center. Depths range from five to 40 ft. The reef features beautiful coral grottoes, walls, caves and tunnels and tame fish. If you've yet to befriend a fish, this area offers the proper social climate. Good visibility and light currents are the norm here.

Boat Sites

☆☆☆☆ **Sand Bar** at Stingray City in North Sound is home to several tame stingrays. Depths are shallow to 12 ft. Boat tours departing from Georgetown or Seven Mile Beach are either a half- or full-day tour.

Stingray City is the most photographed dive site in the Caymans, if not the entire Caribbean. Pictured in all the tourist board ads, the subject of endless travel articles and an Emmy-award film by Stan Waterman, this gathering of Southern stingrays in the shallow area of North Sound is a marine phenomenon which has thrilled divers since their discovery by two dive instructors, Pat Kinney and Jay Ireland, early in 1986.

Today, the 20-member cast of rays are big celebrities, luring curious visitors—as many as 150-200 per day—from across the globe. Feeding time occurs whenever a snorkeling boat shows up.

Grand Cayman Snorkeling Tours & Rentals

Ambassador Divers, at Ambassadors Inn in George Town offer s snorkeling trips, gear rental, video rental, trips to Stingray City. ☎ 800-648-7748 or 345-949-8839, fax 345-949-8839. Write to P.O. Box 2396 GT, Grand Cayman, BWI.

Bob Soto's Diving Ltd. at the Treasure Island Hotel and the Scuba Centre, near to Soto's Reef has snorkeling trips, photo and video services, gear rentals, and comfortable, custom dive boats. ☎ 800-262-7686 or 345-949-2022; fax 345-949-8731. Write to P.O. Box 1801, Grand Cayman, BWI.

Capitol's Surfside offers trips for scuba and snorkeling. ☎ 800- 543-6828 or 345-949-7330, fax 345-949-8639.

Capt. Marvin's Aquatics' large boats carry 40 divers. Located in West Bay. Snorkeling trips, Stingray City tours, courses and gear rental. ☎ 345-945-4590, fax 345-945-5673. Write to P.O. Box 413, West Bay, Grand Cayman, BWI.

Celebrity Divers in George Town features snorkeling and Stingray City tours. ☎ 345-949-3410. No credit cards.

Clint Ebanks Scuba Cayman Ltd. on West Bay Road offers Stingray City tours, and snorkeling trips. Gear rental. ☎ 345-949-3873, fax 345-949-6244.

Crosby Ebanks C & G Watersports at Coconut Place Tropic Center specializes in dive and snorkeling trips to Stingray City. ☎ 345-945-4049, fax 345-945-5994.

Dive Inn Ltd. greets divers and snorkelers with friendly, personalized service. Boats carry 12 passengers. Gear, photo and video rental. ☎ 800-322-0321 or 345-949-4456, fax 345-949-7125.

Don Foster's Dive Cayman, a full-service facility based at the Holiday Inn, Radisson Resort and Royal Palms on Seven Mile Beach, offers snorkeling excursions, waverunners and sailboats. ☎ 800-83-DIVER, or 972-722-2535, fax 972-722-6511 E-mail: dfdus@airmail.net.

Eden Rock Diving Center touts unlimited shore diving on GeorgeTowns waterfront, with guided tours of Eden Rocks Reef and Devil's Grotto. Photo, video and snorkel gear rentals. ☎ 345-949-7243, fax 345-949-0842.

Ocean Frontiers, Cayman's newest operation, caters to East End diving. Snorkelers welcome on the 12-passenger boats. PADI courses. Gear and photo rentals. ☎ 345-947-7500, fax 345-947-7500.

Off the Wall divers offer personalized dive/snorkeling tours. No credit cards. ☎ 345-947-7790, fax 345-947-7790.

Parrots Landing Watersports Park, a half-mile south of downtown Georgetown, has excellent shore diving on four beautiful, shallow reefs 30 yards from their dock and a wall dive 115 yards out. Seven 20-passenger

Seven Mile Beach, Grand Cayman

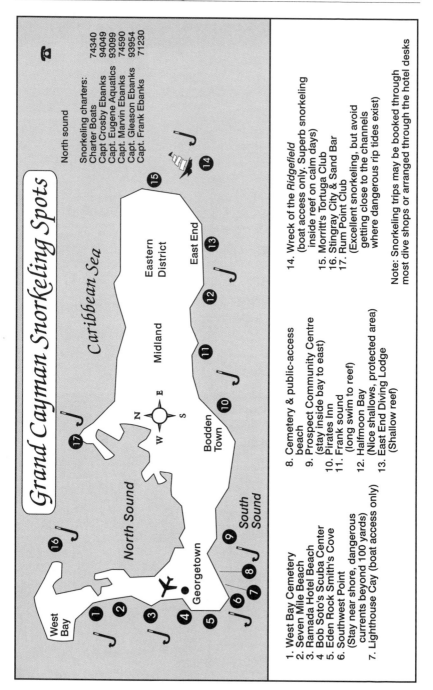

Grand Cayman Snorkeling Spots

Caribbean Sea

North Sound

South Sound

West Bay

Georgetown

Bodden Town

Midland

Eastern District

East End

North sound

Snorkeling charters:
Charter Boats   74340
Capt. Crosby Ebanks   94049
Capt. Eugene Aquatics   93099
Capt. Marvin Ebanks   74590
Capt. Gleason Ebanks   93954
Capt. Frank Ebanks   71230

1. West Bay Cemetery
2. Seven Mile Beach
3. Ramada Hotel Beach
4. Bob Soto's Scuba Center
5. Eden Rock Smith's Cove
6. Southwest Point
   (Stay near shore, dangerous
   currents beyond 100 yards)
7. Lighthouse Cay (boat access only)

8. Cemetery & public-access
   beach
9. Prospect Community Centre
   (stay inside bay to east)
10. Pirates Inn
11. Frank sound
    (long swim to reef)
12. Halfmoon Bay
    (Nice shallows, protected area)
13. East End Diving Lodge
    (Shallow reef)

14. Wreck of the *Ridgefield*
    (boat access only. Superb snorkeling
    inside reef on calm days)
15. Morritt's Tortuga Club
16. Stingray City & Sand Bar
17. Rum Point Club
    (Excellent snorkeling, but avoid
    getting close to the channels
    where dangerous rip tides exist)

Note: Snorkeling trips may be booked through
most dive shops or arranged through the hotel desks

dive boats visit the South Wall, West Wall and Northwest Point. A 60-ft sailing catamaran, *The Cockatoo*, sails from North Sound to Stingray City. Squid is provided for snorkelers to hand feed the rays. Park shuttle boats and busses will pick you up anywhere along Seven Mile Beach. The park offers complete air/accommodation/dive packages with your choice of any hotel or condo on the island. ☎ 800-448-0428 or 345-949-7884. Write to P.O. Box 1995, Grand Cayman, BWI.

Peter Milburn's Dive Cayman Ltd. has been on the island for 18 years. Their 14-passenger boats make three dive/snorkel trips daily. Dive gear rental. No credit cards. ☎ 345-945-5770, fax 345-945-5786.

Quabbin Dives, located in Georgetown, offer trips and rentals. Large boats carry 30 divers and snorkelers. ☎ 345-949-5597, fax 345-949-4781.

Red Sail Sports, across from the Hyatt Regency and at the Westin Casuarina on Seven Mile Beach, offers snorkel and dive trips, dinner sails and cocktail cruises. Waterskiing and parasailing. ☎ 800-255-6425 or 345-947-5965, fax 345-947-5808.

Resort Sports Limited, at Beach Club colony and Spanish Bay Reef hotels, offers Stingray City trips and snorkeling tours. ☎ 345-949-8100, fax 345-949-5167.

Sunset Divers at Sunset House is best known for its Underwater Photo Centre, operated by Cathy Church. The Centre offers 35mm and video camera rental, processing and photo instruction for all levels. ☎ 800-854-4767 or 345-949-7111, fax 345-854-7101. Write to P.O. Box 479, Grand Cayman, BWI.

Treasure Island Divers at the Treasure Island Resort, offers snorkeling trips and sail cruises to all four sides of Grand Cayman. Their 45-foot boats offer freshwater showers, marine heads and a sundeck which shades the bottom deck. ☎ 800-872-7552 or 345-949-4456, fax 954-351-9740. Write P.O. Box 30975 SMB, Grand Cayman, BWI.

Snorkel sails, glass-bottom boat rides, submarine rides, dinner cruises, fishing and more are booked through **Charter Boat Headquarters** in the Coconut Place Shopping Center on West Bay Road. ☎ 345-947-4340,

Where to Stay on Grand Cayman

Grand Cayman has accommodations and packages for every budget and every need. For a complete list of guest houses, cottages and condos contact the Cayman Islands Department of Tourism, 6100 Blue Lagoon Drive, Suite 150, Miami, FL 33126, ☎ 800-346-3313 or 305-266-2300, fax 305-267-2932. New York, ☎ 212-682-5582, fax 212-986-5123. United Kingdom, ☎ 071 491-7771, fax 071-017-1409. Canada, ☎ 800-263-5805 or

416-485-1550, fax 416-485-7578. Grand Cayman, ☎ 345-949-0623, fax 345-949-4053. Web site: www.caymans .com.

Seven Mile Beach Resorts

Treasure Island Resort, a 25-acre beachfront luxury hotel features 280 spacious air-conditioned rooms. ☎ 800-203-0775 or 345-949-7777, fax 345-949-8672.

Hyatt Regency offers 236 ultra-luxurious rooms. Red Sail Watersports on premises. Handicap accessible. ☎ 800-233-1234 or 345-949-1234, fax 345-949-8528. Major credit cards.

Holiday Inn is beachfront with a dive shop on premises. Newly renovated. Handicap accessible. ☎ 800-421-9999 or 345-945-4213. Major credit cards.

Radisson Resort, a huge 315-room luxury resort, five minutes from town features a pool, beach bar, restaurant and nightclub. Don Foster's Diving on premises. All major credit cards. ☎ 800-333-3333 or 345-949-0088, fax 345-949-0288.

Westin Casuarina Resort offers 343 luxurious guest suites on a lovely stretch of Seven Mile Beach. ☎ 800-228-3000 or 345-945-3800, fax 345-949-5825. Write to P.O. Box 30620, Seven Mile Beach, Grand Cayman, BWI.

Georgetown Area

Coconut Harbour, south of Seven Mile Beach, offers suites with mini kitchens and shore diving on Waldo's Reef out front. Parrot's Landing Dive Shop on premises. ☎ 800-552-6281 or 345-949-7468, fax 345-949-7117. Write to P.O. Box 2086 GT, Grand Cayman, BWI.

Indies Suites, a beachfront 41-suite hotel, features Indies Divers on premises offering snorkeling trips to Stingray City, the North and West Walls, gear rental. ☎ 800-654-3130 or 345-947-5025, fax 345-947-5024.

Sunset House, a 59-room resort owned and operated by divers for divers sits south of Seven Mile Beach. Good snorkeling from the beach! ☎ 800-854-4767 or 345-949-7111, fax 345-949-7101. Write to P.O. Box 479, George Town, Grand Cayman, BWI.

CAYMAN BRAC

Often called the loveliest of the islands, Cayman Brac (*brac* is Gaelic for bluff) is rumored to be the resting place of pirates' treasure. Its most striking feature is a 140-foot-high limestone formation covered by unusual foliage, including flowering cactus, orchids and tropical fruits such as mango and papaya. Rare species of birds, including the endangered green, blue and red Caymanian parrot, inhabit the island, which is a major flyway for migratory birds. Resident brown booby birds soar the cliffs.

Best Snorkeling Sites of Cayman Brac

Several excellent shore-entry points exist off the north and south shores. Wind conditions determine which area is calm. Usually, if the north shore spots are choppy, the south shore is calm. Check with area dive shops for daily conditions.

☆☆☆ **WindSock Reef and the Wreck of the *Tibbetts*,** in White Bay off the northwest coast, is the Brac's most popular beach-entry snorkeling spot. A spur and groove reef encircles gardens of elkhorn, pillar corals, sea fans, orange sponges and gorgonians. Expect good visibility and usually calm seas. Typical inhabitants are stoplight parrot fish, blue tangs, midnight parrot fish, sergeant majors, turtles, grey angels, grunts, trumpet fish and triggerfish. Shore area depths range from four to 20 ft.

Further out lies the wreck of the ***Tibbetts***, a 330-ft Russian destroyer built for the Cuban Navy that was renamed the *Captain Keith Tibbets* and deliberately sunk on September 17, 1996. The vessel, the Cayman's most exciting new dive attraction, can be reached from shore if you don't mind a 200-yard swim.

Fore and aft cannons, a missile launcher and machine gun turrets remain on the ship. Snorkelers may easily view the top of the radar tower at 12 feet and the bridge at 32 feet below the surface. The mast of the *Tibbetts's* wreck

Wreck of the Tibbetts

breaks the surface and is easily spotted from the beach. Check with area dive shops before venturing out. Visibility usually 100 ft or better.

To reach White Bay, travel the North Shore Rd (A6) west from the airport to Promise Lane. Turn left. The beach entry point is behind the closed Buccaneer Inn Hotel.

☆☆ **Stake Bay**. Find this spot by turning off the North Shore Rd at the Cayman Brac Museum. Reef terrain, depths and fish life are similar to White Bay. Sea conditions usually calm, but will kick up when the wind is out of the North.

☆☆ **Creek** lies off the north shore. A turn towards the shore from Cliff's Store on the North Shore Rd (A6) will lead to the Island Dock. Enter from the beach area left of the dock, facing seaward. Dense patches of elkhorn predominate. Depths are shallow to 30 ft. Angels, small turtles, and sergeant majors swarm the reef. Wind speed and direction determines the conditions, though seas are usually calm with a light current.

Additional entry points are found at the boat launching areas where cuts through the dense coral have been blasted. Parking is available along side the north road.

South Shore

☆☆ **Sea Feather Bay**, located off the South Shore Rd. at the Bluff Road crossing, provides haven for pretty wrasses, turtles, blue parrot fish, grouper, indigo hamlets, squirrelfish, porkfish, blue tangs, and rockfish. Reef terrain comprises long stretches of dense elkhorn interspersed with tube sponges, fire coral, rose coral and gorgonians. After a big storm, this area becomes a wash-up zone for some strange cargo such as rubber doll parts and unusual bottles which may come from Jamaica or Cuba. Expect some surge and shallow breakers. Visibility good, though silt may churn up the shallows following a storm.

Experienced snorkelers may want to dive the barrier reef at the south western tip of the island. Water entry is best by boat but if you enjoy a long swim you can get out to the reef from either the public beach or one of the hotel beaches.

Where to Stay on Cayman Brac

Brac Aquatics offers reef tours and gear rentals. ☎ 345-948-1429, fax 345-948-1527.

Brac Reef Beach Resort and Reef Divers offers comfortable air conditioned rooms. ☎ 800-327-3835 or 813-323-8727; fax 345- 948-1207. E-mail: refz79a@ prodigy.com. Write to P.O. Box 56, Cayman Brac, BWI.

Brac Caribbean Beach Village offers 16 beachfront condo units. ☎ 800-791-7911 or 345-948-2265, fax 345-948-2206.

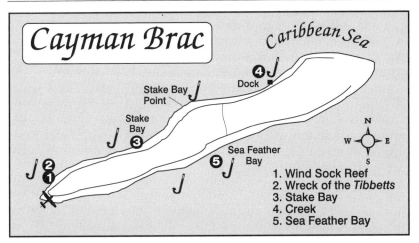

Map of Cayman Brac — Caribbean Sea

Dive sites:
1. Wind Sock Reef
2. Wreck of the *Tibbetts*
3. Stake Bay
4. Creek
5. Sea Feather Bay

Labels shown: Dock (4), Stake Bay Point, Stake Bay (3), Sea Feather Bay (5), Wind Sock Reef (1), Wreck of the *Tibbetts* (2)

Compass: N, E, S, W

Brac Haven Villas has six, one-bedroom condos. ☎ 345-948-2478, fax 345-948-2329. Write to P.O. box 89, Stake Bay, Cayman Brac, BWI.

Divi Tiara Beach Hotel and Peter Hughes Dive Tiara cater almost exclusively to divers and snorkelers. This first-class resort features spacious, air-conditioned rooms, auto rentals, sailboards, bicycles and paddleboats. ☎ 800-367-3484 or 919-419-3484, fax 919-419-2075. Write to Divi Resorts, 6340 Quadrangle Drive, Suite 300 Chapel Hill, NC 27514.

There are other facilities such as **"Soon Come,"** a charming two-bedroom, beachfront, modern house for rent on the isolated south shore. Close to all the best south-side snorkel spots. ☎ 212-447-0337, fax 212-447-0335. E-mail: CLofting@aol.com.

LITTLE CAYMAN

Populated by fewer than 70 people, Little Cayman retains a rural and unhurried ambiance. Its grass runway, unpaved roads and limited phone service attest to its long-standing reputation as a great get-away vacation spot. Activities include diving, snorkeling, fly fishing and counting iguanas. Bring aspirin, bug repellent, decongestants, and suntan lotion from home.

Best Dives of Little Cayman

Little Cayman offers several superb snorkeling spots with visibility often exceeding 100 ft. Ground transportation to beach-access sites is easily arranged through the dive operators. For the ultimate in free diving head out to Bloody Bay and Spot Bay off the north shore where the seas are calm, and the marine life spectacular. The boat ride takes about 25 minutes. Average depth on top of the North Wall is 25 feet.

Note: The Western half of the wall is called the "Bloody Bay Wall" and the eastern half "Jackson Wall."

☆☆☆☆☆ **Bloody Bay Wall** is one of the top five dives in all the Caymans. The "Wall" peaks as a shallow reef at 15 ft and drops off to an unfathomed bottom. Bright orange and lavender tube sponges, pastel gorgonians and soft corals flourish in the shallows. An extremely friendly six-foot barracuda named Snort may join your dive—flashing his pearly whites while cheerfully posing for videos and still photos. Eagle rays blast by the wall along with slow-moving turtles and huge parrot fish. Spotted morays peek from the walls. Sea conditions are usually calm although a stiff wind will churn the surface. Super snorkeling in the shallows. Boat access.

☆☆☆☆ **Little Cayman Wall**, off the island's west end, starts shallow with a blaze of yellow, orange and blue sponges at 15, ft then drops off to unknown depths. Soft corals, big barrel sponges decorate the wall. Great for snorkeling. Boat access.

☆☆☆ **Point of Sand,** off the southeast end of Little Cayman, is excellent for experienced and beginning snorkelers. A gentle current flowing from west to east maintains excellent visibility. The bottom is sandy with many coral heads scattered about. Marine life is fine and the site is accessible from the shore. Ground transportation can be arranged from the resorts.

☆☆☆ Good snorkeling for beginners at **Mary's Bay** starts 50 yards from the beach—inside the barrier reef. There is no current and visibility runs about 30 to 50 ft. A host of fish and invertebrates are found in the shallows. Depth averages three to eight ft. The bottom is turtle grass requiring booties or other submersible footwear. An old shack on an otherwise deserted shore marks the spot.

☆☆ **Jackson Point**, aka School Bus, is for experienced snorkelers only. Swim out about 75 yards from the beach where you'll see a small wall towering from a sandy bottom at 40 ft to 15 ft. Hundreds of fish, rays and turtles congregate in the shallows. Corals and sponges carpet the area. Swimming another 50 to 60 ft brings you to a much larger wall which drops off to extraordinary depths.

☆☆ **Jackson Bay** resembles Jackson Point except for the bottom of the mini wall which drops off to a depth of 50 to 60 ft. Beach access.

☆☆☆ **Bloody Bay Point,** recommended for seasoned snorkelers, requires a 100-yard swim out to the reef. The bottom eases down to about 30 ft before the drop-off to The Great Wall begins. Well worth a visit for the spectacular coral and marine life.

☆ **Preston Bay,** just east of the lighthouse, provides another good shore-entry choice for beginning snorkelers. Maximum shoreline depth is six ft and visibility 30 to 50 ft. Swarming fish and a white sandy bottom offer endless photo opportunities.

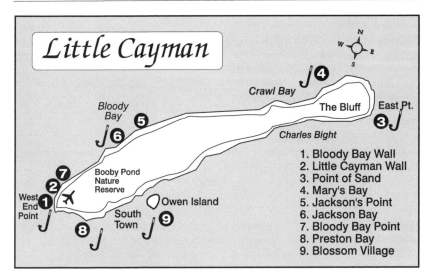

☆☆ **Blossom Village,** a lovely, shallow reef, displays crowds of reef fish and critters amidst staghorn and brain corals at depths from four to eight ft. Boat access. A light current maintains 50-100 ft visibility.

Where to Stay on Little Cayman

Little Cayman dive operations are smaller than those on Cayman Brac and Grand Cayman.

Little Cayman Beach Resort features air-conditioned rooms, fresh water pool, restaurant, and a full-service dive/photo operation. Windsurfers, sailboats and bicycles. ☎ 800-327-3835 or 813-323- 8727, fax 813-323-8827.

Southern Cross Club, a fishing and diving resort comprised of five double cottages, warmly welcomes divers. Snorkelers mix with scuba groups. ☎800-899-2582 or 345-948-1098 or in the United States 317- 636-9501. E-mail: scc@candw.ky. Website: http://scubacentral.com/scc.html. Write to: Southern Cross Club, Little Cayman, Cayman Islands, BWI.

Sam McCoy's Diving and Fishing Lodge, on the north shore, offers rustic accommodations for up to 14 divers (seven rooms). Rooms in the main lodge are air-conditioned with private bath. Twenty-ft fiberglass runabouts are used for reef trips. Shore diving from Jackson's Point. ☎800-626-0496 or 345-948-0026, fax 345-948-0057. Or write to Carl McCoy, P.O. Box 711, Georgetown, Grand Cayman, BWI.

Pirates Point Resort features rustic guest cottages and a guest house on seven acres of secluded white beach. Owner Gladys Howard offers friendly service. Snorkelers join scuba divers on tours. ☎ 800-327-8777 or 345-948-1010, fax 345-948-1011.

Travel Tips

Getting There: Cayman Airways provides scheduled flights from Miami, Houston, Atlanta, Tampa and Orlando to Grand Cayman with connecting flights to Cayman Brac and Little Cayman. Northwest, United, American and Air Jamaica fly nonstop from gateway cities into Grand Cayman. During peak season (Dec 15- April 15) charter flights direct from many major snowbelt cities to Grand Cayman are available from Cayman Airways. Flight time from Miami is 1½ hrs. Grand Cayman is a regular stop on many cruise lines as well.

Island Transportation: Rental cars, motorbikes, and bicycles are available on Grand Cayman and Cayman Brac. Friendly and informative taxi drivers are stationed at hotels and other convenient locations.

Driving: As in England, driving in the Cayman Islands is on the left. A temporary license is issued for a few dollars to persons holding US, Canadian or international licenses.

Documents: Proof of citizenship and an outbound ticket (birth certificate, voter's registration certificate) are required from US, British, or Canadian citizens. No vaccinations are required unless you are coming from an epidemic area.

Customs: The penalties for trying to bring drugs into the Cayman Islands are stiff fines and, frequently, prison terms. No spearguns or Hawaiian slings permitted into the country.

Currency: The Cayman Island Dollar, equal to US$1.20.

Climate: Temperatures average about 80°F year round. The islands are subject to some rainy periods, but generally sunny and diveable.

Clothing: Casual, lightweight clothing. Some nightclubs require that men wear a jacket. Wetskins or shorty wetsuits are useful to avoid abrasions as are light gloves for protection against the stinging corals. Snorkelers should wear protective clothing against sunburn.

Electricity: 110 V AC, 60 cycles. Same as US.

Time: Eastern Standard Time year-round.

Tax: There is a 6% government tax on accommodations. A service charge of 10 to 15% is added to hotel and restaurant bills. Departure tax is US$10.

Religious Services: Catholic, Protestant, Baptist, Mormon and non-denominational churches are found on Grand Cayman.

Additional Information: *United States:*—The Cayman Islands Department of Tourism, 6100 Blue Lagoon Drive, Suite 150, Miami, FL 33126-2085. ☎ 800-G-CAYMAN or 305-266-2300, fax 305- 267-2932. *New York:*—420 Lexington Ave, Suite 2733, New York NY. ☎ 212-682-5582, fax 212-986-5123. *United Kingdom*—6 Arlington Street, London, SW1A 1RE United Kingdom. ☎ 0171-491-7771, fax 0171-409-7773. *The Cayman Islands*—Write to Box 67, Grand Cayman, Cayman Islands, BWI. ☎ 345-949-0623; fax 345-949-4053. Website: www.caymans.com.

Cozumel & Akumal

Vacationers based on Cancun can easily arrange for bus trips to Akumal and boat trips to neighboring Isla Mujeres and Cozumel.

ISLA MUJERES

A lovely, snorkeling-depth reef aprons the south end of **Isla Mujeres**, a small island between Cancun and Cozumel, which can be easily reached via ferry from either spot. When you arrive, enter from the shore at Playa Garrafon, four miles from town. This spot—El Garrafon ("the carafe")—is one of the most populated (by fish and swimmers) in the Caribbean. Just wade out from the beach with some cracker crumbs and you'll immediately be surrounded by crowds of friendly fish. Ideal for first time snorkelers. The beach has a dive shop, showers, refreshment stands & shops.

COZUMEL

Cozumel, Mexico's largest island, lies 12 miles off the Yucatan Peninsula, separated by a 3,000 ft-deep channel. Dense jungle covers most of this island's interior, but its surrounding coast sparkles with miles of luxuriant, white sand beaches.

Noted for its incredible water clarity and marine life, Cozumel's fringing reef system is fed by warm, fast-moving Yucatan currents (a part of the Gulf Stream) as they sweep through the deep channel on the west side of the island. These currents bring a constant wash of plankton and other nutrients that support thousands of exotic fish. Most reef dive sites have too strong a current for snorkeling, but protected areas exist near the shore that are suitable. Visibility remains a constant 70 to 100 ft year round, except during and after major storms.

Tourist activity centers around San Miguel, the island's cultural and commercial center which boasts an impressive seaside shops, cantinas and restaurants. An ultra-modern cruise-ship terminal accommodates daily-arriving ocean liners and ferries from the mainland. Most resorts scatter along the west coast where calm waters prevail.

When to Go

The best time to visit Cozumel is from December till June. Water and air temperatures average 80°F year round with hotter conditions from June to October. Summer and fall often bring heavy rains or hurricanes.

Best Snorkeling Sites of Cozumel

Good snorkeling may be found all along Cozumel's east coast beaches. The reefs off the beaches at both the **Scuba Club Galapago Resort** and **Playa San Francisco** have some nice stands of elkhorn and brain coral with a constant show of juvenile tropicals and invertebrates.

Snorkelers should avoid the strong currents associated with drift diving on the outer reefs and stick to the inner reefs on calm days. Cozumel is for experienced ocean snorkelers only.

☆☆☆ **Paraiso Reef North** is a popular shallow dive just north of the cruise ship pier in San Miguel. The reef is accessible by swimming straight out 200 yds from the beach at the Hotel Sol Caribe or by dive boat. The remains of a twin engine airplane, sunk intentionally as part of a movie set, rests at 30 ft creating a home for a vast array of fish life. Huge green morays, eagle rays, turtles, yellowtail, French angels, schools of pork fish, butterfly fish, and queen trigger fish may be found. Check with the local dive shop before entering the water.

☆☆☆ **Chancanab Lagoon**, south of the cruise ship pier at Laguna Beach is protected from wind and waves. Ideal for snorkeling, depths range from very shallow to about 30 ft. Schools of grunts, angel fish, damsel fish, trumpet fish, turtles, and snapper dart between the clumps of coral. Seafans and soft corals adorn the reef. Visibility runs about 75 ft, sometimes better. Snorkeling gear may be rented from shops on the beach. Changing rooms, freshwater showers and lockers are available. Small admission fee. A botanical garden and restaurant are on the premises.

Cozumel Snorkeling Tours & Rentals

NOTE: To telephone or fax any of the Mexican listings from the U.S., dial 011 52 + 987 + the five digit number. In Mexico just dial the last five digits.

Most of the dive shops offer three to seven day, reduced-rate dive packages where you pay to go out with scuba divers. Before forking over your money, ask if refunds are given for missed dives and whether you can get that in writing. Some snorkelers prefer to pay each day rather than risk missing the boat or discovering the currents are too strong for snorkeling and losing the price of a trip. Strong currents frequently rule out snorkeling on the reefs.

Dive Palancar at the Diamond Resort has trips aboard a 44' custom dive boat to Palancar and Santa Rosa Reefs. Beach diving tours. Dive and snorkeling courses. English speaking guides. Boats on time. Check for currents before signing up for a tour. ☎ 800- 247-3483, (011) 52-987-23443 ext. 895.

Dive Paradise offers personalized tours for divers and snorkelers. Boats carry a maximum of seven people. Snorkelers join scuba trips. Shaded boats.

☎ (011) 52-987-21007, fax (011) 52-987-21061. E- mail: applep@cozumel.czm.com. mx. Write to: 601 Melgar, Cozumel, Quintana Roo, Mexico 77600.

Hotel packages are offered by Landfall Productions ☎ 800-525-3833.

Where to Stay in Cozumel

Hotel Presidente Inter-Continental, two miles south of town at the Chancanab Lagoon, resort features a large pool, tennis, restaurants and entertainment. Good snorkeling off the beach. ☎ 800-346-6116 or 800- 298-9009.

Casa Del Mar an affordable dive resort, across the street from the beach, offers 196 air-conditioned rooms, telephones, on-site dive shop, snorkeling reef in front of hotel, sand beach, shopping arcade, gardens, pool, and restaurant.

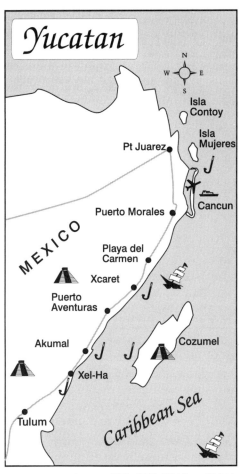

The hotel's bar is built from salvaged shipwrecks. ☎ 800-435-3240 or (011) 52-987-21900. Website: www.iminet.com/mexico/ coz202.html

Diamond Resort, located ten minutes from the best reefs, is a first-class, all-inclusive dive resort. On site, Dive Palancar provides boat tours and gear sales. Kayaks and paddle boats. Reasonable rates. ☎ 800-433-0885, (011) 52-987-23443, fax (011) 52-987-24508 or 713-680-2306. E-mail: divetours@aol.com. Website: www.dsi-divetours. com.

Fiesta Inn Cozumel offers 180 clean, air-conditioned deluxe rooms—all with satellite color TV, telephones, balconies, purified drinking water, large swimming pool, Jacuzzi, tennis court, karaoke bar and on site, Cafe La Fiesta. Decent snorkeling exists off the resort beach. ☎ 800-525-3833. E-mail: lndfall@aol.com. ☎ 800-FIESTA-1 or (011) 52-987-22899, fax (011) 52-987- 22154.

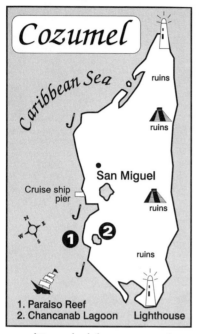

Cozumel

Caribbean Sea

ruins

ruins

San Miguel

Cruise ship pier

ruins

ruins

1. Paraiso Reef
2. Chancanab Lagoon   Lighthouse

Fiesta Americana Cozumel Reef features 172 deluxe ocean-and reef-view rooms and suites with satellite TV, on-site scuba shop, lighted tennis courts, custom charters, gym and jogging trail, two restaurants, gift shop, poolside snack bar, car, bike and moped rentals and purified water. Snorkeling trips. Vacation packages through Landfall. ☎ 800-525-3833, E-mail lndfall@aol.com. Hotel direct ☎ 800-FIESTA-1 or (011) 52-987-22622, fax (011) 52-987-22666. Website: www.fiestamexico.com.

Paradisus Cozumel, (formerly known as the Melia Mayan Paradisus) sits on Cozumel's longest stretch of natural beach. Located 2.5 miles from town on the Northeast side of the island, this all-inclusive hotel offers air-conditioned, deluxe ocean-view and garden view rooms. For diving and snorkeling trips, guests must travel to the Paradisus Beach & Dive Club on the southern side of the island. Hotel guests receive complimentary use of non-motorized sports equipment —kayaks, Sailfish, wind surfers and "spyaks" and lunch at no additional charge. ☎ 888-341-5993, (011) 52-987-20411, fax (011) 52-987-21599. E-mail: paradisu@cancun.rce. com.mx.

Scuba Club Galapago, (formerly the Galapago Inn) is both casual and elegant, with thatch-roofed huts lining the beach, a pool with three mosaic sea turtles, air-conditioned rooms (each with a refrigerator and spacious closet), gourmet dining and an on-site dive shop. Just off shore is a nice snorkeling reef. ☎ 800-847-5708; fax 713-783-3305. Vacation packages through Landfall ☎ 800-525-3833. Website: www.galapago.com.

AKUMAL

Akumal ("place of the turtle") lies 60 miles south of Cancun on Mexico's Yucatan Peninsula in an area known as the Tulum Corridor. Laid back and off the beaten track, this tiny resort community originated as a section of a large coconut plantation. It wasn't until 1958 that Mexican treasure divers salvaging a sunken Spanish galleon discovered great sport diving opportunities along the offshore barrier reef. Pristine corals and sponges, frequent turtle sightings, silky white, sand beaches and terrific beach snorkeling have popularized Akumal with a discriminating group of visitors. Three dive operators serve the area.

Drawbacks exist for those who like "pampered" tours—the boats are open with ladders—no platforms, no sun canopies. On the other hand, most sites lie close to shore, a five- to ten-minute boat ride. Spear fishing is prohibited.

Akumal dive operators also offer snorkelers freshwater tours to jungle pools or "cenotes," which are sunken limestone caverns with dazzling stalagmites and stalactities. These inland adventures combine a jungle trek through nature's most exotic gardens.

When to Go

The best time to dive Akumal is October through April. Weather is very hot in May and June and rain is heavy during July, August and September.

Best Snorkeling Sites of Akumal

Akumal's best snorkeling sites are inside a barrier reef that parallels the shoreline along Akumal Bay, neighboring Half Moon Bay and nearby Yalku Lagoon. Uncrowded beaches, secluded bays and a healthy marine population make Akumal delightful for family snorkeling vacations.

The reef structure comprises three distinct systems running parallel to one another at progressively deeper depths. The inner reef, where most snorkeling takes place is a network of patch reefs with depths from three to 35 feet with huge stands of elkhorn and formations of boulder, brain and plate corals. Frequent sightings of loggerhead, green and hawksbill turtles that nest along Yucatan beaches, highlight many dives.

Snorkelers exploring from the beach can swim up to the breakers on the reef. Conditions inside are normally calm with depths from three to 20 ft.

☆☆☆ **Akumal Bay's** best snorkeling is off the beach in front of the Club Akumal Caribe. Depths range from three feet to 20 feet with coral heads leading out to the breakers at the barrier reef. A variety of corals, sea fans, sponges, reef fish, occasional moray eels, barracudas, jacks, grouper, sting rays, parrot fish and turtles inhabit the bay. Bottom terrain is sandy with coral heads scattered about. Bay conditions inside the barrier reef are almost always tranquil.

☆☆☆ **Half Moon Bay**, about three minutes down the interior road from Akumal Bay, resembles Akumal Bay in terrain and marine life. This is a residential area, but anyone can use the beach.

☆☆☆☆ **Yalcu Lagoon**, at the end of the interior road, a short drive from Half Moon Bay, features several partially submerged caves, throngs of fish and crystal clear, tranquil water. Freshwater mixing with seawater provides nutrients and aquatic plants that attract rich marine life. Big parrot fish, angels, Spanish hogfish, rays, juvenile turtles and spotted eels nibble on the plants around the rocks. A natural entrance from the sea ensures a constant mix of nutrients. The outlying barrier reef protects this magnificent natural aquarium from wind-driven waves and rough seas.

Enter the lagoon from the head of the bay or climb down the big rocks anywhere along the shore. Guided boat and beach-entry snorkeling tours of Yalcu are offered by the dive shop at Club Akumal Caribe.

Inland Cenote

☆☆☆☆ **Nohoch Nah Chich**, listed in the *Guinness Book of World Records* as the world's longest underwater cave system, is also featured in the PBS TV series, *The New Explorers* as one of Yucatan's most exciting caverns. Visitors snorkel in the shallow fresh water amidst brilliant white stalactites and stalagmites. Unlimited visibility and an openness to the caverns offer breathtaking views.

Joining a jungle walk and snorkeling expedition to Nohoch Nah Chich involves a mile-and-a-half trek through impressive flora. Horses or donkeys carry your gear. Be sure to apply sun protective lotions and bug repellent and wear a hat that will shade your face. Not suitable for young children or people with severe disabilities or medical problems.

Snorkeling up and down the coast. . .

Several sheltered bays and secluded beaches with good shore-entry snorkeling exist along the coast. About six miles south of Akumal, the dirt road turnoff at KM 249 leads to ☆☆ **Chemuyil**, a quiet, horseshoe-shaped cove of tranquil water edged by a lovely, powder-white beach. A shallow snorkeling reef crosses the mouth of the bay. A small beach bar (the Marco Polo) serves fresh seafood, cold beer and soft drinks. Full camping facilities and a few tented "palapas" for overnight rental are available.

About 20 miles south of Akumal lies ☆☆ **Xel-Ha** (pronounced shell ha), the world's largest natural aquarium, covering 10 acres of lagoons, coves and inlets teeming with exotic fish. Platforms above the rocky limestone shore provide sea life viewing for non-swimmers. Unlike Akumal, this spot is packed with tourists. Busloads mobbed with avid snorkelers arrive by the moment in season.

A small admission fee is charged. On site showers, shops, a maritime museum, seafood restaurant and Subway sandwich shop serve visitors. Snorkeling gear is available for rent. Despite the crowds, most snorkelers, especially those touring with children, immensely enjoy this spot. Venture across highway 307 to visit some small ruins.

☆☆ **Xcaret** (Scaret), Mayan for "little inlet", about 40 miles north of Akumal, is a private ranch turned aquatic theme park. Once a Mayan port, this novel playground now features dolphin swims and snorkeling through "the underground river," which flows through a series of open- ended caves.

A mix of fresh and saltwater nourishes sea plants, which in turn feed armies of fish that entertain between 400 and 500 snorkelers per day. The effect is like drifting through a very big, very pretty, shaded pool stocked with fish. Holes in the "roof" of the caves filter light into a spectrum of colors.

Topside features include a wild-bird aviary, butterfly pavilion, saltwater aquarium, botanical garden and a couple of Mayan temple ruins, the Museum of Mayan Archaeological Sites with scale models of 26 Mayan ceremonial sites found on the Yucatan peninsula. There are three

Green Moray Eel

Photo © Jon Huber

restaurants, two snack bars, one cafeteria, showers, lockers, photo center, horse shows, gift shops and a sundeck with spectacular ocean views. Crowded, but very user friendly.

The Mayans prized Xcaret for their belief that its waters could purify bodies and souls, thus it became important as a "sacred bath" spot before crossing the sea to Cozumel to worship Ixchel, Goddess of Fertility.

We can't guarantee the fertility or soul-purifying prospects, but most snorkelers find Xcaret a fun day or half-day diversion. Michael Cherub, a snorkeling researcher returning from Xcaret, claims relief from back pain!

Akumal Snorkeling Tours & Rentals

Akumal Dive Center at Club Akumal offers boat tours. ☎ 800-351-1622, (011) 52-987-59025, fax 915-581-6709. E-mail: clubakumal@aol.com.

Mike Madden's Cedam Dive Centers operate from four locations—Club Oasis Puerto Aventuras, Beach Club Hotel Puerto Aventuras, Robinson Club Tulum and Club Oasis Aventuras Akumal. Tours include snorkeling trips to Nohoch the world's longest underwater cave (the Indiana Jones Jungle Adventure). ☎ (011)-52-987-35147, fax (011) 52-987-35129. E-mail: mmaden@cancun.rce.com.mx. Website: www.cedamdive.com. Note: The trip from Cancun to Cozumel by boat takes about 50 minutes.

Where to Stay in Akumal

Hotel Club Akumal Caribe features a variety of air-conditioned accommodations and an on-site dive shop. On the main beach choose from spacious Maya bungalows with garden views or first class hotel rooms facing the pool and ocean. Also on the main beach is the Cannon House Suite with two bedrooms, two baths, living room and kitchen.

Two bedroom condos on Half Moon Bay have one king size bed, two twins, kitchens and living rooms. Rates are low.

Contact the reservation office for additional information: In the US, ☎ 800-351-1622, in Canada ☎ 800-343-1440, in Texas, ☎ 915-584-3552, in Mexico, ☎ 95-(800) 351-1622. E-mail: club akumal@aol.com.

Travel Tips

Helpful Phone Numbers: Police, *Cozumel:* ☎ 20092; hospital, Cozumel ☎ 20140.

Getting There: Direct flights to Cozumel and Cancun from the US are offered by , American Airlines ☎ (800) 733-4300), Continental, United, Northwest, Mexicana and Aero Mexico. There are additional domestic flights from Acapulco, Cancun, Guadalajara, Mexico City, Merida, Monterey, and Veracruz. Cruise ships from Miami: Norwegian Caribbean Lines, Holland America, Carnival. Cozumel island also can be reached by bus ferry, car ferry and hydrofoil from Cancun. Isla Mujeres is reached by bus ferry, car ferry and air taxi from Cancun. AeroCozumel and Aerocaribe fly between the islands. Cozumel is a 40- to 60-minute boat trip from Cancun.

Island Transportation: Taxi service is inexpensive and readily available. Mopeds, cars and Jeeps may be rented in town or at the airport. Book rental cars in advance of your trip.

Departure tax: $12.

Driving: On the right.

Documents: US and Canadian citizens need a tourist card. To obtain one, you must show a valid passport or birth certificate with raised seal. Citizens of other countries should contact their nearest Mexican consulate for regulations. The tourist card is necessary to leave the country as well and may be obtained from the Mexican consulate or your airline prior to departure.

Customs: Plants, flowers and fruits may not be brought into Cozumel. Persons carrying illegal drugs will be jailed. You may bring three bottles of liquor and one carton of cigarettes. Dogs and cats should have a current vaccination certificate. Divers carrying a lot of electronic or camera gear, especially video equipment, should register it with US Customs in advance of the trip.

Water: Drink only bottled or filtered water to avoid diarrheal intestinal ailment. Also avoid raw vegetables and the skin of fruit and foods that sit out for any length of time.

Currency: The exchange rate of the Mexican peso fluctuates a great deal. At this writing US$1 = 5.5 nuevos pesos. Banks are open weekday mornings. Major credit cards and traveler's checks are widely accepted in Akumal, Cancun and Cozumel.

Climate: Temperatures range from the low 70's in winter to the high 90's in summer, with an average of about 80° F. Winter months bring cooler weather; summer and fall, chance of heavy rain.

Clothing: Lightweight, casual. Wetsuits are not needed, but lightweight (1/8") short suits or wetskins are comfortable on deep wall dives.

Electricity: 110 volts; 60 cycles (same as US).

Time: Central Standard Time.

Language: Spanish; English widely spoken.

For Additional Information: *In New York,* Mexican Government Tourist Office, 405 Park Avenue, Suite 1400, New York, NY 10022. ☎ 800-446-3942 or 212-421-6655, fax 212-753-2874. *In California,* 10100 Santa Monica Blvd., Los Angeles, CA 90067. ☎ 310-203-0821; *In Florida,* 128 Aragon Avenue, Coral Gables, FL 33134 ☎ 305-443-9160. *In Canada,* Mexican Government Tourist Office, Suite 1526, One Place Ville Marie, Montreal, Quebec, Canada H3B 2B5 ☎ 514- 871-1052, fax 514-871-1052. *In the U.K.,* Mexican Government Tourism Office, 60/61 Trafal-gar Square, 3rd Floor, London, England WC2N 5DS. ☎ 44-71-734-1058, fax 44-71-930-9202. Website: www.mexico-travel.com\.

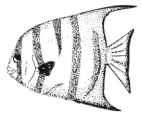

Curaçao

Curaçao, the largest of five islands that make up the Netherlands Antilles, which include Bonaire, Saba, Saint Maarten and St. Eustatius, is a dry and hilly island completely surrounded with rich coral reefs. Its coastline sparkles with beautiful sand beaches, secluded lagoons and coves.

Watersports and tourist activity center around the main resort and beach area off Willemstadt, the capital city, which boasts superb shopping, fine restaurants and a safe environment.

Like its sister islands, Aruba and Bonaire, Curaçao lies far south of the hurricane belt and offers clear skies and good diving year-round. Most dives require a boat. The reefs and wrecks are "a stone's throw from shore," but the "shore" adjacent to the best reefs is often formed of jagged, razor-like, ironshore cliffs. Seas along the south coast—locale of the Curaçao Underwater Park—are usually calm in the morning, but may kick up a three- or four-ft surge in mid-afternoon.

The Curaçao Underwater Park, established in 1983 by the Netherlands Antilles National Park Foundation (STINAPA), stretches 12½ miles from the Princess Beach Hotel to East Point and features more than 20 dive sites marked by numbered mooring buoys. Within the park, snorkelers find crystal-clear water and spectacular seascapes. The reefs are in pristine condition with many yet to be explored.

Best Snorkeling Sites

☆☆☆ **Kalki Beach**, a sheltered cove just south of Westpunt on the northern tip of the island, is Curacao's favorite beach-entry site. A short swim out brings you over hard corals and rocks alive with parrot fish, blue tangs, grunts, small barracuda, anemones and encrusting sponges.

☆☆☆☆ **Jan Thiel Reef**, just outside of Jan Thiel Bay off Willemstadt, has lush, shallow gardens at 15 ft with massive gorgonians, two-foot lavender sea anemones, seafans, long, purple tube sponges, pastel star, leaf, fire, pencil and brain corals. Fishlife is superb with walls of grunts, trumpetfish, parrot fish, angels and small rays. Added buoyancy from a snorkeling vest or shorty wetsuit will help you to stay clear of the fire coral. Swim out from Playa Jan Thiel, just east of the Princess Beach Hotel. The beach has changing facilities and is a favorite for picnics. Admission fee.

Facing: *Christ of the Abyss, Key Largo, Floric*

Hanauma Bay, O'ahu, Hawaii
Photo © Robert Coello, Hawaii Visitors and Convention Bureau

Snorkeling off Andros, Bahamas
Photo © Small Hope Bay Lodge

Facing page, *Molokini Crater Island, Hawaii* © Robert Coello, Hawaii Visitors Bureau

Muraled Building, Route 1, Key Largo, FL.
Photo © Jon Huber

Queen Angelfish (Holacanthus ciliaris)
Photo © Jon Huber

Facing: *Bahamas* Photo © Jean Michel Cousteau's Out Islands Snorkeling Adventures

South Shore, Bermuda
Photo © Bermuda Department of Tourism

*Snorkelers demonstrate proper technique of touching a manatee,
using just one open hand.*

Photo © Francois Fournier

Facing page *Saba Reef Scene* Photo © Joan Borque, Sea Saba

Squirrel Fish (Holocentrus coruscum)
Photo © Jon Huber

Snorkeler over Elkhorn Corals, Bonaire
Photo © Jon Huber

Facing, **Willemstad, Curaçao** Photo © Jon Huber

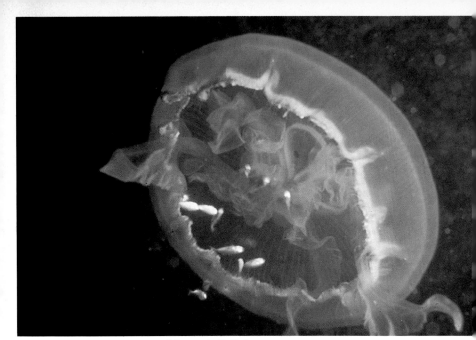

Moon Jellyfish (Aurelia aurita)
Photo © Jon Huber

West Punt, Curaçao
Photo © Jon Huber

Facing: *Tube Sponges, Bahamas Out Islands*

Spanish Hogfish (Bodianus rufus)
Photo © Jon Huber

Smooth Trunk Fish (Lactophrys triqueter)
Photo © Jon Huber

✮✮✮ **Sandy's Plateau** (aka *Boka Di Sorsaka*), is part of a marked snorkeling trail that can be reached by swimming out from Jan Thiel Bay. It is an excellent spot for novice divers and snorkelers. The terrain, a combination of walls and steep slopes, supports radiant lavender and pink star corals, yellow pencil corals and orange tube sponges. Lush stands of elkhorn coral grow to within 10 ft of the surface. Dense coral flows around an undercut ledge from 10 to 30 ft. Soldierfish, trumpetfish and schools of sergeant majors hover at the ledge.

Nearby, just offshore to the Curaçao Seaquarium, lies the wreck of the ✮✮✮ **S.S. Oranje Nassau**, a Dutch steamer that ran aground on the Koraal Specht over 80 years ago. Also known as *Bopor Kibra,* Papiamento for broken ship, this is a favorite spot for free diving. The seas are always choppy over the wreck. Entry is best from the diveshop docks adjacent to the seaquarium. Check with the divemaster for the day's conditions.

This area is known for outstanding corals. Depths start shallow with large pillar and star corals, seafans, huge brain coral, and gorgeous stands of elkhorn. It then terraces off to greater depth. Fish life includes swarms of blue chromis and creole wrasses, French angels, barracuda and jacks. Sea conditions are choppy and recommended for advanced snorkelers with some ocean experience.

The mooring for ✮✮✮ **PBH** sits straight out from the Princess Beach Hotel's beach. This reef starts shallow enough for snorkeling then drops off. Arrow crabs, octopi, and hordes of juvenile fish swim the shallow terrace.

✮✮✮ **Bullen Bay**, just north of the park, is an outstanding dive with a protected shallow area for snorkeling. Yellow pencil corals and pretty white sea plumes highlight the reef. Average shallows' depth runs 10 ft. Boat access.

Beaches

Beautiful, white-sand beaches surround Curaçao, from popular hotel beaches to intimate secluded coves. Along the southern coast, you'll find free public beaches at West Point Bay, Knip Bay, Klein Knip, Santa Cruz, Jeremi Bay and Daaibooi Bay. Knip Bay is the largest and loveliest swimming beach on the island. Fish watching is good along the adjacent cliffs.

The main private beaches, which charge a small fee per car, are Blauw Bay, Jan Thiel, Cas Abao, Barbara Beach and Port Marie.

Be careful of the tree with small green apples that borders some beaches. This is the manzanilla and its sap will cause burns and blisters on wet exposed skin. Its fruit is poisonous.

Snorkeling Tours & Rentals

Reef snorkeling trips may be booked through the following operators. Snorkelers join scuba divers on the dive boats.

Coral Cliff Divers, Coral Cliff Hotel at Santa Martha Bay. Owner/Manager Marlies Feijts. ☎ (011) 5999-8642822, fax 8642237.

Curaçao Seascape, on the beach at the Curaçao Caribbean Hotel, has fast, comfortable, custom dive boats and friendly service. Snorkelers welcome. Manager, Eva Van Dalen. ☎ (011) 5999-4625000, fax 4625846.

Habitat Curaçao Dive Resort, Rif St. Marie. Albert Romijn, Manager. ☎ 5999-8648800, fax 8648464.

Peter Hughes/Princess Dive Facility, at the Princess Beach Resort & Casino, Holiday Inn Crowne Plaza Hotel, offers reef trips and certification courses. Lex Kleine, Manager. ☎ In US 800-932-6237. Curaçao (11) 5999-4658991, fax 4655756. E-Mail: dancer@winnet.net.

Red Sail Sports, at Sonesta Beach Hotel, Piscadera Bay. Staff carries gear and tanks. Towels provided. In US ☎ 800-255-6425. Curaçao (011) 5999-7368800, fax 4627502.

Scuba Do Dive Center, at Jan Thiel Beach & Sports Resorts. Contact H. Ferwerda. ☎ 5999-7679300, fax 7679300.

Underwater Curaçao, adjacent to the Seaquarium, at the Lion's Dive Hotel is a PADI Five star facility. Their double-decker dive boats can easily accommodate large groups. Underwater Curaçao's services include round-trip mini-van service from your hotel or cruise ship.☎(011) 5999-4618100, fax 4618200.

Where to Stay

Curaçao Caribbean Hotel & Casino is a huge beachfront hotel with Seascape Diving on premises. ☎ 800-545-9376 or 203-831-0682, fax 203-831-0817. Write to P.O. Box 2133, Curaçao, NA.

Habitat Curaçao, on the southwest coast in St. Marie, offers restaurant, pool, satellite TV, tennis courts and a variety of watersports. ☎ 800-327-6709 fax 305-438-4220. Curaçao (011) 5999-8648800 fax 8648464. E-mail: maduro@netpoint.- net.

Holiday Beach Hotel & Casino is located on Coconut Beach facing the Curaçao Underwater Park. The 200- room hotel has a complete dive shop, beach, casino, two restaurants, pool, tennis courts and handicapped facilities. ☎ 800-444-5244 (US & Canada). Curaçao (011) 5999-4625400, fax 4625409.

Lions Dive Hotel & Marina is a luxurious, 72-room, oceanfront dive complex adjacent to the Curaçao Seaquarium. Rooms overlook the Curaçao

Marine Park and the *Orange Nassau*. The resort features three restaurants, fitness center and dive shop, ☎ 800-451-9376 (US), fax 4618200.

The Princess Beach Resort & Casino, overlooks a long white-sand beach. Luxury accom modations, swimup bar, shopping, restaurant and casino. Snorkeling off the beach. ☎ 800-332-8266, (011) fax 4614131.

Sonesta Beach Resort & Casino has a beachfront location with 248 rooms. Casino, three restaurants, fitness center, pool, satellite TV, tennis courts and watersports. ☎ (011)5999-7368800 or fax (011) 5999-4627502.

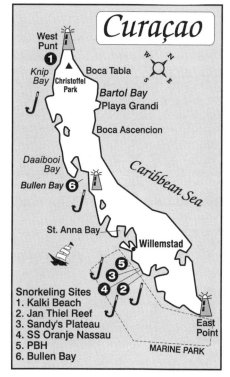

Snorkeling Sites
1. Kalki Beach
2. Jan Thiel Reef
3. Sandy's Plateau
4. SS Oranje Nassau
5. PBH
6. Bullen Bay

Travel Tips

Helpful Phone Numbers: Police, ☎ 114; Taxi Service, ☎ 616711; Island Bus Service, ☎ 684733.

Getting There: ALM Airlines flies from Atlanta four times a week (Thursday, Friday, Saturday and Sunday), and daily from Miami. Connecting flights are available from most major cities on Air Aruba, American Airlines and Guyana Airways..

Driving: Traffic moves on the right. A US driver's license is accepted. Car rentals: Budget, ☎ 683198; National, ☎ 683489 or 611644; Jeep Car Rental, ☎ 379044; Love Car Rental, ☎ 690444; 24-Hour Car Rental, ☎ 689410 or 617568. Curaçao also has an excellent bus system to transport visitors around the island.

Language: The official language is Dutch, but English and Spanish are spoken as well. Most residents speak Papiamento, a blend of Portuguese, Dutch, African, English, French and some Arawak Indian.

Documents: Passports are not required for US and Canadian Citizens. Travelers will need proof of citizenship and a return or continuing ticket. A passport or birth certificate is necessary for reentering the US.

Customs: Arriving passengers may bring in 400 cigarettes, 50 cigars, 100 cigarillos, 2 liters of liquor. There is a duty-free shop at the airport.

US residents may bring home, free of duty, $400 worth of articles, including 200 cigarettes, and 1 quart liquor per person over 21 years of age plus $25 worth of Edam or Gouda cheese for personal use.

Airport Tax: For international flights, $10; for inter island flights, $5.65.

Currency: The guilder, or florin, is the Netherlands Antilles' unit of money. The official rate of exchange is US $1 = 1.77 N.A. florin. However, US dollars and major credit cards are accepted throughout the island.

Climate: Curaçao's tropical climate remains fairly constant year round. The average temperature is 80° F and less than 23 inches of rain fall annually. The island is outside of the hurricane belt and its cooling trade winds average 15 mph.

Clothing: Snorkelers should bring wetskins or long-sleeve shirts to protect from the sun. Wetsuits are comfortable when making several deep dives, but warm ocean temperatures makes them unnecessary baggage for the average sport diver. Topside dress is casual, lightweight. Topless sunbathing is practiced on some beaches. Jackets are required for a few restaurants.

Electricity: 110-128 volts, A.C. (50 HZ), which is compatible with American electric razors and blow dryers. Adaptors are not needed. The Lions Dive Hotel has 220 volts.

Religious Services: Protestant, Catholic, Jewish, Episcopal, Seventh Day Adventist.

Additional Information: Curaçao Tourist Board, 475 Park Avenue South, Suite 2000, New York NY 10016, ☎ 800-332-8266 or 212-683-7660, fax 212- 683- 9337. *In Miami*, 330 Biscayne Boulevard, Suite 808, Miami, FL 333132, ☎ 305- 374-5811, fax 305-374-6741.

In Curaçao: The Curaçao Tourism Development Foundation, 19 Willemstad, Netherlands Antilles; ☎ 011-5999-4616000, fax 011-5999-4612305. E-mail Curaçao @ix.netcom.com. Website: www. interknowledge.com/Curaçao/index/html.

Dominica

Dominica, the largest island in the Windward chain, sits off-the-beaten-track between Martinique and Guadeloupe. It is ideal for the snorkeler who also enjoys rugged rainforest hikes and a wilderness environment. Narrow strips of black-sand beaches that encircle the island rise to a mountainous interior where simmering volcanic pools, exotic rain forests and thundering rivers harmonize.

The island's most outstanding feature is water with more than 365 rivers, thermal springs, pools, and waterfalls fed by 350 inches of rainfall per year in the interior and 50 inches on the drier west coast. Thankfully, all of the resorts and snorkeling sites lie off the "dry" western shores.

Subsea terrain, too, is unique with hot springs bubbling up through the sea floor amidst shallow wrecks and walls of critters.

Roseau, the capital and main city, is a busy area which may be seen in its entirety by way of a half-hour walk. Most interesting are some old French Colonial buildings, botanical gardens at the south end and the Old Market on the waterfront where island crafts are offered.

Visitors arriving by cruise ship at the Cabrits National Park, on the north west tip of Dominica, step off the 300-ft pier and are immediately surrounded by twin waterfalls and a lush garden.

When to Go.

The best time to dive Dominica is during the driest season, February through April, though expect the possibility of "liquid sunshine" (rain) all year. Whenever you go, plan on doing combat with a ferocious mosquito population, especially at dawn and dusk.

Best Snorkeling Sites

None recommended for children.

☆☆☆☆ **Soufriere Pinnacle** rises from the depths of Soufriere Bay to within five feet of the surface. A favorite of macro-photographers, the pinnacle is a cornucopia of crabs, shrimp, lobster, octopi, anemones, starfish, tree worms, and gorgonians. Calm seas and light currents invite all levels of diver and snorkeler. The site is four miles off the southwest shore—a 15-minute boat ride.

☆☆☆☆ **Coral Gardens**, a short trip from Castaways Beach, is a shallow reef with depths from 15 ft. Good for free diving and surface snorkeling, the reef is vibrant with corkscrew and pink anemones, arrow crabs, violet Peterson shrimp, flourescent crinoids and flamingo tongue snails. Spotted and green moray eels, sting rays and scorpion fish hide in the shadows.

☆☆☆ **Scotts Head Dropoff** lies five miles off Scotts Head, a fishing village at the southern tip of the island. Snorkelers will find large sponges and lavish soft corals along the reef's shallow ledge, which starts at five ft. Conditions are light to moderate. Good visibility. Boat access

☆☆ **Champagne** is a shallow site highlighted by sub-aquatic, freshwater, hot springs which emit a continuous profusion of hot bubbles. A fun dive, it's like jumping into a giant glass of hot club soda. Near shore with dependably calm conditions, the site covers an area of about 300 square ft. Depths range from near the surface with 10 ft the average. The bottom is uninspiring brown weeds ruffled by schools of tiny sprat, reef fish and lobster. A few divers report the bubbles to be too hot for comfort! Boat access.

☆☆☆ **Canefield Barge**, an overturned barge rests on patches of shallow reef. Depths from five ft, hordes of friendly reef fish and calm seas make this a good choice for snorkelers. Basket stars, anemones, hydroids and iridescent sponges cover the wreck. Boat access.

☆☆☆ **Point Guinard Caves**, an area of shallow reefs, grottoes and caves, are fun for all level snorkelers. Expect to find sea horses, blood stars, octopi, crabs, lobster and hordes of sponges. Boat access.

Beach-entry Snorkeling Sites

The best shore entry snorkeling spots are Scotts Head on Sourfriere Bay in the southwest and Douglas Bay in the northwest which has a reef less than 200 feet from the shore. Point Guignard off the southwest coast is another popular spot. On the north and northeast coasts try Woodford Hill Bay, Hodges Bay, Grand Baptiste Bay and Hampstead Beach. Check with dive shops for wind and water conditions before snorkeling.

Snorkeling Tours & Rentals

Dive Dominica at Castle Comfort Lodge is a full service dive center. Snorkelers join scuba divers. Whale and dolphin-watching cruises. Beach diving in front of the lodge. ☎ 888-262-6611 or 809-448-2188, fax 809-448-6088. E-mail: dive@tod.dm. Website: www.delphis.dm /dive. html.

Anchorage Dive Centres offers reef, wreck and whale watching aboard two fast boats. Hotel packages. ☎ 809-448-2638; Fax: 809-448-5680. Write to P.O. Box 34, Roseau, Dominica.

Dive Castaways features personal tours to their own special sights. ☎ 800-223-9815 or 809-449-6244, fax 809-449-6246. Write to P.O. Box 5, Roseau, Dominica. E-mail: castaways@mail.tod.dm. Website: www.delphis.dm/castaways.htm.

Nature Island Dive caters to small groups with a variety of water and landsports including kayaking and mountain biking. Dive boats visit Soufriere, Scotts Head Reserve and local reefs. Snorkelers join scuba divers on a space-available basis. ☎ 809-449-8181, fax 809-449-8182. E-mail: walshs @ tod.dm.

Vacation Packages

Landfall Productions, run by dive instructors and underwater photo pros, Karen and Dennis Sabo, offer group and individual tours to Dominica. ☎ 800-525-3833, fax: 510-794-1617. E-mail: lndfall @aol. com. Write to 39675 Cedar Boulevard, Suite 295, Newark, CA 94560.

Paradise Expedition & Trading Co. Ltd packages vacations from the US. Write to: Six Lincoln Park Plaza, Lincoln Park, N.J. 07035. ☎ 800-468-4748; Fax: 201-696-2335.

Island Trails arranges guided snorkeling tours for groups. ☎ 800-233-4366.

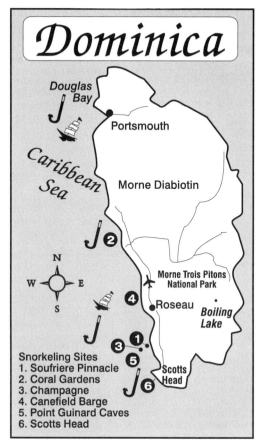

Dominica

Douglas Bay

Portsmouth

Caribbean Sea

Morne Diabiotin

N
W — E
S

Morne Trois Pitons National Park

Roseau   Boiling Lake

Snorkeling Sites
1. Soufriere Pinnacle
2. Coral Gardens
3. Champagne
4. Canefield Barge
5. Point Guinard Caves
6. Scotts Head

Scotts Head

Where to Stay

Anchorage Hotel & Dive Center, one-mile south of Roseau, features 32 air-conditioned, clean, modern rooms, cable TV, phones, squash court, pool, bar, restaurant, and full-service PADI dive center. Whale- and dolphin-watching cruises. ☎ 809-448-2638, fax 809-448-5680. E-mail: anchorage @mail.TOD.dm.

Castle Comfort Diving Lodge is a cozy 10-room inn. Five rooms have ocean-view balconies. All are air-conditioned and have ceiling fans. Great meals! Friendly service. Good snorkeling off the shore. In the US reserve through Landfall, ☎ 800-525-3833. Hotel direct: ☎ 809-448-2188, fax 809-448-6088. E-mail: dive@tod.dm.

The Castaways Beach Hotel, a charming 27-room waterfront resort surrounded by botanical gardens, features modern, spacious guest rooms with ceiling fans and air conditioning. A beachfront terrace overlooks the sea. Adjacent dive shop. ☎ 888-CASTAWAYS or 809-449-6244/5, fax: 809-449-6246. E-mail: castaways@ mail.tod.dm. Website: www.delphis.dm/castaways.htm.

Travel Tips

Helpful Phone Numbers: Police ☎ 999, Ambulance ☎ 999, Tourist Board: 809-448-2351/82186, Canefield Airport ☎ 449-1199, American Eagle ☎ 445-7204, Liat ☎ 448-2421, Air Guadeloupe ☎ 448-2181, Cardinal Airlines ☎ 449-0322.8922.

Airlines: Reaching Dominica requires a stop in San Juan, Antigua, St. Lucia, St. Maartin or Guadeloupe. From most European and North American cities, it can be reached in a day's journey without an overnight stay. Liat, Air Guadaloupe, Air Martinique and Nature Island Airways are the carriers from the larger islands into Dominica. Gateway islands are served by American Airlines (☎ 800-433-7300).

Island Transportation: All areas may be reached via bus and taxi services.

Baggage: Only one carry-on bag is permitted and it must fit under your seat. International baggage allowances prevail on flights to Dominica and may not exceed a total of 44 pounds.

Driving: On the left. A local license is required and may be obtained from the airport or at the Traffic Department, High Street, Roseau (Mon. to Fri.).

Documents: US and Canadian citizens need a passport or proof of citizenship bearing a photograph. A return or onward ticket is also required.

Currency: The Eastern Caribbean Dollar $2.67 to US $1.

Language: English is the official language. Creole or French patois is widely spoken.

Climate: Frequent rain. Average temperatures range from 75°F to 90°F.

Clothing: Lightweight casual cottons. No swim suits or short shorts in shops or stores. In winter, a shorty or wetsuit jacket is recommended.

Electricity: 220/240 volts, 50 cycles. A converter is necessary for US appliances.

Time: Atlantic Standard Time, one hour ahead of Eastern Standard Time and four hours behind GMT.

Valuables: Lock everything up as you would at home. Avoid taking valuables to the beach.

Departure Tax: $12 US.

Religious Services: Roman Catholic, Anglican, Methodist, Pentecostal, Berean Bible, Baptist, Adventist and Baha'i Faith.

Additional Information: *US*—Caribbean Tourism Organization, 20 East 46th St., N.Y., N.Y. 10017-2452 USA, ☎ 212-475-7542, fax: 212-697-4258. *London,* —Dominica Tourist Office, 1 Collingham Gardens, London SW5 OHW, ☎ 071 835-1937; Fax: 071 373-8743. *Dominica,* National Development Corp., P.O. Box 73, Roseau, Commonwealth of Dominica, W.I. ☎ 809-448-2351/82186; Fax: 809-448-5840. Website: frenchcaribbean.com/DominicaActivSports.html.

Florida Keys

A wealth of topside attractions, fabulous resorts and restaurants combined with spectacular offshore coral reefs attract more than a million divers and snorkelers to the Florida Keys each year. Key Largo, the jumping off point to the Keys lies 42 miles south-southwest of Miami. All points from Key Largo to Key West connect to the mainland and to each other by the Overseas Highway, a continuation of US Route 1.

Dive shops offering snorkeling tours line the 100-mile route from Key Largo to Key West. Whether you choose to stay in Key West for its wealth of topside attractions, Key Largo for the John PenneKamp Marine Sanctuary or the middle keys, you won't be disappointed. Patches of finger-like, spur and groove reefs parallel the islands from Key Biscayne to Key West and are inhabited by more than 500 varieties of fish and corals. Shallow depths, ideal for underwater video and still photography, range from just below the surface to an average maximum of 40 feet. There are shallow shipwrecks, such as the wreck of the *San Pedro*, an underwater archaeological preserve off Islamorada, miles of coral canyons and pinnacles, the famous Statue of Christ in Key Largo, and every imaginable fish along the entire coast.

The reef lies between four and eight miles offshore. There are no beach-entry reef sites, but small boat rentals and guided snorkeling trips are offered throughout the Keys.

Before venturing off shore, be sure to pick up a copy of the rules and regulations for boaters and divers. Everything living is protected in Florida's marine parks. Wearing gloves, touching corals and feeding fish are prohibited. Spear fishing is outlawed. Certain foods eaten by humans can be unhealthy and often fatal to fish. Touching corals may kill them or cause infection or disease which can spread to surrounding corals. The entire area has recently gained status as **The Florida Keys National Marine Sanctuary**, an underwater park administered by the National Park Service.

When to Go

The official high season in the Keys runs from mid December to mid-March, but many snorkelers prefer springtime—March, April and May—for the usually dry skies and warm seas. The rainy season starts the end of June and continues till late mid October. Winter, especially January and February bring an occasional drop in air temperature.

The best time to tour the outer reefs

Good snorkeling on the Florida Keys shallow reefs depends on good weather conditions. High winds that churn up surface swells also stir up the sandy bottom. You might plan a reef trip the morning after a storm and find visibility as low as 25 ft, yet return in the afternoon to calm seas and visibility in excess of 100 ft.

When storms rule out trips to the outer reefs, visit the Content Keys, a sheltered area which is almost always calm, located on the Gulf side of Marathon. The corals and sponges don't rival the outer reefs, but the fish life is good and there are some nice hard corals and encrusting sponges.

In Key Largo you might explore the swimming lagoon at John Pennekamp State Park. There are some old cannons and a sunken car. This artificial reef attracts numerous fish and crustaceans. An occasional manatee has been spotted too.

Places to Avoid

Snorkeling is unsafe in the brackish and fresh waters of the Everglades—home to alligators. There is a crocodile sanctuary on the northernmost tip of Key Largo which must be avoided. Alligators and, even more so, crocodiles are unpredictable and despite a sluggish appearance must be considered extremely dangerous to humans. If you're unfamiliar with the area, stick to the ocean, avoid the bays, especially in the northern keys.

Dolphin Swims

An opportunity to swim with the dolphins awaits you in any one of three Florida Keys facilities. You must be at least 13 years old, know how to swim and attend an orientation session with a dolphin trainer. Advance reservations are a must. Cost starts at $75.

Dolphins Plus Inc. 147 Corrine Place, Key Largo 33037; ☎ 305-451-1993.

Theatre of the Sea, (MM 84), Islamorada FL 33036; ☎ 305-664-2431.

Dolphin Research Center, (MM 59), Grassy Key, Marathon Fl 33050; ☎ 305-289-1121.

Best Snorkeling Sites

The Upper Keys — Key Largo to Islamorada

Conditions on the reefs vary with the wind, from flat calm with no current to high seas with strong currents. Two to four-ft seas are the norm with a light current. The inner reefs are always calmer, but visibility isn't as good. Check with individual snorkeling tour companies or dive shops for daily weather and sea conditions.

☆☆☆☆ **The Statue.** Key Largo's most popular dive, underwater wedding site and perhaps the one which symbolizes the area, is a nine-foot bronze replica of **"Christ of the Abyss"**, created by sculptor Guido Galletti for placement in the Mediterranean Sea. The statue was given to the Underwater Society of America in 1961 by industrialist Egidi Cressi.

The statue rises from a sandy bottom at 25 ft to just nine feet from the surface. Huge brain corals and elkhorn formations surround the base. Stingrays and barracuda inhabit the site.

Exercise caution when using your own boat. A buoy marks the statue's location, but swells may make it difficult to find without sophisticated navigation equipment. Extreme shallows in the area make running aground a threat.

☆☆☆☆ More easily found is **Molasses Reef**, marked by a huge, lighted steel tower in the southeast corner of the park. Noted as the area's most popular reef dive, it holds the distinction of having had two shiploads of molasses run aground on its shallows.

The reef provides several dives, depending on where your boat is moored. Moorings M21 through M23 are for scuba diving. M1 through M20 are shallow and better for snorkeling.

Be sure to check the current at Molasses before entering the water since an occasional strong flow makes the area unsafe. Depths vary from very shallow to approximately 40 ft.

☆☆☆☆☆ Slightly northeast of Molasses stands **French Reef**, an area many consider the prettiest in the park with ledges carpeted in pink and lavender sea fans, tube sponges, soft corals and anemones. Shallow depths range from areas where the reef pierces the surface to 20 ft.

Despite pristine reefs and a robust fish population, a long boat ride prevents most dive operators from frequenting **Carysfort Reef**, located in the northeast corner of the park.

If you are fortunate enough to catch a trip out there, expect a good display of fish and the possibility of one huge, resident barracuda, tamed by a local dive master, swimming up to within an inch of your mask. This unique, engaging plea for a handout makes the toothy guy tough to ignore, but sanctuary officials discourage fish feeding so try to resist sharing your lunch. Instead, explore the reef's healthy display of staghorn, elk horn and star corals at depths varying from very shallow.

☆☆☆☆ South of Pennekamp Park lies **Pickles Reef**, a shallow area rich with marine life, sea fans and boulder corals. Residents of the wreck include parrot fish, schools of grunt, sergeant majors, moray eels and angels.

☆☆☆ Another popular site frequented by Islamorada dive shops is **Alligator Reef**, home to walls of grunts, parrotfish and groupers and an occasional nurse shark. There are some nice stands of elk horn and brain corals.

Key Largo Boat Tours
(use area code 305)

Snorkeling trips to the park are offered by the following tour operators: **Coral Reef Park Co.**, MM 102.5 (inside Pennekamp State Park, (☎ 451-1621), the **Sun Diver Station Snorkel Shacks**, MM 103 bayside (☎ 451-2220) or at the Best Western docks, MM100 oceanside (☎ 451- 9686), **Silent World Dive Center**, mm 103.2 (☎ 451-3252), **Upper Keys Dive and Sport Center** (☎ 853-0526), **It's a Dive** (☎ 453-9881), **Scuba-Do Charters**, MM 100 (☎ 451-3446), **Sharky's Inc**, MM 106 Plaza (☎ 451-5533), **Divers City**, MM 104 Oceanside (☎ 451-4554), **Ocean Divers** MM 100 (☎ 451-1113), **The Keys Diver**, MM 100 (☎ 451-1177), and aboard the **HMS Minnow**, MM 100 Holiday Inn docks (☎ 541-7834), **American Diving Headquarters, Inc.** at MM 105.5 (☎ 451-0037. Snorkel tours usually leave the park docks at 9:00 am, noon and 3:00 pm.

Captain Corky's Divers' World at MM 99.5 offers custom snorkeling charters, including three- and five-day live-aboard trips. ☎ 451-3200. Write to P.O. Box 1663, Key Largo, FL 33037.

Islamorada

Offshore Islamorada, on the Atlantic side, lies the remains of the 287-ton Dutch ship, **San Pedro**, one of Florida's oldest artificial reefs. Remains of the ship rest in a sand pocket 18 feet below the surface offering shelter to a host of sea creatures amidst the ballast stones and coral overgrowth. Visibility

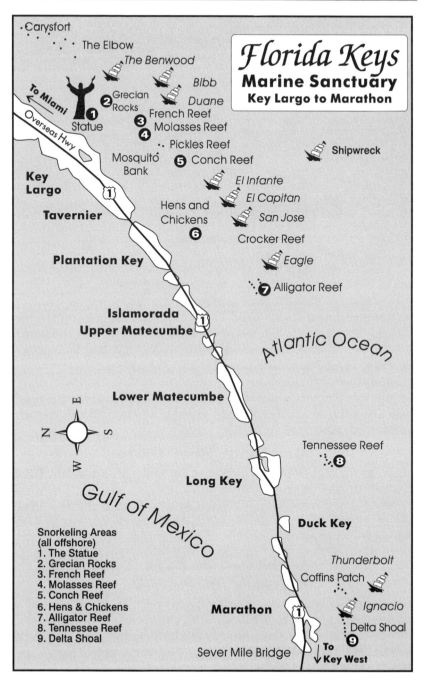

Carysfort

The Elbow

The Benwood

Bibb

Grecian Rocks

Duane

French Reef

Molasses Reef

Statue

To Miami

Overseas Hwy

Pickles Reef

Mosquito Bank

Conch Reef

Shipwreck

Florida Keys
Marine Sanctuary
Key Largo to Marathon

El Infante

El Capitan

San Jose

Crocker Reef

Eagle

Alligator Reef

Key Largo

Tavernier

Hens and Chickens

Plantation Key

Islamorada
Upper Matecumbe

Atlantic Ocean

Lower Matecumbe

N E S W

Tennessee Reef

Long Key

Gulf of Mexico

Duck Key

Snorkeling Areas
(all offshore)
1. The Statue
2. Grecian Rocks
3. French Reef
4. Molasses Reef
5. Conch Reef
6. Hens & Chickens
7. Alligator Reef
8. Tennessee Reef
9. Delta Shoal

Thunderbolt

Coffins Patch

Ignacio

Marathon

Delta Shoal

Sever Mile Bridge

To
Key West

Fort Jefferson.

can't compare with the offshore reefs, but it is an interesting dive nonetheless. Residents include gobies, damsels, moray eels and groupers.

The ship carried 16,000 pesos in Mexican silver and numerous crates of Chinese porcelain when she wrecked in 1733. For tours contact the Long Key State Park office at ☎ 664-4815. Boaters use LORAN coordinates 14082.1, 43320.6. The wreck lies approximately one and one-quarter nautical miles south from Indian Key. Be sure to tie up to the mooring buoys to prevent anchor damage.

Islamorada dive shops visit Molasses, Alligator and Tennessee reefs—all named for a ship wrecked at the site and in depths ranging from extremely shallow to about 40 feet.

Islamorada Boat Tours

Sign up for an Islamorada snorkeling trip at the **Holiday Isle Dive Center**, MM 84.9. ☎ 664-4145.

Daily reef and wreck tours are also offered at **Bud n' Mary's Dive Center**, MM 79.8,(☎ 664-2211) and **World Down Under**, MM 81.5, ☎ 664-9312.

The Middle Keys

Marathon - Big Pine Key

Dive sites in the Middle Keys— from Long Key Bridge Key to the Seven Mile Bridge— are similar to, but often less crowded than those in Key Largo.

Sombrero Reef and Looe Key National Marine Sanctuary both offer superb reef snorkeling. Depths range from two to 35 feet. Corals and fish life are similar to Molasses and French Reef.

☆☆☆☆ **Sombrero Reef**, Marathon's most popular ocean dive and snorkeling spot offers good visibility and a wide depth range from the shallows to 40 feet. Cracks and crevices shot through the coral canyons that comprise the reef overflow with lobster, arrow crabs, octopus, anemones, and resident fish. A huge light tower marks the area. Boaters must tie up to the mooring buoys on the reef.

☆☆☆ Slightly north of Sombrero lies **Coffins Patch**, which has good snorkeling areas with mounds of pillar, elk horn, and brain corals at depths averaging 20- to 30-ft.

Middle Keys Boat Tours
(use area code 305)

Marathon Divers, MM 54,(☎ 289-1141) offers daily reef trips. In Big Pine Key book a tour with Underseas Inc. at MM 30.5. (☎ 872-2700).

Excursions to the island where PT 109 was filmed can be arranged through **Strike Zone Charters** (☎ 800-654-9560 or 872-9863). On the four and one-half hour trip, owners Mary & Larry Threlkeld include snorkeling gear and a fish fry on the beach. Write to Strike Zone Charters, Dolphin Marina, MM 28.5, Rt. 1, Box 610 D,Big Pine Key, FL 33043.

The Lower Keys
From Big Pine to the Dry Tortugas

Dive trips from The Lower Keys—Big Pine Key, Sugar Loaf Key, Summerland Key, Ramrod Key, Cudjoe Key and Torch Key take off to reefs surrounding **American Shoal** and **Looe Key National Marine Sanctuary**.

The **Looe Key** reef tract, named for the *HMS Looe*, a British frigate that ran aground on the shallow reefs in 1744, offers vibrant elk horn and staghorn coral thickets, an abundance of sponges, soft corals and fish. Constant residents include Cuban hogfish, queen parrotfish, huge barracuda, and long snout butterfly fish. A favorite dive site of the Lower Keys, Looe Key bottoms out at 35 feet. Extreme shallow patches of seagrass and coral rubble provide a calm habitat for juvenile fish and invertebrates.

Diving off Key West includes offshore wreck dives and tours of **Cotrell Key, Sand Key** and the **Western Dry Marks**. Huge pelagic fish and graceful rays lure divers to this area.

☆☆☆☆ **Sand Key**, marked by a lighthouse, lures snorkelers to explore it's fields of staghorn coral. Depths range from the surface down to 45 ft.

☆☆☆ **Cosgrove Reef**, noted for its large heads of boulder and brain coral, attracts hordes of large fish and rays.

☆☆☆☆☆ Seldom visited, though pristine for diving, are the **Marquesa Islands**, 30 miles off Key West. Extreme shallows both enroute and surrounding the islands make the boat trip difficult in all but the calmest seas and docking impossible for all but shallow draft cats and trimarans. Check with Lost Reef Adventures (☎ 296-9737) for trip availability.

✰✰✰✰✰ **The Dry Tortugas**, an uninhabited island group lying 70 miles off Key West, sit in the midst of a pristine shallow reef tract, ideal for snorkeling with vibrant staghorn thickets, hordes of fish and critters. On calm days, both high-speed ferry and seaplane tours depart for Garden Key, site of the Fort Jefferson Monument. Seaplane tours are half day, the ferry departs Key West 8am and returns 7pm. Bring a picnic lunch, cold drinks and snorkeling equipment.

Spanish explorer Ponce de Leon discovered these island in 1513 and named them Las Tortugas, meaning the Turtles, for the throngs of turtles around the islands. The latter day name, Dry Tortugas, came about as a way to warn sea travelers that the islands have no fresh water.

In any case, the great numbers of loggerhead turtles are gone, but not all, most snorkelers spot at least one or two.

You reach the area by charter boat or seaplane (☎ 294-6978), and should carry in all of your gear. Check with Key West dive shops for the availability of trips (see also Aerial Tours chapter). For the very adventurous, overnight camping trips can be arranged. The trips are expensive, at this writing $130 for the seaplane trip and $75 for the ferry. Seaplane-snorkel tours to the Dry Tortugas can be booked Key West Seaplane, Junior College Rd. Phone: ☎294-6978. Or try the **Yankee Freedom**, a 100-ft, high-speed ferry with an air-conditioned cabin, spacious sun deck, complete galley, complimentary breakfast and full bar. ☎ 294-7009 or 800-634-0939.

✰✰✰✰✰ **The Marquesas**, equally magnificent in reef life, are approachable only in periods of exceptionally calm seas by private boat. Navigation information is available though the US. Coast Guard.

On the 30-mile crossing to the Marquesas you can spot sharks and rays as they dart under the boat along the sandy bottom. Armies of tulip shells with resident hermit crabs guard the remote island beaches.

Key West and Lower Keys Tours

Key West offers a unique variety snorkeling excursions. Sail-snorkel cruises visit secluded islands surrounded with beautiful coral reefs, often including lunch and refreshments.

Captain Ron Canning cruises with several local pods of dolphins and offers dolphin-watch, snorkeling excursions aboard the luxury catamaran, **Patty C,** ☎ 294-6306. Prior reservations a must.

On neighboring Stock Island, personalized charters can be arranged aboard the six-passenger trimaran, **Fanta Sea**. ☎ 296-0362.

History buffs will want to book a snorkel trip on Key West's largest tall ship, the 86-ft, wooden windjammer **Appledore** (☎ 296-9992). Half-day reef trips depart at 10:30 am and 3:30 pm.

The 65-ft schooner, **Reef Chief** (☎ 292-1345) offers custom snorkeling charters.

Sail-racing fans will delight in touring the out-islands aboard the **Stars & Stripes**, a huge 54-ft., 49-passenger replica of the racing catamaran famed by Dennis Conner. This ninth version was designed especially for cruising the shallow channels and reefs of Key West. See the Stars & Stripes at Land's End Marina (☎ 294-7877 or 800-634-MEOW). You can book a tour at Lost Reef Adventures, 261 Margaret Street, Key West.

Three more fabulous catamarans, the 60-ft. Fury, Queen Conch and **Reef Express** offer sail-snorkel tours out of Key West. The Fury (☎ 294-8899)departs from the Truman Annex (West end of Greene St.) at 9:30 am and 1:00 pm; it visits Sand Key, Rock Key, Eastern Dry Rocks and Western Sambo—all coral reef out-islands. The Queen Conch (☎ 295-9030) departs Conch Harbor Marina off N. Roosevelt Avenue, and includes equipment, soft drinks, lunch and snorkel gear.

The **Reef Express** offers three-hour trips departing the end of William St. Trip includes sanitized snorkel gear, instruction, flotation devices and cold soft drinks.

Sunny Days, a large sailing catamaran departs the dock at the end of William St. Three and one-half hour trips depart at 9 am and 1 pm. Includes gear, instruction and cold sodas. Beer and wine after snorkeling.

Reef Raiders Dive Inc. offers snorkeling trips aboard the 53-ft cata- maran, El Gato departing 9:30 and 1:30. Beer, wine and soda included on all tours.

Witt's End Charters (☎ 305-304-0139) at Land's End Marina offers personalized weekend to ten-day charters aboard the beautiful 51-ft sailing yacht, Witt's End. Includes meals, captain and chef who also happens to be a Coast Guard certified captain, snorkel gear, dive compressor, and fishing equipment. Expert snorkeling instruction. Optional wedding packages. Reservations a must. Write to Captains Witt, P.O. Box 625, Key Largo FL 33037.

Tips for Boaters

Be sure to display a divers flag if you are snorkeling from your own boat. Strong currents may be encountered on the outside reefs. Check before disembarking. One person should always remain on board.

Be aware of weather, sea conditions and your own limitations before going offshore. Sudden storms, waterspouts and weather-related, fast moving fronts are not uncommon. Nautical charts are available at marinas and boating supply outlets throughout the Keys.

Key Largo and Looe Key National Marine Sanctuaries provide mooring buoys to which you should attach your boat rather than anchor. If no buoys are available, you should drop anchor only in sandy areas. The bottom in sandy areas appears white.

In protected areas of the Keys, destruction of coral formations through grounding or imprudent anchoring can lead to penalties and fines of up to $50,000. Minor damage to coral fines start at $150. Give yourself plenty of room to maneuver. For Key Largo National Marine Sanctuary use chart 11451 or 11462, and for Looe Key National Marine Sanctuary use chart 11442 or 11445.

Where to Stay

For a complete list of home rental agencies, resorts, motels and campgrounds call ☎ 1-800-FLA-KEYS or write to P.O Box 1147, Key West, Florida 33041. Website: www.fla-keys.com.

Following are a sampling of popular Florida Keys accommodations. All can book you a reef tour. None allow pets, but those that do are available from the tourist board listed above. MM denotes Mile Marker number.

Key Largo

Amy Slate's Amoray Lodge on Florida Bay offers 16 attractive apartments. Snorkeling trips leave from the resort dock. Walking distance to several good restaurants. Sundeck, no beach. ☎ 800-426-6729 or 305-451-3595, fax 305-4453-9516.

Holiday Inn, Key Largo, MM 99.7, is adjacent to a large marina. Restaurant, pool. ☎ US 800-THE-KEYS or 305-451-2121.

Kelly's Motel, MM 104.5 sits in a sheltered cove on Florida Bay. Boat dock and ramp. Reef trips. ☎ 305-451-1622 or 800-226-0415.

Ocean Pointe, MM 92.5, oceanside, features suites, heated pool, tennis, marina with rental slips. Suntan beach. ☎ 800-882-9464 or 305-3000, fax 305-853-3007.

Sheraton Key Largo, MM 97, bayside, offers a nice sandy beach and watersports shack that rents a variety of equipment and offers reef trips. Guest rooms are wonderful. Good restaurants. ☎ 800-325-3535 or 305-852-5553, fax 305-852-8669.

Islamorada

Plantation Key to Long Key

Cheeca Lodge offers pampered seclusion, oceanside, at MM 82. The luxurious resort offers a wealth of activities and a staff of expert instructors.

Dive shop on premises. Daily, afternoon snorkeling trips take off for Cheeca Rocks, a nearby shallow reef. ☎ 800-327-2888 or 305-664-4651.

Holiday Isle Resort encompasses an entire beach club community with every imaginable watersport and activity. Guests choose from rooms, efficiencies or suites. ☎ 305-664-2321, US 800-327-7070, fax 305-664-2703.

Marathon

Holiday Inn of Marathon, MM54, oceanside, has 134 rooms, restaurant and bar. Abyss Dive Shop on property. boat ramp and marina. Pool. No beach. ☎ 800-224-5053, 800-HOLIDAY or 305-289-0222.

Hawks Cay Resort and Marina offers 177 spacious rooms and suites. Heated pool, saltwater lagoon with sandy beach, 18-hole golf course nearby, marine mammal training center featuring dolphin shows for guests. Boat slips for large and small craft. ☎ 800-753-7000, FL 800-432-2242.

Buccaneer Resort, MM48.5, bayside has 76 units, beach, cafe, boat dock and charters. Fantasea Dive Shop on premises offers reef trips. Snorkelers join scuba tours. ☎ 800-237-3329 or 305-743-9071.

Big Pine Key

Dolphin Marina Resort, MM28.5, oceanside, is the closest marina to Looe Key Marine Sanctuary. Twelve simple motel rooms. Snorkel and sunset cruises daily. ☎ 800-942-5397.

Little Torch Key

Little Palm Island. Located on an out island, this deluxe resort offers all recreational facilities. Ultra luxurious suites include private balcony, fans, AC, refrigerator, wet bar and whirlpool. Launch transfers to the island are provided. No TV or phones. ☎ 800-GET LOST or 305-872-2524.

Key West

Key West has three main resort areas - Old Town, the center of activity and where you'll find the island's most post, oceanfront resort complexes, South Roosevelt Blvd., which runs along the south shore parallel to the Atlantic Ocean, and North Roosevelt Blvd., the commercial strip packed with fast food joints and strip malls that run along the island's northern, Gulf shores. Since the island is just two miles wide and four miles long, no matter where you stay, you can travel to any point within a matter of minutes.

For a complete list of Key West accommodations call ☎ 800-LASTKEY.

Days Inn Key West offer 134 rooms and suites, some with kitchens. This motel is on the highway at the beginning of Key West as you enter from Stock Island. Pets welcome. ☎ 800-325-2525 or 305-294-3742.

Fairfield Inn by Marriot, 2400 N. Roosevelt Blvd. has 100 rooms, heated pool, Cable TV. Handicapped accessible. ☎ US 800-228-2800 or 305-296-5700.

Holiday Inn La Concha Hotel, 430 Duval St. Renovated in 1986, this charming resort features 160 elegant rooms, a restaurant, fitness room, shops and the best view of the city from the rooftop lounge. Walk to all attractions,. ☎ 800-745-2191 or 305-294-3282. Handicapped access.

Holiday Inn Beachside, 1111 N. Roosevelt Blvd. Located directly on the Gulf of Mexico, this resort offer 222 room, 79 with water views, large fresh water pool, watersports, beach and snorkeling trips. Convenient to both sides of the islands and Stock Island. ☎ 800-HOLIDAY or 305-294 -2571.

Hampton Inn, 2801 Roosevelt Blvd. Located on the Gulf, Hampton Inn features 157 units, island decor, freshwater pool, cable TV, Jacuzzi, sun deck. Handicapped accessible. ☎ 305-294-2917, US 1-800-HAMPTON.

Hyatt Key West Resort and Marina, 610 Front St. Oceanfront, this stunning 120-room landmark resort sits two short blocks from Duval and the heart of Old Town. Pool, three restaurants, private sandy beach and marina. ☎ 800-233-1234 or 305-296-9900.

Marriott's Casa Marina Resort, 1500 Reynolds St. Billed as the island's largest oceanfront resort, featuring 314 rooms, tennis, water sports, private beach, two pools, whirlpool and sauna. Handicapped accessible. ☎ 800-235-4837 or 305-296-3535.

Marriot Reach Resort, 1435 Simonton St. Elegant resort located on a natural sand beach. Features 149 rooms with with ocean view. Handicapped accessible. US ☎ 800-874-4118 or 305-296-5000.

Southernmost Motel in the USA, 1319 Duval. Features two pools, jacuzzi, tiki bar poolside, walking distance to shops, night life, across from beach pier on ocean. ☎ 800-354-4455 or 305-296-6577.

Travel Tips

Getting There: All major national and international airlines fly into Miami Airport. Connecting scheduled flights land in Marathon and Key West.

Driving: From the North, take Florida Turnpike to Exit 4-Homestead-Key West. From Tampa, take I-75 south to Naples, then east to Miami and the Turnpike Extension. Or take 41 South, then east to the Turnpike Extension, and finally south to US 1.

From Miami Airport: Take LeJeune Road south to 836 west. Then take the Turnpike Extension to US 1 south, which runs the length of the Florida Keys to Key West.

Climate: Sub-tropical. In winter temperatures range from 75° to 85° F. Fall brings chance of a hurricane. Summer temperatures range from 85°to 95°F.

Dress: Lightweight, casual. Wetskin or light wetsuit needed in winter.

Florida Springs

King's Bay, Crystal River, on Florida's central west coast is *the* place to swim with manatees. In fact, it's the only area that doesn't restrict snorkelers from getting close. These gentle giants inhabit the Crystal River Wildlife Refuge between mid October and May. Nearby Rainbow River and Homosassa River are also excellent manatee watching spots.

Visibility isn't always terrific as the manatees dig up the bottom eating mud grasses, but every encounter is memorable. The clearest spot, and a favorite for photography, in the west coast spring area is Three Sisters Spring, which has a white-sand bottom. Three Sisters is not an official part of the sanctuary, but is on the list currently being considered.

Snorkeling in the chilly, 72°F springs water requires wearing at least a 1/8th inch wetsuit. Dive shops offers rentals (see page 127).

About the West Indian Manatee

Florida's manatees are a highly endangered species. Population studies indicate that there may be as few as 800 manatees in Florida waters. Many are killed or severely injured by power boats. Habitat destruction puts these docile creatures in jeopardy.

It is illegal to harass, harm, pursue, hunt, shoot, would, kill, annoy or molest manatees. When you enter their areas, stay on top of the water and wait for them to come up to you. If they do not, you must settle for viewing them from a distance.

There are seven sanctuaries in this area. Some prohibit touching or getting within 50 ft of the manatees. The one place where interaction is allowed is Crystal River.

Contributor and manatee rescue worker, Francois Fournier suggests joining a guided tour. The guides are trained professionals concerned with

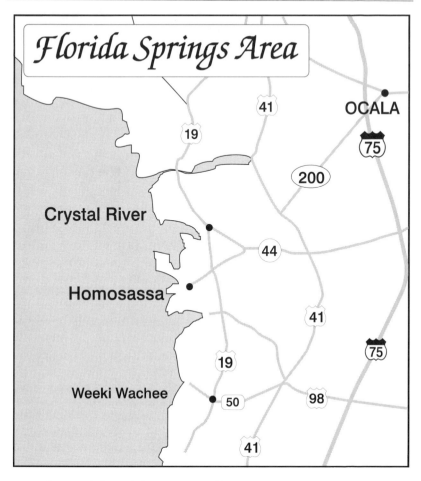

Florida Springs Area

41

19

OCALA

75

200

Crystal River

44

Homosassa

41

75

19

Weeki Wachee

50

98

41

your safety and that of the manatee. Plus, they will teach you the proper and legal way of interacting with the endangered manatee, thus making your experience very enjoyable.

Rescue and Rehabilatation Program

After the Marine Mammal Protection Act of 1972 and the Endangered species Act of 1973 were passed, marine specialists at Sea World, Orlando, were approached to aid in the rescue of beached or stranded marine mammals. In cooperation with the Department of the Interior, the National Marine fisheries Service, the Florida Department of Natural Resources and the Florida Marine patrol, Sea World developed the Beached Animal Rescue and Rehabilitation Program in 1973. Since that time, animal care specialists have responded to hundreds of calls to aid sick, injured or orphaned manatees, dolphins, whales, otters, sea turtles and a variey of birds. The marine life park bears all costs of the rescue program, including those for research, transportation and rehabilitation.

As a result of research conducted by Sea World's animal husbandry staff in aviculture, animal care and aquarium departments, valuable baseline data is being established and shared with scientists worldwide. Food preferences, responses to antibiotic therapy, the safest transportation equipment and the swiftest rescue techniques have been documented by the staff. Sea Word is the largest of two facilities in the state that are authorized to rescue, care for and release manatees.

If your vacation includes a trip to Orlando, be sure to plan a stop at SeaWorld where you can view the recovering manatees.

Snorkeling Tours and Rentals

Bird's Underwater features excellent guided snorkel tours in Crystal River and a Manatee Awareness Program. Owners Bill "Bird" and Diana Oestreich are both licensed Coast Guard captains and scuba instructors. Diana has been working with manatee snorkel programs for nine years and brings a wealth of delightful experiences to every tour. Early morning tours depart from the dock behind Cracker's Restaurant on N. Highway 19 inCrystal River (next to Best Wester Resort). ☎ 352-563-2763. E-mail: bird@xtal wind.net. Website: http://www.xtalwind.net/~bird/. Write to: Bill & Diana Oestreich, 8585 Pine Needle trail, Crystal River, FL 34428.

American Pro Diving Center in Crystal River offers guided snorkel tours to Crystal River, Rainbow River and Homosassa daily during the manatee season. Special packages combining two or more areas are offered as are discount hotel reservations. They also offer a Snorkeling Encounter with Manatee course. ☎ 800-291-DIVE or 352-563-0041. Write to: 821 S. E. Hwy 19, Crystal River, FL 34429. Web site: http://gmient.com/ampro.

A good spot to view manatees without getting wet is the **Homosassa Springs Wildlife Park**, where you can go below the water's surface in their floating observatory. The park is located at 4150 South Suncoast Boulevard, Homosassa, FL 34446.☎ 352-628-2311

Where to Stay

Best Western Crystal River Resort, 614 N.W. Hwy 19, Crystal River, FL 34428 (next to Crackers on Rte 19), offers comfortable rooms and convenient access to manatee tours.☎ 352-795-3171 or 800-435-4409.

Bay View Efficiencies, also next to Crackers) offers simple accommodations with easy access to manatee tours. ☎ 352-563-5004.

Econo Lodge Crystal Resort, adjacent to the Crystal Lodge Dive Center features guest rooms and studios with kitchenettes. Located on US Hsy19. Private dock, launching ramp, tours, fresh water pool. ☎ 352-795-9447.

Plantation Inn & Golf Resort sits 400 yards from the main spring at Crystal River. Dive shop on premises. ☎ 800-632-6262 or 352-795-4211. Write to: P.O. Box 1116, Crystal River, FL 34423.

For additional information on Campgrounds, boat rentals, fishing, marinas and accommodations, contact the Nature Coast Chamber of Commerce at Crystal River at ☎ 352-795-3149.

Guadeloupe

Named for Our Lady of Guadeloupe by Christopher Columbus in 1493, this charming French island is blessed with miles of beautiful white-sand beaches and spectacular coral reefs.

Guadeloupe is actually two main islands connected by a bridge across the River Salee and several out-islands. From the air it resembles the wings of a butterfly. Basse-Terre, the western wing, is mountainous, highlighted by the still-active volcano, Mt. Soufriere. Travelers touring this portion of the islands will find rain forests, bamboo trees, hot springs, postcard waterfalls, and a profusion of tropical flowers, fruits, almond and palm trees. Grande-Terre, the eastern wing of Guadeloupe, is flat, dry, and home to modern resorts, beautiful beaches, sugar cane fields and unlimited topside tourist attractions.

English is NOT widely spoken. Non-French-speaking visitors to Guadeloupe should pick up a French phrase book and familiarize themselves with the language. Also, snorkelers should bring their own equipment.

Topless sunbathing, snorkeling, scuba and swimming are *de rigueur* on Guadeloupe.

Best Snorkeling Sites

Pigeon Island, a mountain in the sea off Basse-Terre's west coast is the prime snorkeling area. The area consists of two land masses, North Pigeon and South Pigeon. The waters surrounding it come under French Government protection as an Underwater Natural Park—the Cousteau Marine Sanctuary. Boat tours take off from Malendure.

☆☆☆☆☆**North Side Reef.** You'll find superb seascapes for photography on the north side of North Pigeon Island. Huge clusters of tube sponges, some six feet tall, and enormous green and purple sea fans grow on the ledges and outcrops of the wall. The reef begins in the shallows and drops off to a maze of small canyons and outcrops. Divers are befriended by large gray snappers. They are tame and may be handfed. Large curious barracuda circle overhead, trumpet and damsel fish adorn the lush thickets of coral. Star and brain corals abound. North Side Reef is a super dive for novices as well as experienced divers. Seas are calm, visibility excellent.

☆☆☆☆☆ **Pigeon Island's West Side Reef** is the best snorkeling area in the Cousteau Marine Sanctuary. Its shallow walls ruffle with enormous feather dusters, sea plumes, sea rods, huge sea fans and sponges. Barrel sponges (large enough to camp in) thrive among clumps of elkhorn and enormous brain corals. Puffer fish and unusual golden moray eels are inhabitants. Expect calm seas and exceptional visibility.

Additional snorkeling sites are found among the lagoons and bays of Les Saintes, the east coast of BasseTerre, and off-shore Gosier (the south coast of Grande Terre). Check out Mouton Vert, Mouchoir Carré, and Cay Ismini. They are close by the hotels in the bay of Petit Cul de Sac Marin, near Rivière Salée, the river separating the two halves of Guadeloupe. North of Salée is another bay, Grand Cul de Sac Marin, where the small islets of Fajou and Caret also offer decent snorkeling. St. Francois Reef on the eastern end of the south shore of Grande-Terre is a good, shallow, patch reef area as is Ilet de Gosier, off Gosier.

Snorkel Tours & Rentals

Chez Guy is directly opposite Pigeon Island on Malendure Beach in Bouillante on Basse-Terre, with a branch on Les Saintes. Operator and master diver Guy Genin has three fast, comfortable boats for daily snorkeling excursions to Pigeon Island. The boats have wide hydroplanes that double as diving platforms. Chez Guy also offers a one-week, all-inclusive package, which includes boat trips, equipment and accommodations with breakfast and dinner at Guy's guest house, the Auberge de la Plongée. ☎ (011) 590-98-8172, fax: (011) 590-98-8358. Or book through your travel agent.

Aqua-fari Club is based at La Créole Beach Hotel in Gosier, a bustling resort area 15 miles east of Point-à-Pitre, Guadeloupe's largest city. ☎ (011) 590-84-2626.

Another well-organized watersports center is **Nauticase** at the Hotel Salako, ☎ (011) 590-84-2222.

Where to Stay

If your tongue doesn't curl comfortably around conversational French, head for one of the bigger hotels where English is spoken. Or if getting to know people is one of the reasons you travel, stay at a Relais Créole, a small family-owned inn. Most of the hotels are situated on Grande-Terre (one-hour drive to Malendure). Among the small hotels close to Pigeon Island on Basse-Terre are Raphael Legrand's charming 12-room **Auberge De La Distillerie** at Tabanon near Petit-Bourg. This fully air-conditioned inn is a short ride from Pigeon Island dive operators. ☎ (011) 590-94-2591, fax 590-94-1191. The adjacent restaurant, Le Bitaco, is popular with the locals and noted for Creole dishes. Freshwater pool.

Hotel Paradis Créole is a small dive lodge operated by Les Heures Saines divers. Bungalow-studios or rooms can be packaged with boat tours and meals. ☎ (011) 590-98-7162 or 590-98-8663, fax (011) 590-98-7776.

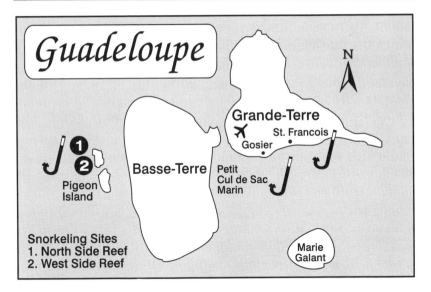

La Sucrerie du Comte has opened on the site of an old rum distillery. With 26 comfortable bungalow rooms, La Sucrerie is by the sea at Sainte Rose in the north of the western wing of Basse-Terre. ☎ (011) 590-28-6017. Write to: Comte de Loheac, Sainte-Rose 97115, Guadeloupe, FWI.

Le Domaine de Malendure, on Basse-Terre overlooking Cousteau's Reserve, offers 50 deluxe, air-conditioned, hillside cottages with TV, telephone and 1½ baths. Restaurant, pool and swim-up bar. Snorkeling tours to Pigeon Island. ☎ 800-742-4276.

La Créole Beach Hotel, located on the beach at Gosier, offers large, well appointed rooms. Aqua-Fari Dive Shop on premises offers tours to the coral reef surrounding Gosier Island and to Pigeon Island. ☎ (011) 590-90-4646, fax 590-90-1666. In the US ☎ 800-742-4276.

Meridien Guadeloupe, just east of Gosier at St. Francois, features 265 four-star beachfront rooms. Despite the boom in tourism, the town of St. Francois manages to retain its fishing village look. On the road east of it are beachside bistros serving lobster and seafood. Dive shops here offer daily trips to the offshore reefs of Grande-Terre and excursions to Pigeon Island. ☎ (011) 590-88-5100, fax (011) 590-88-40-71.

Sailboats, crewed or bareboat, are plentiful. For rentals or tours try **Vacances Yachting Antilles** at Marina Bas-du-Fort, Pointe-A-Pitre. ☎ 90-82-95. Full-day picnic sails on the trimaran, *La Grande Voile* ☎ 84-4642, or catamaran, *Papyrus*, can be arranged through your hotel. ☎ 90-9298.

Travel Tips

Getting There: Connections from Miami on Air France and from San Juan, take American Eagle (☎ 800-433-7300). Inter-island flights can be arranged at Le Raizet Airport. Water ferries to Iles des Saintes are available from the city of Pointe-à-Pitre, Basse-Terre, or Trois Rivieres on the south coast.

Island Transportation: All major car rental agencies are at the airport. Reservations should be made before arriving in Guadeloupe to insure getting a car. Bus service in Mercedes vans is available between cities. The cities are clearly marked on the outside.

Driving: Right side of the road. The main roads between major cities are clearly marked. A wonderful tourist map is available from the tourist office in Pointe-à-Pitre.

Documents: For stays of up to three months Canadian and US citizens require a return ticket and two forms of I.D.— either a passport or proof of citizenship such as a birth certificate or voter's registration card with some type of photo. A passport is recommended. British citizens require a passport.

Currency: French franc. 5 FF=US$1.00.

Climate: Temperatures range from 75 to 85° F. Water temperatures are warm year-round so you won't need a wetsuit, although a wetskin or $^1/8$ - inch shortie wetsuit is comfortable in mid-winter.

Clothing: Casual light clothing. Most beaches are topless.

Equipment Required: Bring all of your own scuba gear except for tanks and weights. Most operators have Scubapro tanks, which do not require any special regulator adaptor.

Electricity: European adaptors required.

Time: Atlantic Standard (EST + 1 hr).

Language: French, local Creole dialect.

Tax: A service charge of 10 to 15% is included on most hotel and restaurant tabs.

Religious Services: Catholic, Protestant, Jewish.

Additional Information: French West Indies Tourist Board, 444 Madison Avenue, NY NY 10022. ☎ 900-990-0040 (95¢ per minute). Website: www. guadeloupe.com

Hawaii

Hawaii, one of the world's best vacation spots, offers visitors a tropical paradise with palm-studded beaches, fields of wild orchids, sugar cane and pineapple. Inland, glistening mountains slope down to endless, white sand beaches.

Explorers to underwater Hawaii find a magical world of lava tubes, tunnels, archways, cathedrals, and caves carpeted with vibrant corals and sponges.

Giant sea turtles, eagle rays, squid, Hawaiian turkeyfish, dolphins, whales, crustaceans, octopus, tiger cowries and tame morays abound in the islands' crystal waters. In fact, thirty percent of it's marine life exists no where else in the world. Sunken tanks and Jeeps, abandoned after World War II, lie motionless on the ocean floor, camouflaged now with layers of coral and barnacles.

Oahu

Oahu is the gathering place for vacationers, and Waikiki Beach, with miles of high rise hotels creating a luminescent skyline, is the undisputed capital. Honolulu, the cultural center, vibrates with concerts, dance performances, and live theater. Outside Honolulu, small countryside communities dot a vast expanse of open country. The Nuuanu Pali Lookout provides a panoramic view of the windward side of the island. Expert body surfers test their skills at the uncrowded beaches. At Makapuu Point daring hang-gliders soar from towering cliffs. On the leeward side of Waianae Range, small towns and wide beaches line the coastline. North shore snorkeling is excellent during summer when the seas are calm.

Best Snorkeling Sites of Oahu

☆☆☆☆ **Hanauma Bay** Marine Life Conservation District, on the southeast shore of Oahu, is the most popular snorkeling site in all of Hawaii. This state marine preserve hosts more than one million visitors each year. Formed from an ancient volcanic crater, the bay is lined with a shallow inner reef that starts at 10 ft and slopes down to an outer reef. To get there, take H-1 east from Waikiki, which becomes 72. You won't miss it. Beach access.

☆☆☆ **Rainbow Reef**, just west of Waikiki Beach, is a favorite dive site for beginners. The reef begins at 10 ft and slopes to 30 ft. Also known as Magic Island, Rainbow Reef shelters hundreds of tame tropicals, including

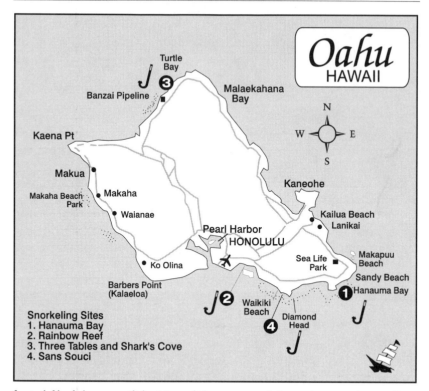

fantail file fish, parrotfish, triggerfish, surgeon fish, and porcupine puffers. All demand hand feeding. Beach access.

☆☆☆ **Three Tables and Shark's Cove**, part of the Pupukea Marine Life Conservation District north of Waimea Bay, takes is name from a trio of flat rocks which break the surface close to the beach. Starting at a depth of 15 ft, snorkelers can explore large rock formations, caverns, and ledges. Beach access is easy, however, this spot is diveable only during summer months. Extremely rough surf and strong currents exist from October through April. Check sea conditions with local dive shops.

☆☆ **Sans Souci Hotel**, just east of Waikiki has good snorkeling out front.

Oahu Snorkeling Tours & Rentals

Snorkel Bob's Oahu, rents snorkel gear from basic to the very best. In addition, they have prescription masks available. Snorkel Bob's shops are located on Hawaii, Kauai, Maui, and Oahu. Gear rented on one island may be returned on another. 700 Kapahuli Ave., Honolulu, HI 96816. Tel: 808-735-7944. E-mail: SnorkelBob@snorkelbob.com. Website: www. snorkel bob.com.

Where to Stay on Oahu

For a complete list of accommodations contact the Oahu Visitors Association at 800-OAHU-678 or 1-800-GO-HAWAII. Waikiki accommodations are nearest the beach-snorkeling sites.

Nahua Condominium Suites offer low-cost units with parking. pool, TV, phone, TV, kitchens. ☎ 800-446-6248, fax 310-544-1643.

The Outrigger Waikiki, on the beach, features air-conditioned suites, beauty salon, health club, spa, lounge, parking, phone, pool, TV. ☎ 800-688-7444 or 303-369-7777, fax 303-369-9403. E-mail: reservations@ outrigger.com. Website: www.outrigger.com.

The Royal Hawaiian Hotel, has luxurious, air-conditioned guest rooms, beauty salon, lounge, parking, parking, phone, pool, restaurant, TV. High. ☎ 800-325-3535.

Maui, The Valley Isle

Two mountain ranges, the West Maui mountains and Haleakala, cover most of Maui. Haleakala rises to 10,000 ft. Hiking here, especially at sunrise, is more of an "encounter" than a sport. Visitors enjoy wandering along the "road to Hana," a remote town on the windward side of Haleakala, which passes bamboo forests, waterfalls and gardens of wild fruits and flowers. On the northwest side of Maui you can explore Lahaina, an old whaling village. Lahaina Harbor is a bustling sailing port where you can see yachts from all over the world.

Maui County offers snorkelers an endless variety of sites. It is also a jumping-off point for snorkeling tours to the islands of Lanai, Molokai, Molokini and Kahoolawe. At these out-island dive sites, you'll see strange creatures rarely seen elsewhere, docile 50-foot whale sharks and, during the winter months, humpback whales. Snorkel-tour operations are located in the main resort areas of Wailea/Kihei and Lahaina. Trips to Molokini and other nearby sites take 15 to 30 minutes; trips across the channel to Lanai and Molokai can take 1½ hours.

Best Snorkeling Sites of Maui

☆☆☆☆☆ **Molokini Crater**, a crescent-shaped island two miles from Maui, is by far this island's most popular dive and snorkel site. Expect to see as many as 30 to 40 dive boats anchored here at one time.

Formed by the top of an old volcanic crater, this area is unique because it combines many ecosystems within a small area—deep water, shallow reef, flowing and still waters, with their natural complements of marine animals. Good visibility.

Marine life and sub-seascapes fascinate photographers and explorers alike. You can snorkel inside or outside the crater in the shallows or along the walls. Whales, porpoises and unusual marine animals are common at Molokini Crater. Plan a morning trip to the crater. Stronger currents are encountered in the afternoon.

☆☆☆**Grand Canyon**, off the southern end of Lanai, is an enormous underwater canyon with walls of lava where huge turtles and rays glide along the bottom and parrotfish of all colors, triggerfish and surgeonfish hover near the ledges. Shrimp and squirrel fish hide in the crevices. Depths start at 20ft. Boat access.

☆☆☆☆ **First and Second Cathedrals**, also off Lanai, has coral encrusted pinnacles rising from 60 ft to just below the surface. Snorkel trips tour this area only during morning hours, since afternoon currents can be treacherous. Visibility is excellent during periods of calm water and weather. Boat access.

☆☆ **Black Rock** sits on the northwest shore of Maui off Kaanapali Beach. Snorkelers enjoy exploring the cove created by a peninsula. The bottom is sandy and the lava walls of the peninsula are inhabited by a wide variety of fish. Visibility is good. Depths shallow. Maximum 20 ft.

Maui & Lanai
HAWAII

Snorkeling Sites
1. Black Rock
2. Molokini Crater
3. Sharkfin Rock
4. Grand Canyon
5. First and Second Cathedrals

☆☆☆☆ **Sharkfin Rock**, off the south shore of Lanai, is a large rock formation that protrudes from the water like a shark's fin. The rocks top a vertical wall that drops to 90 ft. This is a popular site for feeding lemon butterfly fish. Around the ledges you'll find orange stonycup coral and, nearby, moray eels and nudibranches.

Maui Snorkeling Tours & Rentals

Ed Robinson's Diving Adventures. Ed Robinson has been diving and photographing the reefs off Maui since 1971. His photographs have appeared in over a hundred publications including *National Geographic, Oceans* and *Islands* magazine.

Although the shop does not offer dedicated snorkeling trips, snorkelers accompanying divers are welcome on dive boats for a ride-along fee. The captains will try to accommodate snorkelers needs. P.O. Box 616, Kihei HI 96753. ☎ 800-635-1273, fax: 808-874-1939. E-mail: robinson @maui. net. Website: www.maui.net/~robinson/erda.html

Dive Maui/Offshore Adventures offers dedicated snorkel trips and scuba tours. Owner Leslie Sternberg knows of many dive spots right off the beach where guests can join huge turtles and hundreds of different reef fish. Depths range from 10 ft. to 60 ft. Weather and sea conditions determine site selection. 900 Front St., Lahaina, HI 96761. ☎ 808-667-2080. E-mail: offshore@ maui.net. Web site: www.maui.net/~offshore/

Kelii's Kayak Tours. For a different adventure, try a kayak-snorkeling tour from Kelii's Kayak Tours. Trips lasting from two and one-half to five hours leave from the north, south and west shore of Mauii. 158 Lanakila Place, Kihei, HI 96753. ☎ (888) 874-7652. E-mail: kelii@maui.net. Website: www.maui.net/~kelli/KKT/KKT.html.

Snorkel Bob's Lahaina, 161 Lahainaluna Rd., Lahaina, HI 96761. 808-661-4421 and **Snorkel Bob's Napili**, 5425 C Lower Honoapiilani Hwy., Lahaina, HI 96761. ☎ 808-669-9603 offer gear rentals, maps and tips. (See Snorkel Bob's Kona for complete description).

Where to Stay on Maui

All major hotels will arrange snorkeling trips. Your travel agent can suggest hotels or other accommodations to suit any pocketbook. For a complete list of resorts contact the Maui Visitor Bureau ☎ 1-800-525-MAUI or 808-244-3530, fax 808-244-1337. Write to P.O. Box 580, 1727 Wili Pa Loop, Wailuku, Maui, Hawaii 96793.

Stouffer's Wailea Beach Hotel sits on the southwest coast where beach snorkeling is great year round. This luxury resort features five beautiful beaches, restaurants, tennis and golf. Reserve through your travel agent or write Wailea, Maui HI 96753. ☎ 808-879-4900. Expensive.

Sheraton Maui Hotel on Kaanapali Beach in Lahaina is near Black Rock, a favorite reef and wall dive for snorkelers and divers. The hotel features a lovely garden, restaurants, and Polynesian show in the lounge. ☎ 800-325-3535 or see your travel agent. Expensive.

Kaanapali Beach Resort encompasses 10 resort hotels and condominiums, golf, tennis, shopping, all on a three-mile beach adjacent to Lahaina. ☎ 800-245-9229.

HAWAII, The Big Island

Located 120 miles southeast of Oahu (40 minutes by air), Hawaii is the largest island of the Hawaiian archipelago. The birthplace of King Kamehameha, the best known ruler of the islands, it is also the location of the islands' only active volcanoes. Molten lava still flows to the sea. More than 20,000 varieties of orchids grow here.

The entire west coast of Hawaii is a diving and snorkeling paradise. Over 50 miles of the shoreline are protected from high winds and swells, and many snorkeling areas can be reached easily from the beach. The most spectacular snorkeling is just offshore and all sites are less than 30 minutes away by boat trip.

Best Snorkeling Sites of Hawaii

☆☆☆☆☆ **Red Hill** is located 10 miles off South Kailua. This area has four different dive sites which range from 15 to 70 ft in depth. Expect visibility from 75 to 100 ft. The fish population is enormous with many varieties of eels, turtles, frogfish, porpoises, shell fish and lobsters. Boat access.

☆☆☆☆☆ **The Aquarium at Kealakekua Bay**, an underwater state park, is a beautiful reef inhabited by thousands of tame fish who enjoy following snorkelers. The shallows can be reached from the beach, but the deeper reefs and drop-offs require a boat. Seas are flat calm, making this a popular site for novices. Divers can spot parrotfish, rudderfish, sergeant majors, bird wrasse, bronze tangs trumpet fish, raccoon butterfly fish, tame moray eels and many more. The bottom is hard coral—lobe, finger, plate, cauliflower, octocorals—and patches of sand. Visibility is best on the outer reef. This is where Captain Cook was killed.

☆☆☆☆ **Kaiwi** lies two miles from Kailua Bay, a five minute boat ride. Depths range from 15 to 50 ft. Snorkelers will see caves, pinnacles and coral encrusted lava arches. Video and still photographers can capture graceful manta and eagle rays or large turtles here. Triton and conch shells are found on the bottom as well as 7-11 crabs. Swarms of fish of all types are in abundance here. Visibility is almost always 75 to 100 ft here and the seas are calm with a small south surge during the summer.

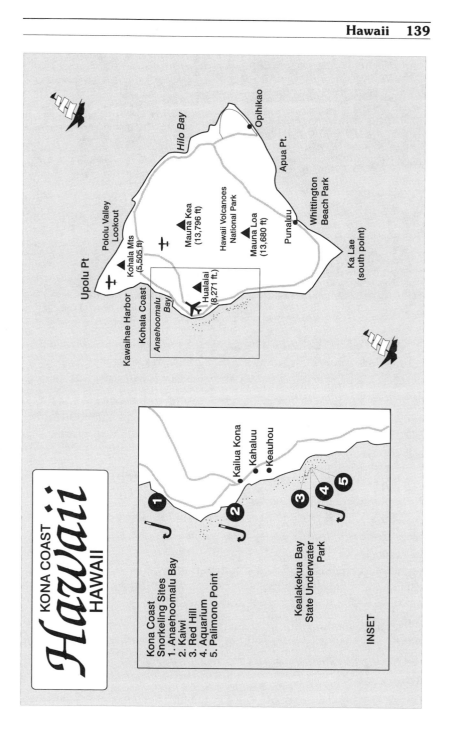

Hawaii
KONA COAST
HAWAII

Pololu Valley Lookout

Hilo Bay

Opihikao

Apua Pt.

Upolu Pt

Kohala Mts
(5,505 ft)

Mauna Kea
(13,796 ft)

Hawaii Volcanoes
National Park

Mauna Loa
(13,680 ft)

Punaluu

Whittington
Beach Park

Kawaihae Harbor

Kohala Coast

Hualalai
(8,271 ft.)

Anaehoomalu
Bay

Ka Lae
(south point)

Kailua Kona

Kahaluu

Keauhou

Kona Coast
Snorkeling Sites
1. Anaehoomalu Bay
2. Kaiwi
3. Red Hill
4. Aquarium
5. Palimono Point

Kealakekua Bay
State Underwater
Park

INSET

Rainbow Diver II

☆☆☆☆☆ **Anaeho'omalu Bay Beach Park**, north of Kealakekua Bay, just past Mile Marker 77, features a lovely sand beach, pretty corals and a lot of fish. Visibility decreases with high winds and heavy surf. Beach access.

☆☆☆☆ **Palemano Point**, off the southern end of Kealakekua Bay is known for vibrant corals. Snorkelers will enjoy photographing rudderfish, yellow tangs, and trumpetfish. Visibility is good, water usually calm. No facilities. Rocky shoreline. Beach access.

Hawaii Snorkeling Tours & Rentals

Eco-Adventures offers dedicated snorkeling trips to 66 sites with depths of 15-30 ft. Kona Shopping Village, 75-5744 Alii Dr., Kailua-Kona, HI, 96740. Kona Coast ☎ 800-949-3483, fax: 808-329-7091. E-mail: warren@eco-adventures.com. Website: www.eco-adventure.com.

Kona Coast Divers offers complete vacation packages. Snorkeler rates include mask, fins and snorkel. Their night manta ray trip includes an u/w light and chem-lite stick. Owners Julie and Jim Robinson operate a full-service dive shop with a well-equipped underwater photography center. 75-5614 Palani Road, Kailua-Kona HI, 96740. ☎ 800-329-8802 or 808-329-8802. E-mail: divekona@kona.net. Website: www.konacoast divers. com.

Jack's Diving Locker doesn't offer scheduled, dedicated snorkeling trips, but will take snorkelers on normal dive trips and will charter boats for the day for snorkeling or swimming with dolphins. 75-5819 Alii Dr., Kailua-Kona, HI 96740. ☎ 800-345-4807. E-mail: divejdl@gte.net. Website: divejdl. com.

Manta Ray Dives of Hawaii/Rainbow Diver II offers dedicated snorkeling trips on glass bottom boats. Non-snorkeling companions or "ride alongs" are welcome. Night snorkeling with mantas and day trips to the "Amphitheater" are favorites. PO Box 3457, Mililani, HI 96789. (800)-982-6747. E-mail: rainbow@rainbowdiver.com. Website: www. rainbowdiver.com.

Red Sail Sports whisks snorkelers aboard their 50-ft sailing catamaran, *Noa Noa*. Captain Gary Hoover, who will take you to wonderful snorkeling spots, can also tell you of his experience as captain of Kevin Kostner's trimaran in the movie *Waterworld*.

The morning snorkel cruise includes a continental breakfast, buffet luncheon, snorkel gear, towels and expert guides. *Noa Noa* also carries a fully-stocked bar. Everything but the bar is included in the basic rate. Contact Red Sail Sports, 909 Montgomery St., San Francisco, CA 94133. ☎ 800-255-6425. E-mail: info@redsail.com. Website: www.redsail.com.

Snorkel Bob's Kona rents snorkel gear from basic to the very best. In addition, they have prescription masks available. Snorkel Bob's shops are on Hawaii, Kauai, Maui, and Oahu. Gear rented on one island may be returned on another. 75-5831 Kahakai St., Kailua-Kona, HI 96740. 808-329-0770. E-mail: SnorkelBob@snorkelbob.com. Website: www. snorkel bob.com.

Where to Stay on Hawaii

For a complete list of accommodations and visitor information, contact the Hawaii Visitor sand Convention Bureau 800-GO-HAWAII or The Activity Warehouse ☎ 800-923-4004. The following resorts are near the beach snorkeling areas.

Hilton Waikoloa Village in Kamuela features a dolphin Quest program for guests. This huge resort offers all amenities, golf, hair salon, tennis, pools, TV. ☎ 800 HILTONS. Website; www.hilton.com/hawaii/waikoloa.

Royal Kona Resort, Kailua-Kona, offers 441 guest rooms, health club, movies, phones, pool, fridges, tennis, TV, AC, lounge, ☎ 800-774-5662 or 808-329-3111, fax 808-329-7230. E-mail: rkr5433@isis.interpac.net. Website: www.interpac.net/~rkona.

Kona Village Resort, Kailua-Kona rents 125 units. Nice beach, beach bar, fitness center, pool, tennis, meeting room. ☎ 800-367-5290.

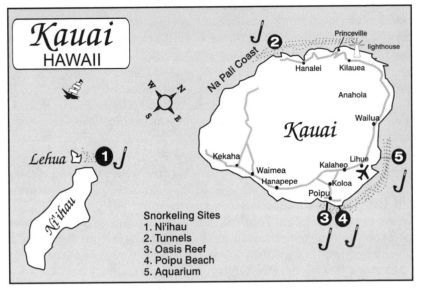

KAUAI, The Garden Isle

Kauai, a tropical oasis famous for its relaxed, rural atmosphere, features postcard waterfalls, beautiful beaches, swimming lagoons (featured in the movie *Bali H'ai* and the TV series Fantasy Island), exotic birds, rain forests, botanic gardens, deep canyons, and lush valleys. It is also the oldest Hawaiian island and the richest in folklore and history.

Because Kauai is so old, its marine life is more unusual and varied than the marine life anywhere else in the state. South shore sites are accessible year-round and offer snorkelers an underwater fantasyland teeming with every kind of fish and coral imaginable. On the north shore, huge surf pounds the beaches during winter months, but summer offers opportunities to explore networks of lava tubes.

Best Snorkeling Sites of Kauai

☆☆☆☆☆ **Niihau** (the Forbidden Island), located 18 miles from Kauai, is privately owned and is populated almost entirely by Hawaiians. It is a cultural preserve dedicated to the traditions and culture of old Hawaii. Residents lead a primitive life style without benefit of electricity, medical facilities or paved roads.

Dive boats regularly tour the magnificent coral reefs surrounding the island. Besides spectacular drop offs and arches, large, open-ocean game fish such as rays and sharks are often sighted here. For advanced, open-water snorkelers only.

☆☆☆ **Tunnels** at Ha'ena Beach State Park sits approximately nine miles west of Princeville on Route 56, across from the Dry Cave. Walk east along the shore and enter from the sandy beach. An outer reef protects this area, providing calm water.

☆☆☆☆ **Oasis Reef**, on the south shore, is protected and diveable all year. A lone pinnacle surrounded by sand rises from 35 ft to just below the ocean surface. This is a gathering place for thousands of fish including false moorish idols, triggerfish, butterfly fish and porcupine puffers. Octopus are found in the flats, lobsters and moray eels reside along the ledges. Depths run from four to 35 ft. Boat access.

☆☆ **Poipu Beach** offers ideal conditions for beginners. No current, depths from three to 20 ft and plenty of fish. Go south on Poipu Rd. from Koala town to Hoowili Rd. Turn right on Hoowili Rd. Parking and full facilities available. Beach access.

☆☆☆☆ **Aquarium**, on the southeast side of Kauai, takes its name from the variety of colorful tropicals in residence. This shallow reef stretches into an expanse of lava ledges and small coral valleys. You'll see several cannons from an 18th-century wreck. Depths from 25 ft.

Kauai Snorkeling Tours & Rentals

Bubbles Below offers advanced snorkelers adventurous summer trips to Niihau. This is great snorkeling for seaworthy, open-water swimmers in good physical condition. 6251 Hauaala Rd. Kapaa, Kauai, Hawaii 96746. 808-822-3483. E-mail: kaimanu@aloha.net. Website: http://aloha. net/~ kaimanu.

Snorkel Bob's has two locations on Kauai. Snorkel Bob's Kapaa, 4-734 Kuhio Hwy., Kapaa, HI. 808-823-9433. And Snorkel Bob's Koloa, 3236 Poipu Rd., Koala, HI. 808-742-2206. (See Snorkel Bob's Kona for description).

Seafun's staff includes a marine biologist who accompanies snorkelers to shore-entry sites selected for interest, clarity, weather conditions and season. A guide is provided for every six snorkelers. Passenger vans pick you up at your hotel and transport you to the various sites. The price includes use of snorkel gear (optical masks are available) and a wetsuit. Video tapes of your dive are available for purchase. PO Box 3069, Likue, HI 96766. ☎ 808-245-4888. E-mail: tours@gte.net. Website: http://home1.gte.net/tours/ konnections/konnect.htm.

Offbeat and Adventure Tours

Oceanic Society Expeditions offers year-round trips to Midway from Kauai. Midway, a remote coral atoll located 1,250 miles west-northwest of Honolulu, opened to the public for the first time in August 1996. You can walk among nesting seabirds, see monk seals, green turtles and spinner dolphins. Midway rivals the Galapagos for the variety of wildlife and their lack of fear of humans. Accommodations are in restored military barracks. Rooms are double occupancy with private bath and cafeteria style meals. Oceanic Society Expeditions, Fort Mason Center, Building E, San Francisco, CA 94123. ☎ 800-326-7491, fax: 415-474-3395.

Where to Stay on Kauai

For a complete list of accommodations on Kauai ☎ 800-245-2824.

Poipu Kai Resort features 350 condo units, health club, spa, tennis, tv. One-, two-, three- and four-bedroom rates are available by the week, month or season. Low to moderate. ☎ 800-688-2254

Poipu Shores rents oceanfront studios, one- and two-bedrom units. Near restaurants and shopping. Moderate. ☎ 800-367-5004

Whalers Cove offers luxury ocean front condos. Panormaic views, pool, spa and tennis. ☎ 800 22-POIPU, fax 808-742-6843. E-mail poipu@ aloha.net. Website www.poipu-inn.com.

TRAVEL TIPS

Getting There: All-expense packages including airfare can greatly simplify planning your trip to Hawaii. Several major airlines fly into Honolulu International Airport from all mainland cities in the United States. The largest carrier is Continental Airlines. Other flights available from United Air Lines, Northwest Orient, Western, American, Delta, Hawaiian Air, World. Frequent daily flights from Honolulu to the other main islands of Hawaii are offered by Aloha Airlines, and Hawaiian Air.

Entry Requirements: Non-U.S. citizens must have a passport and visa. Canadians must prove place of birth with either a birth certificate or passport.

Clothing: A lightweight wetsuit is suggested for snorkeling in Hawaii. Ocean temperatures are 72 to 80 F. Topside is tropical with average air temperatures in the 80's. During winter a light jacket or sweater is recommended. Light casual clothing is appropriate for most activities. Expect lower temperatures in the mountains.

Currency: U.S. Dollar, credit cards widely accepted.

Medical Emergency: If you need emergency medical or rescue services call (Kauai, Oahu, Maui): 911, or "O" for operator. On Lanai 565-6525 (police) 565-6411 (ambulance) or "O" for operator.

Marine Forecasts: Kauai, 245-3564; Oahu, 836-3921; Maui, 877- 3477; Hawaii, 935-9883.

Note: Snorkelers should use a water-resistant sun screen with a high sun protection factor (SAF) rating to prevent painful sunburn.

Additional Information: See your travel agent or call 1-800-GO- HAWAII. Write to Hawaii Visitors Bureau, 2270 Kalakaua Avenue, Honolulu, Hawaii 96815.

The Bay Islands Honduras

Located between 12 and 40 miles off the coast of Honduras, the Bay Islands (Las Islas de la Bahia) serve as a remote outpost set in the middle of the world's second largest barrier reef.

Roatan, the largest of the 70-island chain, is the most populated, with 30,000 residents, and the most developed. It is where you'll find the most dive resorts and creature comforts. Guanaja, next in size, is surrounded by its own barrier reef. Third in size, and a newcomer to this resort-island group, is Utila. The Cayos Cochinos, a mini-cluster of small fishing-village islands boasts one resort on their biggest island, Cochino Grande.

The smaller islands are uninhabited or sparsely populated. Most do not have roads. Phones, faxes and e-mail are newcomers. Surrounding reefs are impressive with brilliantly-colored sponges and corals, towering pinnacles, walls, tunnels, wrecks and caves. Visibility and water clarity are superb. Big turtles, grouper, rays, eels, and pelagics proliferate despite an active fishing industry. And novice snorkelers discover their own special paradise in the small patch reefs that dot the shallow bays throughout the area.

Plan on an entire day to reach the Bay Islands from the U.S. The islands are close to Honduras' coastline, but the mainland airport at San Pedro Sula is 160 miles away. Some flights depart La Ceiba, which is closer. Connections are often erratic. Luggage sometimes arrives late. Sand fleas and no-see-ums are a nuisance and make their presence known as soon as you arrive. Apply repellent beforehand.

Best Snorkeling Sites

The Bay Islands have a number of calm and sheltered areas, but the ordeal of getting there and getting around makes it a poor choice for travel with children.

Roatan

☆☆☆☆☆ The reef at **West End Wall,** which encompasses **Peter's Place** and **Herbie's Place,** starts at the shore and extends out 20 yards where the wall drops off sharply from a ledge at 15 feet. Visibility often exceeds 100 ft. Fishlife is superb, with schools of horse-eye jacks, permits, and schoolmaster. Seas are calm, with an occasional light current. No spearfishing.

Guanaja

☆☆☆☆☆ **The Bayman Drop**, a wall dive off the north shore, has some shallow spots good for snorkeling. Check the current before entering the water. The top of the wall is between 10 and 40 ft. Lots of fish. No collecting or spearfishing.

☆☆☆☆ **Pavilions**, a series of pillar corals and out croppings with soft corals and sponges has hordes of fish and invertebrates. Beware of the fire coral which seems hotter here than other parts of the Caribbean. The site is off Michael's Rock around the point next to the Bayman Bay Club.

Cayo Cochinos

Cayos Cochinos are a group of 13 small islands deemed a Biological Reserve and managed, in part, by the Smithsonian Institution to conduct a scientifitc study of the reef. The park is patrolled by park rangers. Snorkeling from the shore or by boat is outstanding.

Utila

Utila, fringed by yet-unnamed virgin reefs and canyons, offers some of the best shore diving in the Caribbean. Wildlife is exceptional with turtles, eagle rays, southern sting rays and tropicals. Offshore sites are a 15-to-45 minute boat ride. Shore dive areas sit about 150 yards out.

Barbaretta

☆☆☆☆ **Barbaretta Wall** off Barbaretta island, a favorite snorkeling-picnic spot between Guanaja and Roatan, features a wonderland of barrel sponges and soft corals. The wall stretches for a mile.

Pigeon Cays

☆☆☆☆ Pigeon Cays are a small cluster of islands surrounded by shallow, protected reefs, all perfect for snorkeling.

Where to Stay

None of the resorts cater specifically to snorkelers other than allowing them to join dive-tour boat trips. Some resorts offer water-taxi service or have kayaks for getting around the bays. The main après-dive activities are fishing, bird watching and hiking.

Rates are dramatically lower than most Caribbean spots. Group and individual tours from the U.S. are offered by **Landfall Productions** ☎ 800-525-3833, email: lndfall@aol. com, **Rothschild Travel Consul-tants,** ☎ 800-359-0747 and **Tropical Travel** ☎ 800-451-8017 or 281-367-3386, 281- 298-2335.

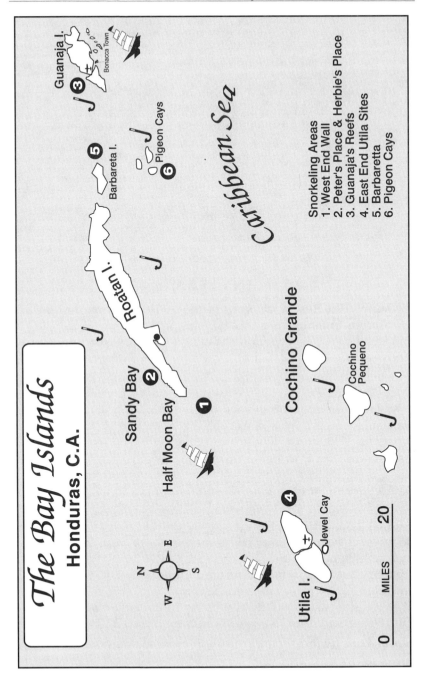

The Bay Islands
Honduras, C.A.

Caribbean Sea

Guanaja I.
Bonacca Town

Barbareta I.

Pigeon Cays

Roatan I.

Sandy Bay

Half Moon Bay

Cochino Grande

Cochino Pequeno

Utila I.

Jewel Cay

Snorkeling Areas
1. West End Wall
2. Peter's Place & Herbie's Place
3. Guanaja's Reefs
4. East End Utila Sites
5. Barbaretta
6. Pigeon Cays

N
E
S
W

0   20
MILES

Dolphins are frequently spotted offshore to Roatan

ROATAN

Anthony's Key Resort features rustic cabins. No beach, but the **Institute for Marine Sciences** is on the grounds and features dolphin swims. Snorkelers join scuba divers on reef trips. ☎ 800-227-DIVE, or 305-666-1997, fax 305-666-2292. E-mail: ark @gate.net Website: www. aventuras. com/anthony.key.

Coco View Resort, on the southside peninsula, is a group of oceanside bungalows, two-story cottages and cabanas that are built over the water. Standard rooms each have one double and one twin bed. Bungalows have two rooms, each with a kingsize bed.

Great wall dives lie a stone's throw from the beach bar. Nearby is a 140-ft tanker wreck, *Prince Albert* in 25 ft of water that can be seen from the surface. Disabled access. ☎ 800- 282-8932, 800-525-3833 or 352-588-4158, fax 352-588-4158. Website: roatan.com/honduras.htm

Fantasy Island Beach Resort sprawls across its own 15-acre island off Roatan's south coast. A small bridge connects the resort to the main island. Built in 1989 by local entrepreneur, Albert Jackson, the resort's 73 guest rooms are luxurious, with air conditioning, phones, refrigerators, full baths and cable TV. There is a full-service dive operation on premises with a fleet of 42-ft custom dive boats. Excellent shore snorkeling. ☎ 800-676-2826 or (011) 504-455191, fax 813- 835-4569. Packages:☎ 800-525-3833.

Inn of Last Resort, Roatan's newest dedicated dive resort, features 30 large guest rooms built of natural woods and decorated with tropical accents. All rooms are air-conditioned. Restaurant. Good shore diving off the resort's beach. ☎ 800-374-8181, (011) 504-45-1838, fax (011) 504-45-1828.

Packages from the US ☎ 800-525-3833. E-mail: lastresort@globalnet.hn. Website: www.dive.com/innlast.html.

The Reef House Resort touts 11 lovely cottages in two wings. All are furnished in tropical decor. Two are air-conditioned, the rest have ceiling fans and the trade winds for cooling. Great shore diving exists off the jetty in front of the resort. Snorkeling trips to neighboring islands and side trips to mainland Honduras Mayan sites and hot springs are offered. ☎ 800-328-8897 or 210-681-2888, fax 210-733-7889, in Roatan 504-45-2142.

Romeo's Dive & Yacht Club sits at the south end of Roatan on Brick Bay. Standard rooms, some air-conditioned, have porches facing the sea. Restaurant and lounge. Use of kayaks and paddle boats. Pool. ☎ 800-535-DIVE or 305-559-0511, fax: 305-559-0558. E-mail: brick bay@aol.com. Packages with air from the US, ☎ 800-525-3833.

Guanaja

Bayman Bay Club is a beautiful waterfront lodge. Guests stay in cottages on a hillside overlooking the reef. The resort features a dive shop, restaurant, gameroom and clubhouse. Sea-kayak snorkeling adventures and guided hikes to the island's lovely waterfall are offered. Good snorkeling is right off the resort's 300-ft dock. Use of kayaks. ☎ 800-524-1823; fax 954-572-1907, or (011)-504- 454179. Write to Terra Firma 11750 N.W. 19th Street, Fort Lauderdale FL 33323. E-mail: reservations@baymanbayclub.com or info@baymanbay club.com. Website: www.baymanbayclub.com.

Posada Del Sol is a luxurious Spanish villa resort on 72 acres of oceanfront greenery and, except for two small villages, is the only developed area on the southeast shore. Handicapped access. ☎ 800-642-3483 or 561-624-3483; Fax: 561-624-3225. E-mail: posadadel@aol.com. Website: www. posadadelsol. com.

Casa Sobre El Mar is a small family-run hotel built on concrete piers over the reef, one-half mile from Guanaja. The effect is like staying on a live-aboard that doesn't rock. Comfortable rooms have private baths and are cooled by sea breezes. No sand flies or mosquitos! Free launch to Guanaja any time. ☎ 800-869-7295 or direct 011-504-45-4269. Write to Casa Sobre el Mar, Pond Cay, Islas de la Bahia, Honduras, Central America.

Utila

Utila Lodge, a two-story, eight-room inn offers good shore diving. Rooms are air conditioned and overlook the sea. Dive shop on premises. ☎ 504-45-3143.

Laguna Beach Resort, the newest and most luxurious dive resort on Utila, has air-conditioned bungalows perched at the water's edge. Full service dive operation offers three dives daily, night dives and unlimited beach diving on the spectacular fringing coral reef which lies about 150 yards off shore. Snorkelers find lots of fish in the turtle grass on the way out. The dock takes you half-way there. Kayaks for guests' use. ☎ 800-66-UTILA (88452) or 318-893-0013, fax 318-893-5024. Direct (011) 504-45-3239. E-mail: awhite@utila.com. Website: http://www.utila.com.

Cayos Cochinos

Plantation Beach Resort, formerly a pineapple plantation, on Cochinos Grand is a delightful 10-room beachfront resort. Rooms are clean and simple. Great snorkeling is a giant stride off the beach. ☎ 800-628-3723 or (011) 504-42-0974, fax (011) 504-42-0974 Write to 8582 Katy Freeway, Suite 118, Houston TX 77024. E-mail: hkinett@hondutel.hn.

Note: If your flight arrives after 4:00 pm on day of arrival or departs before 8:00 am on day of departure, an overnight on the mainland will be necessary.

Travel Tips

Getting There: The best days to travel are Friday and Saturday. *From Miami* —American Airlines (☎ 800-433-7300) has daily flights to San Pedro Sula, Honduras. *From Houston:* Continental Airlines to San Pedro Sula with a stop in Tegucigalpa. Isleña Airlines flies to the Bay Islands every day but Sunday from Tegucigalpa, San Pedro Sula and La Ceiba to Guanaja. Direct flights to Roatan from Miami, Houston and New Orleans are provided by TACA weekly. Water taxis are sent by the one-island resorts to pick you up.

Precautions: Register your cameras and electronic gear with customs before visiting Honduras. Do not bring drugs, plants or flowers into or out of the country.

Language: English on the Bay Islands, Spanish on mainland Honduras.

Documents: A passport, visa, and onward ticket is required to enter Honduras.

Departure tax: US$15-$20 depending on the currency change.

Health: Vaccinations are not required. Check with your own doctor for health precautions. Drinking water comes from mountain wells on the islands. Ask about the water before drinking. Pack a diver's first-aid kit for sea stings and bug bites.

Currency: The lempira (L). L9.22 = US$1.

Climate: Hot and humid. March and April are the hottest months. Rain clouds crop up most afternoons during summer and fall. Coolest months are January and February. Water temperature averages 80° F year-round.

Clothing: Shorts and tee shirts, jeans and sneakers. Long-sleeve shirts and long pants are good for mountain hikes and protection from bugs or sunburn. Snorkelers should wear protective clothing from the hot sun. Divers will find a lycra suit comfortable for deep wall dives.

Electricity: Most resorts have 110 volts, but some have 220. Carry an adaptor to be sure.

For Additional Information: Contact the resorts direct, the tour operators listed under "Dive Resorts," or the Honduras Institute of Tourism, ☎ 800-410-9608. Website: www.islands.com/coral/roatan/roatan.html#how.

Puerto Rico

Beautiful beaches, first-class hotels and easy access from the US make Puerto Rico a favorite all-around vacation spot.

Underwater terrain is diverse, with shallow reefs off Humacao on the east coast, caves and wrecks off Aguadilla on the west coast, and dramatic walls at The Great Trench which starts in the Virgin Islands, stretches the entire length of Puerto Rico's south coast and winds up at Cabo Rojo on the west coast. Marine life is exciting, with manatees in the brackish mangrove areas, pelagics at Mona Island (50 miles southwest), and all species of sea turtles at Culebra. In winter, migrating humpback whales travel the Mona Passage off the west coast. Dolphins frequent the eastern shores. Towering soft corals grow to 20 ft in some spots. Snorkeling is best around the out islands and off the east coast.

Best Snorkeling Sights

East Coast

Snorkeling off Puerto Rico's east coast centers around Fajardo, Humacao and the offshore islands of Icacos, Palominos, Palminitos, Monkey Island, Vieques and Culebra. Outstanding features include towering soft corals and abundance of fish. Many of the mainland dive sights are close to shore, but the visibility is dramatically better offshore. Shore diving is possible off Fajardo, but freshwater runoff near the shore clouds the water and lowers visibility. Spearfishing and coral collecting are prohibited.

Culebra and Vieques

Trips to out islands, Culebra and Vieques, take off from Humacao or Puerto del Rey Marina at Fajardo, north of Humacao. Puerto del Rey is the largest marina in the Caribbean with 700 deepwater slips and service facilities. For ferry schedules, ☎ 787-863-0705. If you wish to ferry an automobile you must reserve space a week in advance.

Culebra, a mini-archipelago with 23 offshore islands, sits mid-point between Puerto Rico and St. Thomas. Shallow coral reefs surround the entire area. Nearby Culebrita is a good spot for snorkeling and photos.

The main five-mile-long island, home to 2,000 people, is a National Wildlife Refuge known for its lovely white sand beaches, sea bird colonies—boobies, frigates, and gulls—and as a nesting ground for all species of Caribbean sea turtles—leatherback, green, hawksbill and loggerhead. The turtles nest from April through July. (Refuge ☎ 787-742-3291).

Expeditions for turtle watching are conducted by Earthwatch, a non-profit organization.

Vieques

Vieques is a popular camping island for locals and day trip for east coast divers and snorkelers. Known for its beautiful beaches, two thirds of the island is owned by the US Navy with a small section still used for military operations and manuvers. The rest is rural. At presstime, plans to build Vieque's first resort were in the works.

Shallow reefs and dropoffs lie within one mile of the shoreline. Many with some very shallow areas. Sea conditions, sometimes rough, vary with the wind. Swells on the leeward side average two to three ft. Vieques subsea highlights are walls, giant barrel sponges, healthy fish populations, and a magnificent phosphorescent bay. Beach dives are possible off the West end at Green Beach with reef depths starting at 10 ft.

Two towns, Esperanza and Isabel Segunda serve Vieques' 8,000 residents. Accommodations are available at Casa Del Frances near Espernaza, ☎ 787-741-3751.

Vieques is a one-hour boat trip from Fajardo or Humacao. Or by air via Sunaire Express from San Juan's international airport.

East Coast Dive Operators

Coral Head Divers (CHD) at the Palmas Del Mar Resort, is an English-speaking, PADI and NAUI Pro Facility offering personalized dive adventures. Service is impeccable.

The shop has two dive boats, a six-passenger, 26-ft dive boat, for nearby sites and a 48-ft, custom dive boat, *Cool Change* for trips to Monkey Island or Vieques. Reservations required. CHD also rents ocean kayaks suitable for exploring nearby snorkeling spots. ☎ 787-850-7208, 800-635-4529, fax 787-285-8507. Write to P.O. Box 0246, Humacao, Puerto Rico 00792.

Snorkeling tours aboard the *Fiesta*, a 48-ft Trimaran and weekly live-aboard charters are offered by **Caribbean Marine Services** on Culebra. ☎ 800- 635-4529 or 787- 850-7208, fax: 787- 285-8507. E-mail: coralheaddivers@worldnet.att.net.

Where to Stay on the East Coast

NOTE: Paradores are country inns that offer quality lodging near places of great natural beauty, historical monuments and points of interest. For a list and rates call the central booking number ☎ 800-443-0266.

Palmas del Mar, located 40 miles southeast of San Juan, is a beautiful 2,700-acre luxury resort with three miles of sandy beach. Rooms feature air conditioning, cable TV, phones, and Caribbean decor. Sports facilities include 20 tennis courts, 18-hole golf course, five swimming pools, fitness center, and equestrian center. Water sports include sailing, deep-sea fishing, snorkeling and diving. **Coral Head Divers** is on the grounds. Rothschild travel offers discounted packages from the US. ☎ 800-359-0747. Contact the hotel at 787-852-6111, fax 787-852-2230. Write to P.O. Box 2020, Humacao, Puerto Rico 00792.

SOUTH COAST

Dive trips off the south coast originate in Ponce, Puerto Rico's second largest city or La Parguera, a sleepy fishing village known for its famed Phosphorescent Bay—one of four bio-luminescent bodies of water in the world. It is also home to the University of Puerto Rico's Marine Science Facility.

A two-and-one-half hour drive from San Juan airport, La Parguera is not yet heavily populated by tourists. Accommodations are modest, local attractions and other activities are limited. No beaches.

Best Snorkeling Sites

☆☆ **Ponce Caja de Muertos** (Coffin Island), **Cayo Ratones, Cayo Caribe** and **Cayo Cardon** form a crescent barrier reef from Ponce west to Tallaboa. All are a 20-minute boat ride from Ponce. Shore dives are possible off Coffin Island, a park administered by the Department of Natural Resources. Depths are from 15 ft.

South Coast Dive Operators

Paraguera Divers Training Center, a PADI and NAUI instruction facility, offers snorkeling trips, jet skis, windsurfing, mangrove-trail tours, Phosphorescent Bay trips, fishing and boat rentals. Major credit cards and travelers checks accepted. ☎ 787-899-4171, fax 787-899-5558. Write to Parguera Divers, P.O. Box 514, Lajas, Puerto Rico 00667.

Marine Sports & Dive Shop, in Ponce, visits Coffin Island. ☎ 787-844-6175.

Where to Stay on the South Coast

Copamarina Beach Resort in Guanica, a new resort halfway between Ponce and La Parguera, offers 70 deluxe, air-conditioned rooms, tennis court, cable TV, direct dial telephone, restaurant and pool. Snorkeling tours are off Gilligan's Island, less than a mile away. ☎ 800-468-4553 or 787-821-0505, fax 787-821-0070. Book through Dive Safaris, ☎ 800-359-0474, fax 212-749-6172. E-mail: rothschild@divesafaris.com.

Parador Posada Porlamar has 19 air-conditioned rooms with kitchen facilities, TV, pool and charming gardens. The dive dock for Parguera Divers is directly in front of the hotel. No beach. Low rates. ☎ 800-359-0747 or 212-662-4858. Write to 900 West End Ave. Suite 1B, New York, N.Y. 10025 or ☎ 800- 899-4015. E-mail: rothschild @divesafaris.com.

Parador Villa Parguera faces Phosphorescent Bay and is next door to the dive dock. This parador (small hotel) features waterfront rooms with private terraces. No beach. ☎ 800-359-0747 or 212-662-4858. Write to 900 West End Ave. Suite 1B, New York, N.Y. 10025. Hotel direct: ☎ 787-899-7777. Route 304, La Parguera, Lajas, PR 00667.

West Coast

West coast waters are too generally too rough for snorkeling other than offshore Desecheo Island.

☆☆☆☆ **South Gardens—Desecheo Island**, 13 miles offshore, is being considered for a marine sanctuary. This popular west-coast dive features a huge fish population, immense barrel sponges, giant sea fans (six ft across) and shallow depths. Sting rays and turtles are frequently sighted. Dives are off the protected southwest tip of the island. Snorkelers will be encircled by curious fish along the rocky shore. Star, brain and staghorn corals form the shallow reef. For experienced ocean swimmers only.

West Coast Dive Operator

Aquatica Underwater Adventures is a PADI/NAUI instruction center offering courses, dive and snorkeling trips, repairs and rentals. Boats depart from Aguadilla or Joyuda Beach. Trips to Desecheo, Aguadila and Isabella Islands. ☎/fax 787-890-6071. Write to: P.O. Box 250350, Ramey, Aguadilla, PR 00604. E-mail: aquatica@caribene.

Where to Stay on the West Coast

Tours below may be booked by your travel agent.

Joyuda Beach Hotel is a beachfront property offering 52 tastefully decorated guest rooms. The dive-boat pier is a short walk away. Joyuda Beach on Cabo Rojo is a quaint fishing and resort community with more than 20 great seafood restaurants. Book through your travel agent or write to P.O. Box 250350, Ramey, Puerto Rico 00604.

Mayaguez Hilton, at Mayaguez, just north of Cabo Rojo, has 145 luxurious guest rooms and suites with full amenities. Two fine restaurants, bar, dance club, casino, olympic pool, and three tennis courts. ☎ 787-831-7575.

Travel Tips

Getting There: *By Air*—Major airlines including American ☎ 800-433-7300, United and USAir fly into San Juan from most major US cities. American has service to Aguadilla from Miami. American has made the Luis Munoz Marin International Airport its hub for all flights from the US to other Caribbean destinations, Europe and Latin America. International carriers include Air Portugal, British Airways, BWIA, Iberia, LACSA, LIAT, Lufthansa and Mexicana.

Island Transportation: *By Road*—Taxis, buses and rental cars are available at the airport and major hotels. All taxi cabs are metered, but they may be rented unmetered

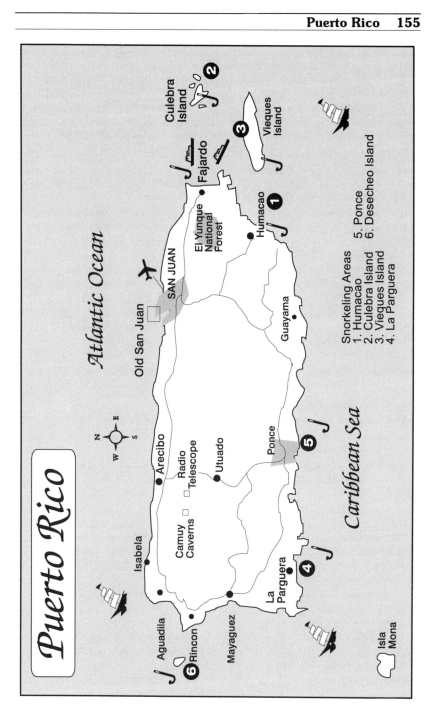

for an hourly rate. "Publicos" (public cars) run on frequent schedules to all island towns (usually during daytime hours) and depart from main squares. They have fixed rates. The "Ruta Panoramica" is a scenic road meandering across the island offering stunning vistas.

By Ferry and Boat Service—Ferries shuttle passengers to and from Culebra and Vieques at reasonable rates. Car transport is available on some. San Juan's harbor can also be crossed by the Catano ferry to the Bacardi Rum plant's free tours.

Driving: On the right. Distance markers are in kilometers.

Customs: US citizens do not need to clear customs or immigration (other citizens do). On departure, luggage must be inspected by the US Agriculture Department, as laws prohibit taking certain fruits and plants out of the country.

Entry Requirements: Since Puerto Rico is a Commonwealth of the United States, no passports are required for US citizens. Visitors do need a valid driver's license to rent a car. If you are a citizen of any other country, a visa is required. Vaccinations are not necessary.

Currency: The US dollar is legal tender and credit cards are widely accepted. Several foreign exchange offices are available in San Juan and at the airport for the benefit of international travelers.

Climate: Temperatures average mid-80's on land and underwater. During winter and on deep dives a light wetsuit is recommended. The rainy season is April to November, but most days have some sunshine. The south coast receives much less rainfall than the north.

Clothing: Lightweight, casual. Bring a light jacket for mountain hikes in winter.

Electricity: 110V AC 60 cycles, same as US

Time: Puerto Rico operates on Atlantic Standard Time, which is one hour ahead of Eastern Standard Time and the same as Eastern Daylight Savings Time.

Language: Spanish is the official language, although many people speak English, which is taught from kindergarten to high school level.

Taxes: The airport departure tax is included in the price of the airline ticket, and there's a 7% government tax at all hotels. Gratuities in restaurants are not included in the bill but 15% is the usual tip.

Religious Services: The majority of Puerto Ricans are Catholic, but religious freedom for all faiths is guaranteed by the Commonwealth Constitution. Catholic services are conducted throughout the island in both English and Spanish. There is a Jewish Community Center in Miramar and a Jewish Reform Congregation in Santurce. There are English-speaking Protestant services for Baptists, Episcopalians, Lutherans, Presbyterians and inter-denominational services.

For Additional Information:

Puerto Rico Tourism Company Offices: *In New York*—575 Fifth Avenue, New York, NY 10017 ☎ 212-599-6262, Toll Free 800-223-6530. *In California*— 3575 West Cahuenga Blvd., Suite 560 Los Angeles, CA 90068. ☎ 213-874-5991. *In Florida* —200 S.E. First St., Suite 700 Miami, FL 33131. ☎ 305-381-8915. *In the UK* —67-69 Whitfield St. London WIP 5RL United Kingdom. ☎ (07-1) 436-4060. *In Canada*— ☎ 416-969-9025. *In Puerto Rico*—Paseo de la Princesa Old San Juan, PR 00901 ☎ 787-721-2400.

$\mathcal{S}aba$

Located 30 miles off the coast of St. Maarten, this tiny, five-mile-square mountain is often visited as a day trip. The smallest of the Netherlands Antilles, Saba rises from the sea like the nose of a friendly dolphin breaking the water's surface. Its cliffs rise sharply from the blue Caribbean, culminating in mist-shrouded 2,855-foot Mount Scenery.

Tiny, white villages cling to the sides of the mountain—Hell's Gate, Windwardside, St. John's, The Bottom—linked by a road that dips and soars, curves and backtracks like a giant roller coaster. Visitors arrive at one end of the road or the other since it begins at the airport and ends at the pier.

Snorkeling is superb, though weather dependent. Most reefs and pinnacles are within 100 yards of shore—five or six minutes by boat. With little fishing, less than 1,000 divers per year and a government long-active in marine management, fish life is spectacular. Water clarity is too. The sea floor is a dense, heavy, black sand—not prone to silting or clouding the water. A constant wash of open-ocean currents supports a rich growth of soft and hard corals on submerged lava rocks and pinnacles. And, it is one of the few destinations left in the Caribbean where you can still find huge turtles and grouper.

When to Go

The best visibility is during winter, though seas can be rough outside the leeward side of the island. Summertime brings warmer 80° water with plankton blooms and lowered visibility, but a tremendous amount of fish life. Water temperature varies from 76° in February to 82° in October. Sea conditions vary. The island is round with no natural harbors and a very small leeward side. Seas are usually calm, but tropical storms can rule out many dive sites.

Saba Marine Park

The Saba Marine Park (SMP) was established in 1987 "to preserve Saba's Marine resources for the benefit and enjoyment of the people, in perpetuity." The project was funded by World Wildlife Fund-Netherlands, the Prince Bernhard Fund, and the Dutch and Saban Governments.

The park encompasses the entire island and includes the waters and the seabed from the highwater mark down to 200 ft and two offshore seamounts. It was set up by Dutch marine biologist, Tom van't Hof, who also established successful marine parks in Bonaire and Curacao.

Park officials maintain a system of mooring buoys and administer the Saba Marine Park Hyperbaric Facility, a four-person recompression chamber operated by a staff of trained volunteers.

Visitors to the marine park are charged a "dollar-a-dive" to help maintain the park and facilities. Spearfishing and collecting of any marine animals are prohibited. Snorkelers must not sit or stand on the corals. Anchoring on corals is prohibited. Vessels entering the park are advised to contact the marine park office on VHF channel 16 for directions on anchoring. For additional information Write to Saba Marine Park, Fort Bay, P.O. Box 18, The Bottom, Saba, Netherlands Antilles.

Best Snorkeling Sites

Saba's entire coastline is excellent for snorkeling. There are three locations for easily entering the water: the Fort Bay Harbor area, Well's Bay/Torrens Point area and Cove Bay near the airport. Snorkeling trips to the outer reefs can be arranged at the dive shops.

☆☆☆ **Torrens Point** off the island's northwest corner is the start of the Edward S. Arnold marked Snorkeling Trail. An outstanding shallow dive spot, depths range from five to 30 ft as you swim from marker one through 11. Black volcanic rocks, small caves and ledges swarm with fish and invertebrates. Pink sponges and lace corals grow in the crevices. Light pouring through the tunnels creates dramatic photo opportunities.

This spot is weather-dependent. Ocean swells from the north, usually during winter months, make exploring the open caves hazardous, especially the areas known as #10, The Rocks, and #9, Into The Alley. Check with a local divemaster before entering the water.

☆☆☆ **Ladder Labyrinth** is an erratic maze of coral-covered mounds off Saba's western, leeward coast. Depths are from 30 ft. The reef is vibrant with enormous lavender sea fans, swaying sea plumes and a carpet of star corals. Within the labyrinth are hundreds of crevices teeming with banded coral shrimp and lobsters. Schools of curious barracuda circle the area. Seas are usually calm. Good for experienced snorkelers. Boat access.

Additional boat-access, snorkeling spots include **Hot Springs, Hole in the Corner, Core Gut** and **Tent Reef**.

Snorkeling Tours & Rentals

Snorkelers join the scuba boats or go in off the shore. Sites are five to 15 minutes from the pier. Expect to sign a waiver before joining a boat trips.

Sea Saba , a PADI training facility with two 40-ft custom dive boats tailors trips to visitors' requests. Snorkelers join scuba divers on the noon trip which is to a shallow site. Owners, Joan and Lou Bourque, have been on Saba for more than 10 years and offer a variety of dive and accommodation packages. E-6 processing, equipment sales and rentals. Joan is an expert

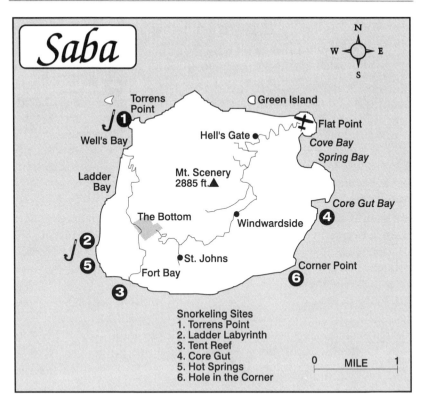

Saba

N
W — E
S

Torrens Point
① J
Well's Bay
Green Island
Flat Point
Hell's Gate
Cove Bay
Spring Bay
Ladder Bay
Mt. Scenery 2885 ft.▲
The Bottom
Windwardside
Core Gut Bay
④
② J
⑤
St. Johns
Fort Bay
Corner Point
⑥
③

Snorkeling Sites
1. Torrens Point
2. Ladder Labyrinth
3. Tent Reef
4. Core Gut
5. Hot Springs
6. Hole in the Corner

0   MILE   1

underwater photographer and entertains visitors with a weekly slide show. ☎ (011)-599-4-62246 or fax (011) 599-4-62362. Write: P.O. Box 530, Windwardside, Saba, NA. E-mail: brqswks@sedona. net or seasaba @aol.com. **Saba Deep** at Fort Bay Harbor, on the southwest side of the island, offers guided snorkeling tours. The shop is part of a dive complex in the newly-restored old harbor master's building with a restaurant, sundeck and dive boutique upstairs. Vacation packages. 888-DIVE SABA, (011) 599-4-63347, fax (011) 599-4-63397. Write to: P.O. Box 22, Fort Bay, Saba, NA. E-mail: diving@ sabadeep.com. Website: www. sabadeep.com/-diving.

Saba Reef Divers (formerly Wilson's) offers gear rentals, guided ocean-kayak tours with snorkeling on request and boat tours to the best snorkeling sites. Snorkelers join scuba groups on the afternoon reef trips. When you book a boat tour, use of snorkeling gear is included. The shop has two locations—Fort Bay at the Pier and Windwardside. Hotel packages with snorkeling are available. ☎ (011) 599-4-62541, fax (011) 599-4-62653. E-mail: sabareef@aol.com. Website: www. dive travel.net/sabadive.

Where to Stay

Accommodations may be reserved through your travel agent, direct or packaged through the dive shops listed above. A government room tax of 5% and a service charge of 10% or 15% is added to your bill.

Captain's Quarters, a former sea captain's home, is set into the hillside at the base of Mt. Scenery in Windwardside. Its 10 rooms are clustered around a pool and outdoor bar, all overlooking the Caribbean. ☎ 212-289-6031 (011) 599-4-62201, fax (011) 599-4-62377. Write: Captain's Quarters, Windwardside, Saba NA. E-mail: sabacq@megatropic.com. Additional packages available through Caradonna tours ☎ 800-328-2288. E-mail: caradonna @aol.com.

Julianas is a group of eight one-bedroom units, one apartment and a separate two-bedroom cottage built in 1989. Owners, Franklin and Juliana Johnson are local residents who maintain the property. ☎ (800) 223-9815 or direct (011) 599-4-62269, fax (011) 599-4-62389. Write: Juliana's, Windwardside, Saba NA.

The Cottage Club, a group of 10 Saban cottages with full kitchens, bath, cable TV, phone, fax and two beds, is a favorite spot for snorkelers. Book through your travel agent or ☎ (011) 599-4-62386, fax (011) 599-4-62476. **Saba Cottages and Private Villas'** vacation packages are offered by Sea Saba. Some cottages are close to everything, others a short walk away. ☎ (011) 599-4-62246, fax (011) 599-4-62362.

Travel Tips

Airlines: International flights connect through St. Maarten via Windward Island Airways (WINAIR), ☎ 800-634-4907. There are also connecting flights between Saba and St. Eustatius.

Ferry: *Style*, a 52-ft, luxury, commuter craft departs Great Bay Marina in St. Maarten on Wednesday, Friday and Sunday for Saba. Returns to St. Maarten at 3 pm. *Voyager I*, a mono-hull ferry holds up to 150 passengers and departs from Bobby's Marina in Philipsburg, St. Maarten on Thursday and Saturday at 8:30 am and arrives at Fort Bay, Saba at 10:00.

Driving: On the right. Rentals are available through Johnson's Rent A Car or your hotel. Beware of hairpin turns, potholes and bumps along "the road."

Seaport: A deep water pier accommodates ships at Fort Bay. Anchorage for yachts at Ladder Bay and Wells Bay.

Documents: US and Canadian citizens require official proof of citizenship: passport, voter registration card, or birth certificate and a return or onward ticket.

Customs: No customs.

Currency: Netherlands Antilles Guilder. US dollars accepted everywhere. Credit cards are widely accepted. NAfl 1.80 = US$1.

Language: Dutch is the official language, but English is widely spoken.

Climate: Air temperature is from 78°F to 82°F year round. Winter evenings may cool to 60°F. Rainfall is 42 inches per year.

Clothing: Casual, lightweight. Sweater or light jacket suggested for winter evenings. Wetsuit needed for winter diving, when water temperatures drop to 75°F. A light wet suit or lycra wet skin is recommended for summer.

Electricity: 110 Volts, 60 cycles (220 volts on request).

Time: Atlantic Standard (Eastern Standard + one hour).

Departure Tax: US $5 within NA, US $10 elsewhere.

Religious Services: Limited.

Additional Information: Saba Tourist Bureau, P.O. Box 6322, Boca Raton FL. 33427 ☎ (800) 722-2394 or (800) SABA-DWI, or 561-394-8580, fax 561-394-8588. Website: www.turq.com/saba.

St. Eustatius (Statia)

St. Eustatius, a tiny island about 38 miles south of St. Maarten and 17 miles southeast of Saba, has the distinction of being home to the first museum you snorkel through. As one of the lesser-known islands in the eastern Caribbean—so small and with a name so long, it is often deleted from maps. Like, Saba, Statia is often toured as a day trip via ferry from St. Maarten.

Statia's topside profile is marked by The Quill, a 2,000-ft extinct volcano, that covers most of the south end. Steep limestone cliffs interspersed with a few stretches of black-sand beach dominate the island's western coast. There are few roads, and donkeys are still used for exploring rocky inland trails. Offshore, lie the ballast stones and rubble of more than 200 sunken 17th-century, wooden trading ships, highlighted by giant golden sea fans and lush, soft corals. Most are close to shore, a few minutes by boat.

Overall, the island is perfect for snorkelers seeking a quiet haven. There is virtually no crime on the island. Doors are rarely locked and the people are extremely friendly.

When to Go

Visibility is best in winter, though seas occasionally get rough. Summer brings calm seas, warmer water and more fish. Water temperature varies from 76° in February to 82° in October.

Sunken Treasure Hunting

The remains and treasures of 17th- and 18th-century sailing ships are played up in many Statia dive articles, but the island's real treasures are her lovely shallow reefs. The ship's wooden hulls rotted away centuries ago. What's left are some wonderful old anchors and piles of stone ballast where small fish play hide and peek.

A few sites have, in fact, given up treasures of jewels and exotic pottery, but any charted wrecks not yet salvaged are buried in the sand and would require extensive excavation work to uncover. Plus, if a diver happens upon an intact artifact, it must go to the St. Eustatius Historical Foundation. Treasure hunting is discouraged—metal detectors are prohibited, as is "fanning" of the bottom to find artifacts. Exceptions which divers may keep are fragments of clay pipe stems or bowls and blue beads (slave beads), Uninhabited shells and broken pieces of dead coral may also be taken.

Best Snorkeling Sites

There are several snorkeling sites around Statia with depths from 3 ft. Visibility often exceeds 100 ft with water temperatures averaging 80°F.

☆☆ **The Snorkeling Museum** is an underwater cannon display established for the St. Eustatius Historical foundation at Oranje Bay in Lower Town through the Golden Rock Dive Center (see *Dive Operators*).

☆☆☆ **False Shoal**, outside of Kay Bay off the southwest shores, is an unusual formation of huge boulders that rise from the bottom at 25-30 ft to within a foot of the surface. Coral cover is minimal, but fish life is superb, with big congregations of tiger groupers, French and queen angels, several species of parrot fish and swarms of reef fish.

☆☆☆☆ **Outer Crooks Reef** is a pretty, shallow reef, five minutes by boat south of the city pier. The reef's ledges form a V shape, which might stand for variety as every imaginable hard and soft coral thrives within its bounds. Fish life, too, is diverse, with schools of smallmouth and striped grunts, black durgons, blue head wrasse, coneys, rock hinds, banded and four-eyed butterflyfish, rock beauties, blue tang, bar jacks, damsels, fairy basslets, princess parrots, queen parrots, stoplight parrots, Spanish hogfish, sharknose gobies, spotted drum, honeycomb cowfish, burrfish, and huge porcupine fish—some over three ft long.

There are also secretary blennies. It takes a sharp eye to spot these tiny fish, but if you can, try watching them for a few minutes. You'll see them dart out for food that's drifting by, then quickly shoot tail first back into their holes. They are unafraid of divers and make great subjects for close-up photography.

Invertebrate include flamingo-tongue snails, small crinoids, corkscrew anemones, giant anemones, pistol shrimp, pederson shrimp, thor shrimp, feather dusters, fire worms, crabs and spiny lobster. At night, divers have spotted rare copper lobsters and orange-ball anemones.

Outer Crooks is a best pick for getting reacquainted with the water and your gear after a long dry spell. Maximum depth, 40 ft.

☆☆ **City Wall** is 40 yards out from shore in front of Dive Statia and the hotels in Lower Town. The rock wall parallels the shore from 75 yards south of the Golden Era Hotel to the pavilion at Smoke Alley. This was the old sea wall for Lower Town back in the days of sailing ships. Storms, erosion, a freak earthquake and wave action have since repositioned the shoreline and the wall underwater. The top is at six ft, the bottom at seven to 13 ft. In many areas the wall is folded or crumpled, forming deep crevices where fish and creatures stand guard. There is not much coral cover, but reef fish are plentiful and invertebrate life is good. Watch out for sea urchins. The deepest point of the wall is 12 ft.

☆☆☆ **North Point** is an outstanding site at the north point of the island. The area is strewn with huge boulders, some up to 40-ft tall. The boulders

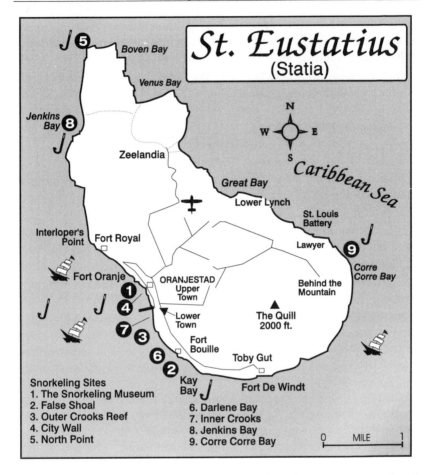

St. Eustatius
(Statia)

Caribbean Sea

Boven Bay

Venus Bay

Jenkins Bay

Zeelandia

Great Bay

Lower Lynch

St. Louis Battery

Interloper's Point

Fort Royal

Lawyer

Corre Corre Bay

Fort Oranje

ORANJESTAD
Upper Town

Behind the Mountain

Lower Town

The Quill
2000 ft.

Fort Bouille

Toby Gut

Kay Bay

Fort De Windt

Snorkeling Sites
1. The Snorkeling Museum
2. False Shoal
3. Outer Crooks Reef
4. City Wall
5. North Point
6. Darlene Bay
7. Inner Crooks
8. Jenkins Bay
9. Corre Corre Bay

0   MILE   1

are covered with corals, sea fans and gigantic barrel sponges—up to five ft across. Fish life is extraordinary. Huge two-ft French and gray angels swim by. Spotted eagle rays and reef sharks cruise the area. Good for experienced snorkelers.

☆☆ **Darlene Bay** is excellent for snorkeling when the seas are calm. The dive (or snorkel) boat anchors in a sandy area offshore of the shallow reefs or will drift with you as you swim among lava outcrops and fingers. Maximum depth is 20 ft. The lava and corals come up to the surface at the bay's south end. Good fish life—turtles, sea fans, sea whips and branching corals.

It is easiest to reach this site by a five-minute boat ride. It is a most difficult hike for a shore entry, with large rocks and loose gravel to negotiate, but if you are very rugged, you can reach it by heading south along the coast for half an hour after passing the ruins of Crooks Castle.

Additional good snorkeling is found at **Inner Crooks**, just north of Crooks Castle (max. depth 18 ft); **Jenkins Bay** (max. depth 25 ft) on the northwest corner of the island; and **Corre Corre Bay** (max. depth 40 ft), opposite town on the Eastern shores.

Snorkeling Tours & Rentals

Blue Nature Water Sports, Cherry Tree, offers rentals and snorkeling tours. ☎ 011 599-3-82725, fax 011 599-3-82756.

Dive Statia is a full-service facility offering guided reef and wreck trips. Their boats range from inflatables to a 31-ft cabin boat. ☎ 011-599-3-82435, fax 011-599-3-82539. Write P.O. Box 158, St. Eustatius, NA.

Golden Rock Dive Center, Oranjestad, features snorkeling trips and rentals. ☎ 800-311-6658 or (011) 599-3-82946. Website: www.divetrip. com/goldenrock/.

Where to Stay

Statia hotels add a 5%-10% service charge and 7% government room tax. Note: St. Eustatius and Saba are marketed jointly in the USA and offer dual-destination packages that include hotels, dives and more. Contact the Statia Tourist Office, P.O. Box 6322, Boca Raton FL 33427, ☎ 800-722-2394 or 561- 394-8580. E-mail: 10565.536 @compuserve.com.

Dive Saba Travel, 1220 Brittmoore Road, Houston TX 77043, customizes tours with any of the resorts. ☎ 800- 883-7222 or 713- 467-8835, fax 713-461-6044.

Island Trails offers guided hiking/snorkeling tours. ☎ 800-233-4366.

King's Well, offers eight lovely rooms on Orange Bay, each with a fridge and cable TV. Great views! Low rates Walk to the beach and Dive Statia. ☎ 800-692-4106, direct 011 599-3-82538. The hotel pub, a favorite après-dive meeting place, serves steaks, jaeger and wiener schnitzels.

The Golden Era Hotel offers 20 air-conditioned rooms on Oranje Bay, pool and seaside restaurant. Low rates. Cable TV, phones, fridges. Dive shop next door. ☎ 800-223-9815 or 011-599-3-82345/82545, fax 011-599-3-82445. Canada, ☎ 800-344-0023.

Travel Tips

Helpful Phone Numbers: Police ☎ 599-3-82333; Hospital, ☎ 599-38-2211 Or 599-38-2371; Airport, ☎ 599-3-82361; Tourist Board, ☎ 599-3 82433; Usa Tourist Office: ☎ 800-722-2394 or 561-394-8580, fax 561-488-4294, E-mail: nrhv11f prodigy.com.

Airlines: Windward Island Airways (WINAIR ☎ 800- 634-4907) connects daily from Princess Juliana Airport, St. Maarten. Flight time is 20 minutes. Passengers from the US and Saba are considered "in-transit" and do not need to clear immigration in St. Maarten.

Driving: On the right.

Seaport: Gallows Bay.

Documents: US and Canadian citizens need official proof of citizenship—a valid passport, birth certificate or voter registration card. Others need a passport or alien registration card. You need an onward or return ticket.

Customs: No customs.

Currency: Netherlands Antilles Guilder. American dollars are accepted everywhere on the island.

Language: Dutch is the official language; English is widely spoken.

Climate: Air temperature is from 78°F to 82°F year-round. Winter evenings may cool to 60°F. Rainfall is 45 inches per year.

Clothing: Casual, lightweight. Light wetsuit or wetskin suggested during winter.

Electricity: 110, 60 cycles (same as US).

Time: Atlantic Standard (Eastern Standard + one hour).

Departure Tax: US $5.

Religious Services: Limited.

Additional Information: St. Eustatius Tourist Office, PO Box 6322, Boca Raton FL 33427. ☎ 800- 722-2394 or (561) 394-8580, fax (561) 488-4294. *In St. Eustatius* — ☎ 011-599-3-82433 or (599) 3-82213 or (599) 3-82209, fax (599) 3-82433. E-mail: 105065. 536@compuserve.com. Website: www.turq.com/statia.

St. Lucia

Saint Lucia, (pronounced loó sha), the second largest of the Windward Islands. sits 1,300 miles southeast of Florida and 21 miles from Martinique.

Excellent snorkeling reefs lie off the island's sheltered southwest corner at Anse Chastanet (pronounced "ants-shas-tan-ay") and Soufriere Bay. Within 150 ft of their shorelines lies a 30-mile-long coral reef on a shelf at 10- to 30-ft depths. Outside the coves strong currents rule out snorkeling tours. The entire area is protected as a marine park.

When to Go

Visit St Lucia from January to April, the dry season. The rainiest months are from June through November; August-September are the worst. Annual rainfall varies from 55 inches on the south coast to 140 inches in the interior. Air temperatures average 80°F.

Best Snorkeling Sites

✰✰✰✰ **Anse Chastanet Reef**, which lies off the Anse Chastanet Hotel, has a nice shallow area with a small cavern, sponges, large brain and boulder corals at depths of five to 25 ft. A resident school of squid are joined by goat fish, a frog fish, parrot fish, chromis and wrasse.

✰✰✰✰✰ **Pinnacles** are four spectacular seamounts that rise from the depths to within a few feet of the surface. These coral-covered subsea cliffs are a macro-photographer's dream—alive with octopi, feather dusters, arrow crabs, seahorses, squid, and shrimp. Cleansing currents nurture big barrel and vase sponges and a lattice of soft corals—sea plumes, sea whips and sea fans. Lots of fish. Black corals at depth.

Snorkeling Tours & Rentals

Scuba St. Lucia is a PADI five-star training facility located at Anse Chastanet. The seven-instructor shop offers introductory and advanced open-water and rescue courses plus specialty courses in marine life identification, scuba diving and UW photography. E6 processing and photo rentals are available. Five custom dive boats. Hotel-dive packages with Anse Chastanet Hotel. ☎ 800-223-1108, 758-459-7000 or 758-459-7355. Write to P.O. Box 7000, Soufriere, St. Lucia. W.I.

Where to Stay

St. Lucia has a wide range of accommodations for all budgets, some as low as US$30 per night. For a complete lising call the tourist board at ☎ 800-456-3984 or fax 212-867-2795.

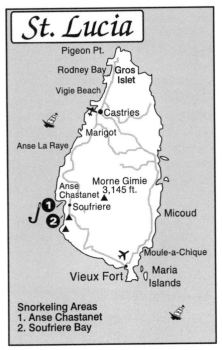

St. Lucia

Pigeon Pt.
Rodney Bay / Gros
Islet
Vigie Beach
Castries
Marigot
Anse La Raye
Anse   Morne Gimie
Chastanet 3,145 ft.
Soufriere
Micoud
Moule-a-Chique
Vieux Fort   Maria
Islands

Snorkeling Areas
1. Anse Chastanet
2. Soufriere Bay

For home rentals contact: **Happy Homes,** P.O. Box 12, Castries, St. Lucia; **Caribbean Home Rentals,** P.O. Box 710, Palm Beach, FL 33480; or **Tropical Villas,** P.O. Box 189, Castries, St. Lucia, ☎ 758-452-8240.

Anse Chastanet Beach Hotel is the islands' premier dive resort and a favorite place for snorkelers to stay—the reef is right off the hotel beach. It 's named for one of the French aristocratic families who settled on the island during the 18th century, the Chastanet family who originated in the Bordeaux region.

"Anse" is antique French for "Bay."

The resort is set amidst a lush 400-acre plantation, and edged by a secluded, quarter-mile-long, soft-sand beach. Some of the 48 rooms are scattered on a hillside, others beachside. Group packages available. ☎ 758-459-7000, fax 758-459-7700. Telex: 0398/6370. Write to P.O. Box 7000, Soufriere, St. Lucia, W.I.

Marigot Beach Club Bay Resort is nine miles from Vigie Airport and Castries on picturesque Marigot Bay. The resort features 47 villas set in the hillside around the bay and marina. The Moorings dive shop on the premises offers bareboat or crewed charters on Beneteau 32s or Bordeaux 104s. For current rates and reservations ☎ 800-334-2435 or 813-538-8760, fax 813-530- 9747. In St. Lucia ☎ 758-451-4357, fax 758-451-4353.

Wyndham Morgan Bay Resort's 250 guest rooms sprawl across 22 green acres on secluded Choc Bay, a short trip from the airport. Luxury rooms have satellite TV, large balconies, high ceilings, and tropical decor. Beach, pool, fitness center. Dive shop on premises. ☎ 800-327-8150. E-mail: nealwatson@aol.com. Website: www.twofin.com/twofin/stlucia.htm.

Travel Tips

Helpful Phone Numbers: Police ☎ 999; St. Jude's Hospital, Vieux Fort, ☎ 454-6041; Victoria Hospital, Hospital Road, Castries, ☎ 452-2421.

Getting There: American Airlines (☎ 800- 433-7300), has service from Miami, New York and other gateway cities with a stop in San Juan. BWIA (☎ 800-327-7401), flies direct from New York and Miami. Air Canada (☎ 800-422-6232), flies from Montreal and Toronto with connections through Barbados. LIAT connects with other Caribbean destinations.

Island Transportation: Car rentals: **Avis, Vide Boutielle,** ☎758-45-24554/22700, fax 758-45-31536; **National** ,Gros Islet, ☎ 758-45-28721, fax 758-45-28577; Dollar, Reduit, ☎ 758-45-20994; and **Budget,** Marisule, ☎ 758-45-20233/28021; fax 758-45-29362.

Cab service is readily available from Hewanorra International Airport at the south end of the island. Taxis are unmetered and unregulated. Be sure to ask the cost *before* getting in the cab and whether it is in EC or US dollars.

Driving: You must be 25 or older and hold a valid driver's license. Buy a temporary St. Lucian license at the airport or police headquarters on Bridge St in Castries. Steering wheels are on the right. Driving is on the left. Drivers should exercise extreme caution while negotiating St. Lucia's rugged mountainous roads and hairpin curves.

Documents: Citizens of the USA, UK and Canada must produce proof of identity. Passports are suggested, but a birth certificate with a raised seal and some form of photo ID will suffice. Visitors must have onward tickets.

Currency: The Eastern Caribbean dollar which is exchanged at the rate of US$1 to EC$2.70 ($2.60 in hotels and stores); US and Canadian dollars are also accepted. Credit cards accepted in many stores, but not all restaurants. Check when making reservations or accommodations.

Climate: In winter temperatures are between 65°F and 85°F. Summer between 75°F and 95°F. Summers are rainy. Light wetsuits are suggested for winter diving.

Clothing: Lightweight and casual. Some of the fancier restaurants at the hotels in Castries require a jacket and tie.

Electricity: 220. Adapters are required.

Time: Atlantic Standard (EST + 1 hr.)

Language: English

Tax: An 8% government tax is added to accommodations. A service charge of 10% is added to restaurants. Note: hotels often calculate the taxes and charges in the rates.

Religious Services: Most of the island is Catholic, but Anglican, Methodist, Baptist, Seventh Day Adventist, and Jehovah Witness faiths are also represented.

For Additional Information: Contact the St. Lucia Tourist Board. *In New York*, 820 Second Ave., New York NY, ☎ 212- 867-2950, fax 212-370-7867. *In Canada*, 151 Bloor St West, Suite 425, Toronto, Ontario, Canada M5S 1S4, ☎ 416-961-4317. *In London*, 10 Kensington Court, London W8 5DL England, 044-71-937-1969, fax 044-71-937-3611; *In St. Lucia*, P.O. Box 221, Castries, St. Lucia, ☎ 758-45- 24094 /25968; fax 758-453-1121. Website: http://info@stlucia.com/.

The Turks and Caicos

Uncrowded beaches, outstanding visibility and exotic marine life beckon snorkelers to the Turks and Caicos. Eight main islands and countless uninhabited cays comprise this archipelago located 575 miles southeast of Miami, at the southern tip of the Bahamas.

The chain caps two major limestone plateaus that step down onto a wide shelf then plunge to sheer coral walls—a backdrop for passing manta rays in spring, humpback whales in winter, dolphins and sea turtles year round. Pristine patch reefs along this shallow shelf begin right offshore.

Most vacationers head for the two main resort islands, Grand Turk, the seat of government, and Providenciales (Provo), though a growing number of travelers are snorkeling Salt Cay and South Caicos.

When to Go

Mid November through April brings the driest weather. Calm seas and the best rates for hotels arrive with summer. Some resorts close down during hurricane season, July through November.

THE CAICOS

The six principal islands of the Caicos, West Caicos, Providenciales, North Caicos, Middle Caicos, East Caicos and South Caicos, and their numerous small cays offer superb snorkeling. Providenciales (Provo) is the most developed island of the Turks and Caicos.

Best Snorkeling Spots of Providenciales

Provo's snorkeling spots are weather dependent. On calm days, the northwest side offers terrific snorkeling conditions. When high winds churn up rough seas, the southern coast becomes diveable. Rent a 4-wheel drive vehicle to explore that area.

There are numerous patch reefs scattered along Grace Bay that are good snorkel sites. Most aren't very large, but all are well populated by fish.

☆☆ **Smith's Reef**, located north of Turtle Cove off Bridge Road at the beginning of Grace Bay, has a snorkel trail that is maintained by the National Trust. The reef trail runs along a shallow shelf through flourishing elkhorn and staghorn corals, vase sponges and pink-tipped anemones. Depths run from eight to 25 ft, with the majority eight to 10 ft. Residents include three turtles, parrot fish, yellow and blue-headed wrasses, queen angels and lots of juvenile fish. There is also a HUGE green moray who pops his head out from the coral now and then, as well as stingrays, small eagle rays and nurse sharks. A large barracuda hangs out and adores getting close to snorkelers.

Beach access. If you can't find the entry point, stop in at Provo Turtle Divers in Turtle Cove for directions.

☆☆☆☆ **The Bight Reef** off Provo's beautiful North shore in the Bight area of Grace Bay lies within walking distance of Beaches Resort and Treasure Beach Villas. To find it, turn off the main road onto Penns Road. This reef, smaller than Smiths and not as deep—maximum depth averages 12 ft, drops off to shallow gardens of teal seafans, iridescent sponges and corals splashed across rows of shallow canyons. A marked snorkeling trail maintained by the National Trust, provides haven for Nassau grouper, moray eels, sea turtles, snapper, sergeant majors, basslets, and schooling grunts. Exceptional visibility. This area is usually calm though sea conditions will vary with the wind. Beach access.

☆☆ **North West Point** at Malcom Roadstead Beach is a good spot to see squid, queen triggerfish and silversides. Strong swimmers can swim out to a nice patch reef about 200 yds off the north end of the beach. Thickets of elkhorn coral swarm with juveniles, stingrays and a few nurse sharks. Beware of boat traffic if you venture out from the shoreline—carry a floating dive flag. This area can get big breakers during the winter months. Beach access.

☆☆☆ French and queen angels, eagle rays, turtles, spotted groupers and lobster congregate at **Eagle Ray Run,** off Fort George Cay. Reef depths range from the surface to about 20 ft. Super. Good Visibility. Boat access.

☆☆☆ **Wheeland Cut**, off Provo's northwest point near Navigation Light, provides a glimpse of small sharks, turtles, lobster, and a host of critters in a garden of dense elkhorn corals. Vase sponges and gorgonians thrive in the light current. Boat access.

☆ **Fort George's Cut** on Provo's northeast end off Fort George Cay, is perfect for beginners. Small cannons manned by small barracuda lie on the bottom. Beach access.

Provo Snorkeling Tours & Rentals

Art Pickering's Provo Turtle Divers offers reef trips from their Ocean Club location. Use of gear included. Friendly and helpful service. ☎ 800-833-1341 or 649-946-4232, fax 649-941-5296. Write to Box 219, Providenciales, Turks & Caicos, B.W.I. E-mail: Provoturtledivers @provo. net. Website: www.provo.net/ptd/.

Flamingo Divers offers snorkelers guided reef trips aboard two 29-ft. custom Delta dive boats, NAUI and YMCA instruction, resort courses and rental gear. Tel: 649-946-4193, fax 649-946-4193. Write to P.O. Box 322, Providenciales, Turks & Caicos, B.W.I.

Dive Provo provides a complete range of services including a full-service photo-video operation. Besides snorkeling gear they rent ocean kayaks, Laser sailboats and Windsurfers. Located at the Ramada Turquoise Reef Resort, Dive Provo offers complete vacation packages. Tel: 800-234-7768 or 649-946-5029. Write to P.O. Box 350, Providenciales, Turks and Caicos Islands, B.W.I.

Turtle Inn Divers tours outlying islands and points off Provo. ☎ 800-359-3483 or 649-941-5389, fax 815-623-6574.

SEATOPIA/DISCOVER DIVING, LTD. offers boat dives and rental gear. ☎ 649-946-6553.

Where to Stay on Providenciales

Note: A few Turks and Caicos' hotels close during summer months. For additional information contact the tourist board. ☎ 800-241-0824 or 649-946-2321/2, fax 649-946-2733.

Turquoise Reef Resort & Casino, a luxury 230-room hotel, features three restaurants, a health club, conference, tennis courts and Dive Provo, a full-service dive and snorkeling center. ☎ 800-992-2015 or 649-946-5555, fax 649-946-5522.

Erebus Inn sits on Turtle Cove, a small resort community where you'll find restaurants, shops, dive shops and beaches. The inn which overlooks the Turtle Cove Marina features two swimming pools, tennis courts, miniature golf, a bar, restaurant, and sun deck. Air-conditioned guest rooms are equipped with cable TV, and phone. ☎ 649-946-4240, fax 649-946-4704.

Turtle Inn Divers Resort, a 30-unit hotel on Turtle Bay, has air-conditioned rooms with cable TV, a restaurant and snack bar. Swim or snorkel to Smiths Reef off the beach. ☎ 800-359-3483 or 649-941-5389.

Treasure Beach Villas offers 18 deluxe beachfront suites. Near beach snorkeling sites. ☎ 649-464-4325, fax 649-946-4108.

Ledeck Hotel & Beach Club, a 27-room hotel located on a lovely stretch of Grace Bay beach, features a Creole restaurant and pool. Air-conditioned guest rooms have color TV. ☎ 800-328-5285 or 649-946-5547, fax 649-946-5770. Write to Box 144, Grace Bay, Providenciales.

Sandals/Beaches Turks & Caicos, an all-inclusive, luxury resort, features a water sports center and all amenities. ☎ 800-BEACHES or 649-946-8000, fax 649-946-8001.

Grace Bay Club, a posh, suite resort features an 18-hole golf course, sail boats and Windsurfers, snorkeling/picnic excursions. All suites have air conditioning ceiling fans, direct dial phones, 33 channel cable TV with VCR,

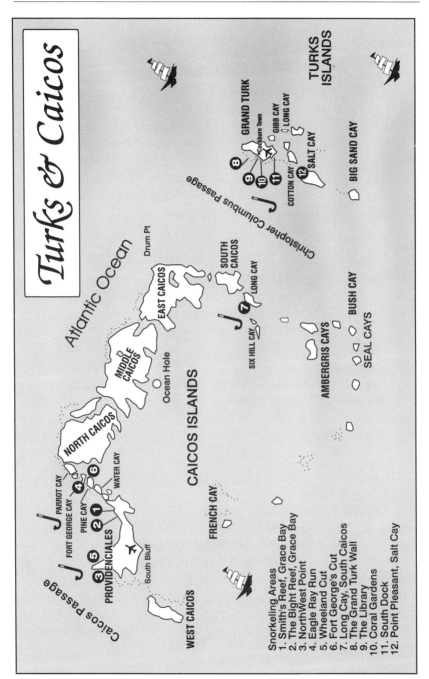

Turks & Caicos

Atlantic Ocean

TURKS ISLANDS

GRAND TURK
Cockburn Town
GIBB CAY
LONG CAY
COTTON CAY
SALT CAY
BIG SAND CAY

Christopher Columbus passage

Drum Pt

SOUTH CAICOS
LONG CAY
SIX HILL CAY

EAST CAICOS

MIDDLE CAICOS

Ocean Hole

NORTH CAICOS

WATER CAY

PARROT CAY
PINE CAY
FORT GEORGE CAY

PROVIDENCIALES

South Bluff

Caicos passage

WEST CAICOS

FRENCH CAY

CAICOS ISLANDS

AMBERGRIS CAYS

BUSH CAY

SEAL CAYS

Snorkeling Areas
1. Smith's Reef, Grace Bay
2. The Bight Reef, Grace Bay
3. NorthWest Point
4. Eagle Ray Run
5. Wheeland Cut
6. Fort George's Cut
7. Long Cay, South Caicos
8. The Grand Turk Wall
9. The Library
10. Coral Gardens
11. South Dock
12. Point Pleasant, Salt Cay

a safe, refrigerators and kitchen facilities. Beautiful beach. ☎ 800-946-5757, fax 800-946-5758. Book direct or through your travel agent.

SOUTH CAICOS

South Caicos, a true beachcomber's paradise, offers a quiet escape from telephones, television and newspapers. About the closest thing to rush-hour traffic you'll find is a herd of wild horses that roam the island's Eastern Ridge. Snorkeling on the outlying reefs and uninhabited cays is magnificent, especially off the western shores where countless coves shelter thick growths of elkhorn and staghorn corals, throngs of fish and crustaceans. Reef trips are through the Harbour Beach Resort, which has three 24-ft skiffs.

Nearby snorkeling islands, **Long Cay** and **Dove Cay** are great for picnic excursions.

Where to Stay on South Caicos

Club Carib Harbor & Beach Resorts has two locations, one overlooking Cockburn Harbour and one at the Beach. The Harbour is good for scuba divers, but The Club Carib Beach Resort is the choice of snorkelers. Choose from eight rooms cooled by ceiling fans (no air conditioning) or a two-room, air-conditioned villa with a kitchen.

Excellent snorkeling lies off the beach. During high tide the water ranges from three ft in shore to six ft 200 yards off shore. There are small reefs within this area with plenty of marine life. At low tide, one can walk in ankle-deep water out to the reef for snorkeling. A two-minute boat ride from the harbour will take you to the marine park. Long Cay and Dove Cay are less than five minutes away. The 16-room resort features a restaurant and bar. Horseback riding. Color T.V. Dive shop on premises operates four boats. ☎ 800-241-0824 or 649-946-3444, fax 649-946-3446 or book through your travel agent.

GRAND TURK

About 3,700 permanent residents populate Grand Turk, capital of the Turks and Caicos Islands. Cockburn Town is its principal municipality. Divers and snorkelers form the tourist population.

This tiny, seven-square-mile island is separated from the Caicos by a 22-mile-wide channel known as the Turks Island Passage. Like the Caicos, Grand Turk is synonymous with superb snorkeling. Its best spots lie along the reef fringing the west coast.

Best Snorkeling Sites of Grand Turk

Good beach snorkeling is found off the **Sitting Pretty Hotel** (formerly the Kittina), the **Arawak Hotel, Guanahani Beach Resort** and the **Salt Raker Inn** where juvenile reef fish (angels, barracudas) shells, and small turtles blast by shallow coral heads.

The Grand Turk Wall, with depths starting at 20 ft, is *the* place to spot huge Nassau grouper, big barracuda, oversized parrot fish, rock beauties, and Spanish hogfish. Yellow and lavender vase sponges envelope broad platforms of pastel gorgonians and colonies of hard corals.

Visibility excels except during the plankton blooms. This springtime "bloom" creates a soupy cloud over parts of the reef, but also acts as a dinner invitation for a circus of manta rays to somersault in. Mini-critters such as cleaner shrimp and octopi work the crevices of the reef. A superb area for video and still photography. For advanced ocean snorkelers only. Boat access.

☆☆☆ **The Library,** (buoy 10) off Cockburn Town, rates as a favorite snorkeling spot along the wall. Huge schools of gray snapper, creole wrasse, sergeant majors, turtles, crabs and scorpion rove around mountains of beautiful red and orange corals and sponges. Depths start at 18 ft. Seas in summer are dependable flat. Winter brings swells.

☆☆ **South Dock** at the south end of Grand Turk is a virtual junkyard of lost cargo from ships inhabited by a flirty community of frog fish, sea horses, batfish, eels, and shrimp and crabs. Sponges cover the pilings. Check with the dockmaster before entering the water.

☆☆☆☆ Snorkeling trips take off to **Round Cay** and **Gibbs Cay**, two out islands surrounded by elkhorn reefs. Bright sponges and gorgonians color abound. At Gibbs, friendly stingrays greet you in the shallows off the beach. They will pose for your pictures while you pet and handfeed them.

Grand Turk Snorkeling Tours & Rentals

Cecil Ingham's Sea Eye Diving features boat and beach dives. Cecil has been operating on Grand Turk for several years and is known for quality service. He is also an accomplished underwater photographer. The shop offers E-6 processing and a full assortment of Nikonos cameras and lenses and excursions to nearby Gibbs Cay. ☎ 800-810-3483, 649-946-1407, fax 649-946-1407.

Oasis Divers also takes snorkelers to Gibbs Cay, where they provide a beachside picnic. On the way to the island, they dive for conch which is served in a salad while burgers are cooking for lunch. Whale watching trips are offered during January, February and March when the Humpback whales pass by Grand Turk on their way to the Silver Banks to breed. Manta ray watch tours are offered in springtime. ☎ 800-892-3995, local 649-946-1128, fax 649-946-1128. E-mail: oasisdiv@caribsurf.com. Website: www.oasis divers.com.

Where to Stay on Grand Turk

For a list of resorts and other accommodations contact the Turks & Caicos Reservation Center at ☎ 800-548-8462 or 305-667-0966. Write to: Franklin International Plaza, 255 Alhambra Circle, Suite 312, Coral Gables, FL 33134. Please note that a few small hotels close during the summer months. Room rates average $100 to $150 in summer; $105 to $225 in winter. Villas and posh resorts are higher. Check with individual resorts for current prices.

The Sitting Pretty Hotel offers modern, spacious suites, a native restaurant, beach bar, sand beach, and freshwater pool. Each room has an efficiency kitchen and air conditioning. ☎ 800-548-8462 or 649-946-2232, fax 649-946-2877.

The Salt Raker Inn, a 150-year-old Bermudian shipwright's home, features lovely guest suites that open onto the sea or gardens. Air-conditioning and ceiling fans. ☎ 800-548-8462 or 649-946-2260, fax 649-946-2432.

The Arawak Inn & Beach Club touts the best beach snorkeling on Grand Turk. A number of nice coral heads thrive in shallows with a good show of fish, all close to the shore. The resort features 15 air-conditioned rooms, a restaurant, phones, TV and pool. ☎ 800-548-8462 or 649-946-2277, fax 649-946-2279.

Guanahani Beach Resort offers 16 spacious, ocean-front rooms with air conditioning, TV, phones, a gift shop and convenient dive facility with storage and rinse area on the beach. Spectacular sunsets. Snorkeling off the beach. Excellent restaurant. ☎ 800-725-2822 or 649-946-2135.

SALT CAY

Salt Cay lies seven miles southeast of Grand Turk. This sparsely-populated island offers beachcombing and snorkeling as the mainstay of activity.

Salt Cay Snorkeling

Point Pleasant, The Turks and Caicos' best snorkeling spot off the northern tip of Salt Cay, will leave you in awe with massive vertical brain corals, giant elkhorn and staghorn gardens all in 15 ft of water. You can swim side by side with big turtles, stoplight parrot fish, pompano, and eagle rays. This fabulous spot is always calm with no currents. Visibility exceeds 100 ft. Beach or boat access.

Where to Stay on Salt Cay

Castaways Beach House offers six simple, beachfront guest rooms for moderate rates. ☎ 649-946-6921, fax 649-946-6922.

Mount Pleasant Guest House has eight comfortable, beachfront rooms with TV. ☎ 649-946-6927 for voice and fax.

Travel Tips

Getting There: American Airlines provides daily service from Miami to Providenciales. Flying time is 80 minutes. ☎ 800-433-7300. Turks and Caicos Airways (TCA) provides scheduled flights to and from Nassau and Freeport in the Bahamas, to Puerto Plata in the Dominican Republic and sometimes to Jamaica ☎ 800-845-2161.

Island Transportation: Taxis. Car rentals available on Grand Turk and Provo.

Driving: Traffic moves on the left side of the roads.

Documents: US and Canadian residents are not required to carry a passport, but will need some identification such as a voter registration card or birth certificate.

Customs: Cameras and personal dive equipment do not require any special paperwork. No spear guns are allowed on the islands.

Currency: The U.S. dollar is legal tender.

Climate: 70 to 90°F year round. Water temperature never below 74° F. Possibility of storms and heavy rainfall in July through November.

Clothing: Lightweight, casual. A lightweight lycra wetskin is a good idea for winter snorkeling or to prevent coral abrasion.

Electricity: 110 volt, 60 cycle

Time: Eastern Standard.

Language: English.

Tax: There is a $15 departure tax. Hotels may add a 15 percent service charge and a 7 percent government accommodation tax.

Religious Services: Roman Catholic, Anglican, Baptist, Methodist, Seventh Day Adventist, Church of God.

For Additional Information: Turks and Caicos Tourist Board, P.O. Box 128, Grand Turk, Turks and Caicos Islands, 800-241-0824, 649-946-2321, fax 649-946-2733.

United States Virgin Islands

The USVI's three main islands —St. Croix, St. Thomas and St. John offer the snorkeling vacationer an enormous variety of reefs and dropoffs, all in gin-clear water, protected from strong winds and waves.

ST. CROIX

The largest of the USVI, St. Croix plays host to over 50,000 visiting snorkelers per year, the main attraction being Buck Island National Park—the most famous snorkeling spot in the world. Many other terrific sites are accessible by beach entry.

Best Snorkeling Sites

☆☆☆ **Buck Island Reef** continues to capture the hearts of Caribbean tourists despite noticeable wear from hurricanes and a daily blitz of snorkelers. Established by President John F. Kennedy as a national monument, this 850-acre sanctuary houses the world's first underwater national park.

As in most national parks, Buck Island has its own rangers, only here they sport swim trunks and patrol in power boats. There are also the standard park guide markers, but at Buck Island they stand at a depth of 12 ft, embedded in the sands along the ocean floor. Each day, catamarans, trimarans, sloops, and yawls unload what the islanders call "the wet set." The Buck Island welcoming committee includes green parrotfish, snappy sergeant majors, grouper, rainbow-striped angel fish and the silvery Bermuda chub. Beginners and experienced snorkelers alike can experience this underwater fantasy in an unusually safe atmosphere. The reefs of Buck Island lie only 100 yds off the coast and no trail is more than 15 ft deep. As snorkelers enter the park, they are welcomed by a blue and white plaque shimmering below the surface. One marker (number 8) next to an unusual round coral full of veins inquires, "What would you name this coral?" The next marker says "You are right. Brain Coral." Arrows and signs guide the swimmer along the underwater trail and give the precise names of coral and other growths below the surface.

More than 300 species of fish are identified. One species that audibly demands attention is the small striped grunt, a fish that can be clearly heard underwater. The National Park Service maintains a careful watch, but one familiar park rule—Don't Feed the Animals—does not apply here. Swimmers can feed the fish as often as they like. Grouper, a favorite fish to hand-feed, come readily at the slightest beckoning.

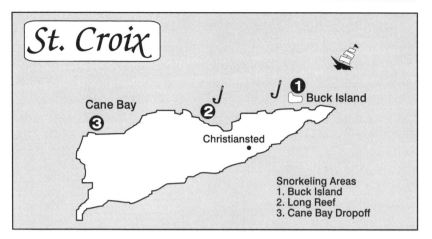

Since the reef park is strictly non-commercial, you are advised to rent gear before heading out. Whether you're coming from St. Thomas, St. Croix or St. John, you can obtain equipment readily on all three islands. And getting there is half the fun. Most hotels on St. Croix offer a shuttle service to Christiansted, where you can select almost any kind of boat imaginable. Charter boats of every description line the docks of the Christiansted harbor. Boats to Buck Island are widely available at low cost.

Make sure you stop over on Buck Island Beach, a pristine stretch of powdery, white sand created in part by parrotfish gnawing on the coral reef and excreting sand. From the beach, a wildlife trail leads 200 ft to an observation tower, which gives a grand view of the lagoon and reef. A trip to Buck will be one of the most memorable experiences of your visit to the Virgin Islands. Boat access.

☆☆☆ **Long Reef**, a six-mile wide shallow area on the outskirts of Christiansted Harbor, offers a variety of reef dives. The bottom terraces gently from the shallows to 80 ft. Hundreds of caves and crevices along the reef shelter French angels, parrotfish, rays, turtles, morays, octopi, lobsters and goatfish. A docile nurse shark makes frequent appearances. Huge brain and elkhorn coral formations prevail. Visibility varies. Boat access.

☆☆☆ **Cane Bay Dropoff** is the favorite beach dive. The reef lies about 140 yards off the beach with depths ranging from the surface to great depths. Inside the reef, calm waters and a decent fish population make this spot a favorite of snorkelers. Light surf along the shore. Light current at the dropoff. Park along the road at Cane Bay Beach.

Additional shore entry dives are best at **Davis Bay** and **Butler Bay**. Visibility close to shore is weather-dependent and decreases when rain and wind churn the bottom. Equipment may be rented at any of the dive shops.

St. Croix Snorkeling Tours & Rentals

All of the dive operators on St. Croix require a C-Card.

Cane Bay Dive Shop, on the beach at Cane Bay, offers "walk in" dives to the Cane Bay drop-off. Snorkeling tours. ☎ 800-338-3843 or 340-773-9913. Write to P.O. Box 4510, Kings Hill, St. Croix, USVI 00851.

Dive St. Croix in Christiansted offers Buck Island trips, camera rentals, and accommodation package tours with several different resorts. ☎ 800-523-3483 or 340-773-3434; fax 340-773-9411. Write to 59 Kings Wharf, Christiansted, St. Croix, USVI 00820.

Virgin Island Divers, located at the Pan Am Pavilion in Christiansted, offers beach and boat dives. ☎ 340-773-6045 or write Pan Am Pavilion, Christiansted, St. Croix, USVI 00820.

Sea Shadows at Cane Bay and Kings Wharf operates two dive boats that tour all the sites around St. Croix. Owners Libby Wessel and Steve Fordyce are beach diving specialists.

Where to Stay on St. Croix

St. Croix offers a wide range of luxury resorts, villas, condominiums, inns and guest houses. Like the neighboring British Virgin Islands, the waters around the USVI are excellent for sailing. Many visitors combine a week of bare boating or live-aboard sailing with sub sea exploring. The following resorts cater to divers .

Christiansted Harbor, St. Croix

The Buccaneer Hotel in Christiansted sprawls across three beautiful beaches with three restaurants, a spa, shopping arcade, eight tennis courts, an 18-hole golf course and all water sports. Snorkeling trips leave from the resort dock for Buck Island. ☎ 800-223- 1108 or 340-773-2100; write P.O. Box 800, Waccabuc NY 10597.

The Waves At Cane Bay offer spacious seaside studios with balconies, pool, beach, restaurant. Snorkeling off the beach. TV, no phones. ☎ 800-545-0603 or 340-773-0463, fax 340-778-4945. P.O. Box 1749, Kingshill, St. Croix, USVI 00850.

Cane Bay Reef Club, features six two-room suites with full kitchens, balcony overlooking the sea. Saltwater pool. PO. Box 1407, Kingshill, St. Croix, USVI 00851 ☎ 340-778-2966.

ST. JOHN

St. John, the smallest and most verdant of the USVI, is the best for snorkeling and beach-front camping. Two-thirds of the 28-square-mile island and most of its stunning shoreline comprise the Virgin Islands National Park, part of the US National Park system.

Best Snorkeling Sites of St. John

☆☆☆ **Trunk Bay** on the island's north shore has a clearly marked underwater trail, with abundant soft and hard corals, yellowtail, damsel fish, and occasional turtles. The shallow reef sits just off beautiful Trunk Bay Beach, a great setting for vacation snapshots. Average depths: 10 to 15 ft.

☆☆☆**Salt Pond Bay,** at the southeast end, is never crowded and is blessed with ample shade trees. Coral reefs stretch from both points of the Bay, offering snorkelers a full day's worth of adventure. Many fish and marine animals make their home here.

☆☆☆ **Chocolate Hole**, located at the east side of the mouth of Chocolate Bay, is distinguised by several rocks sticking up out of the water. The reef sits to the west of these. Depths run from four to 15 ft. Hordes of fish, including grunts, squirrelfish, blue chromis, parrot fish, rays and turtles wander about. Seas are usually very calm unless the wind is from the south. Good for all levels.

☆☆ **Waterlemon Cay National Park** offers terrific fish watching for experienced swimmers. To get there, drive to Annaberg Sugarmill ruins, park and hike down the road to the beach (½ mile). Swim along the east side of the bay to Waterlemon Cay. There are loads of big Caribbean starfish in the sand and walls of fish all around the island, including big yellowtail snapper and jawfish. This spot is usually calm in summer, but choppy in winter when the wind is out of the northeast. Tidal currents may exist.

Trunk Bay, St. John

☆☆ **Caneel Bay Snorkeling Trail** is limited to guests of the Caneel Bay Resort or boaters who enter from the sea, but Caneel Bay's main beach is open to the public and offers some nice fish watching.

☆ **Francis Bay** is easiest by boat, but you can reach it by driving to the Annaberg Sugar Mill, then left to Francis Bay. The last stretch of road is gravel and dirt. Rocks, corals and plenty of fish.

☆☆ **Cocoloba Cay,** a bare rocky site "attached" to St. John by rock, coral and sand, requires boat access. The east side has huge coral formations, some 15-ft high, which died long ago, but now have new coral growing on top, Large coral patch reefs exist along the west side. Depths range from five to 30 ft. Highlights are angel fish, schools of blue tang, spadefish, jacks, pompano and an occasional shark. This area is usually rough, good only on days with the wind from the north or northeast. Experienced ocean swimmers only. Boaters should anchor about 100 yards east of the cay.

☆☆ **Fishbowl Reef**, just south of Cruz Bay, is a nice shallow dive. Divers swim along ledges sparkling with beautiful elkhorn and staghorn coral. Soft corals undulate in the shallows. Many kinds of small reef fish are found hiding in the crevices. Boat access.

St. John Snorkeling Tours & Rentals

Lucy Portlock's **Pelagic Pleasures** (☎ 340-776- 6567) at the Caneel Bay Resort offers boat snorkeling excursions to all the best sites around St. John.

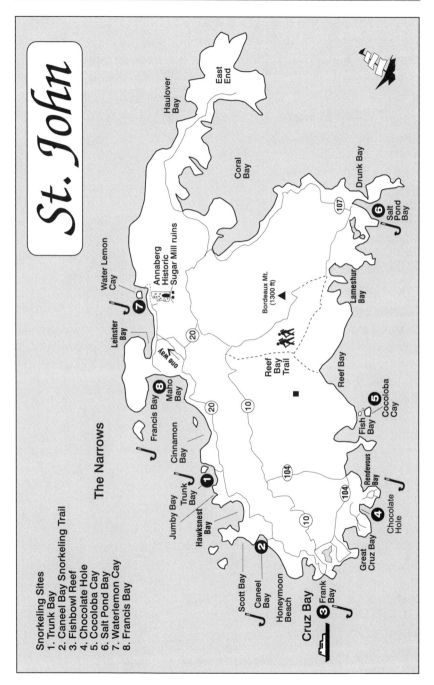

St. John

Snorkeling Sites
1. Trunk Bay
2. Caneel Bay Snorkeling Trail
3. Fishbowl Reef
4. Chocolate Hole
5. Cocoloba Cay
6. Salt Pond Bay
7. Waterlemon Cay
8. Francis Bay

The Narrows

Haulover Bay

East End

Coral Bay

Drunk Bay

Salt Pond Bay

Water Lemon Cay

Annaberg Historic Sugar Mill ruins

Bordeaux Mt. (1300 ft)

Lameshur Bay

Leinster Bay

One Way

Maho Bay

Francis Bay

Cinnamon Bay

Reef Bay Trail

Reef Bay

Cocoloba Cay

Fish Bay

Jumby Bay

Trunk Bay

Hawksnest Bay

Rendevous Bay

Scott Bay

Caneel Bay

Honeymoon Beach

Great Cruz Bay

Chocolate Hole

Cruz Bay

Frank Bay

If you're not staying at Caneel Bay, sign up for tours at Hurricane Alley in the Mongoose Junction Mini Mall.

Coral Bay Watersports Center offers diving rentals, snorkeling gear, sailing, windsurfing, fishing, and parasailing. ☎ 340-776-6857 or write 14 Emmaus, Coral Bay, St. John, USVI 00830.

Where to Stay on St. John

Caneel Bay Resort occupies a 170-acre peninsula that adjoins the Virgin Islands National Park. There are 171 posh guest units in low-profile buildings scattered about the grounds, three restaurants, seven white sand beaches and seven tennis courts. ☎ 800-928-8889 or see your travel agent.

Westin Regency St. John sprawls over 34 exotic acres with a gigantic freshwater pool covering a quarter-acre and offers 280 luxury guest rooms with all amenities. Under 18 stay free. Good snorkeling off the beach. Cruz Bay Watersports (☎ 693-8000) on premises offer snorkeling trips. ☎ 800-228-3000 or 340-693-8000, fax 340-779-4985.

Condos and Apartments

Cruz Bay Villas, high on the mountainside are near town. ☎ 340- 776-6416.

Gallows Point Suite Resort, on the waterfront, features suites with full kitchens, private patios and bathrooms. Pool, gourmet shop and restaurant. Good snorkeling from the beach. ☎ 800-323- 7229, fax 340-776-6520.

For additional rentals try **Tropic Retreats** ☎ 800-233-7944, fax 340-778-3557 or **Island Villas** ☎ 800-626-4512, fax 773-8823.

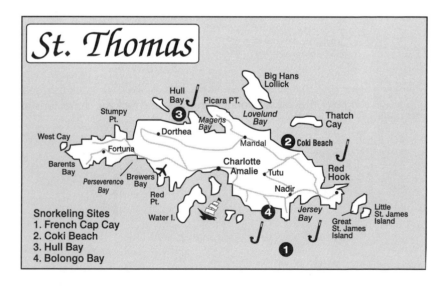

Campgrounds

Camping/snorkeling trips are popular on St. John. Be sure to take your own gear.

Cinnamon Bay Campground, P.O. Box 720, Cruz Bay, St. John, USVI 00830. Cottages, campsites and tents on Cinnamon Bay Beach in a national park. ☎ 800-539-9998 or 340-776-6330, fax 340-776-6458. Windsurfing and sailboat rentals.

Maho Bay Camps, P.O. Box 310, St. John, USVI 00830. Luxury camping, white sand beach, watersports and gourmet restaurant. ☎ 800-392-9004,

ST. THOMAS

St. Thomas is the second largest of the USVI and site of their capital, Charlotte Amalie. Its sheltered coves once harbored some of the most bloodthirsty pirates in Caribbean history.

For those mixing snorkeling and sailing, St. Thomas is the home port to a number of charter operators.

Though some beach-entry diving exists here, the prettiest reefs and clearest waters are found around the outer cays. Some dive shops offer trips to the wreck of the *R.M.S. Rhone*. Cruise ship visitors will find an abundance of snorkeling opportunities.

Best Snorkeling Sites

French Cap Cay lies well south of St. Thomas, but worth the long boat ride for its lovely shallow areas that are filled with large sea fans, lavender, orange, and yellow vase and basket sponges. Expect a light current. Visibility is often unlimited. Good for photography. Experienced snorkelers.

Coki Beach on the north shore of St. Thomas is a favorite beach-entry site. Adjacent to Coral World, an underwater viewing tower, the reef starts at 20 ft. You swim along a sand slope amid schools of snappers, French and queen angels. The reef is also a favorite hiding place for small fish, sea turtles and stingrays. Star coral, sponges, crinoids, and rock are characteristic inhabitants.

Additional good beach snorkeling exists at **Hull Bay** on the north coast and **Bolongo Bay** plus the resort beaches at Sugar Bay Resort, Renaissance Grand Beach, Secret Harbor Beach, Sapphire Beach, Point Pleasant Resort, Marriott's Morning Star Resort, Grand Palazzo, and Carib Beach.

St. Thomas Snorkeling Tours & Rentals

Chris Sawyer Diving Center has three locations, one at the Renaissance Grand Beach Resort at Coki Beach, American Yacht Harbor and the main operation at Compass Point Marina. All gear, including underwater photo equipment, is available for rental. Escorted beach-snorkeling tours. ☎ 800-882-2965 or 340-7757320. Write to 6300 Estate Frydenhoj, St. Thomas, USVI 00802. E-mail: sawyerdive@worldnet.att.net. Website: insightsintl.com/dive.

St. Thomas Diving Club at the Bolongo Bay Beach Club, specializes in dive and snorkel excursions to local and BVI sites. ☎ 340-776-2381.

Where to Stay on St. Thomas

St. Thomas has a seemingly endless variety of accommodations. You'll find charming antique guesthouses and cozy in-town hotels, resorts on secluded beaches, romantic mountain-top villas, condos, and hotels.

Bolongo Bay Beach & Sports Club has 75 air-conditioned beachfront units with telephone, color TV, kitchenettes, and balconies. Nightly entertainment. Sport facilities include four tennis courts, a Sunfish sailboat fleet, resort yacht *Heavenly Days*, snorkeling, volleyball courts and board games. Informal atmosphere. Children under 15 free in room. beach bar. Good snorkeling off the beach. ☎ 800-524-4746 or 340-779- 2844, fax 340-775-3208 or write 50 Estate Bolongo, St. Thomas, USVI 00802.

Renaissance Grand Beach Resort, a deluxe beachfront resort at Pineapple Beach has 315 rooms, two pools, three restaurants, entertainment, and TV. Guided beach snorkeling excursions with Chris Sawyer Diving Center on the property. Write P.O. Box 8267, St. Thomas, USVI 00801. ☎ 800-HOTELS1 or 340-775- 1510, fax 340-775-2185.

Marriott's Frenchman's Reef Resort, a full-service 423-room luxury beachfront resort, offers snorkeling tours, freshwater pool, tennis and seven restaurants. Recently renovated luxury rooms have TV, phones and tropical decor. ☎ 800-524-2000, fax 340-776-3054.

Sapphire Beach Resort, on the northeast coast, offers suites with full kitchens, TV, phone, handicap access, day-long children's program. Under 12 free in room. Dive In! dive shop on premises offers snorkeling tours. Freshwater pool, tennis, three restaurants. ☎ 800-524-2090, fax 775-4024.

Best Western's Carib Beach Resort on south coast Lindbergh Bay, features affordable, ocean-view rooms with private balconies. Two miles from town. Freshwater pool, phones, TV. ☎ 800-792-2742 or 340-774-2525, fax 340-777-4131.

Secret Harbor Beach Resort on Nazareth Bay, the southeast Caribbean side, offers 171 luxury rooms in a tranquil beachfront setting. Children under 13 stay free. Good snorkeling off the beach on a small reef with tropicals, turtles and rays. Aqua Action Dive Shop on premises offers rentals and snorkeling boat trips. ☎ 800-524-2250 or 340-775-6550, fax 775-1501.

Small Hotels and Condos

Blazing Villas, adjacent to Renaissance Grand Beach Resort, features boat and shore snorkeling excursions with Chris Sawyer Diving. Guests use all of Rennaissance Resort's facilities. Suites feature full kitchens or kitchenettes, phones, TV, handicap access, tennis, beach. Under 12 stay free with adults. Add 10% service charge. ☎ 800-382-2002 or 340-776- 0760, fax 776-0760.
Cowpet Bay Villas, one mile from the St. John ferry, faces Great St. James Island where good snorkeling via boat is found. White sandy beach. ☎ 800-524-2038 or 340-775-7531, fax 340-775-7531.

Live-Aboards

Virgin Islands Charter Yacht League will rent you a sailing yacht and teach you how to sail. ☎ 800-524-2061 or 340-774-3944. Advance reservations suggested.

Regency Yacht Vacations offers vacations aboard fully-crewed, liveaboard yachts from 40 to 100 ft. ☎ 800-524-7676, 340-776-5950. Write to 5200 Long Bay Rd, St. Thomas, USVI 00802.

Travel Tips

Getting There: There are daily direct flights from the US mainland, via American Airlines (☎ 800-433-7300) USAir, Delta and Prestige. Other airlines serving the newly expanded Cyril E. King Airport are American Eagle, Air Anguilla and Seaborne Seaplane. Inter-island connections can be made by ferry, seaplane shuttle or one of the island airlines. US citizens must carry a passport if also traveling to the BVI.

Island Transportation: Car rentals and taxi service is readily available on all three islands. Bus service exists on St. Thomas and St. Croix.

Driving: Traffic keeps to the left on all three islands. A US driver's license is required.

Customs: US residents are entitled to take home $1200 worth of duty-free imports. A 10 percent tax is levied on the next $1,000.

Currency: US dollars, travelers checks, major credit cards. No personal checks.

Climate: Year-round temperatures vary from 76 to 82°F.

Clothing: Casual, lightweight, with sweaters for winter; jackets and ties needed for some resorts and eating establishments.

Electricity: 110V AC 60 cycles (same as US).

Time: Atlantic Standard which is one hour earlier than Eastern Standard.

Language: English.

Taxes: No sales tax. 8% hotel tax. Service charge may apply at some restaurants.

Religious Services: All denominations.

For Additional Information: ☎ 800-372-USVI. United States Virgin Islands Division of Tourism, P.O. Box 6400, Charlotte Amalie, USVI 00804. In New York, 1270 Avenue of the Americas, NY NY 10020. ☎ 212-332-2222, fax 212-332-2223. Website: http://www.usvi.net

Sharks

Sharks have generated more sensational publicity as a threat to snorkelers, divers and swimmers than any other animals, even though their bites are among the least frequent of any injuries divers sustain. Two opposing attitudes seem to predominate: either irrational fear or total fascination.

Paul Sieswerda, collection manager of the New York Aquarium, warns against taking either approach to this honored and feared species. Common sense and a realistic understanding of the animals should be used, he says, adding that "anything with teeth and the capability of biting should be treated with the same respect we give to any large animal having potential to inflict injury." The vast majority of sharks are inoffensive animals that threaten only small creatures; but some sharks will bite divers that molest them. Included are such common forms as nurse sharks and swell sharks. These animals appear docile largely because they are so sluggish, but large individuals can seriously injure a diver when provoked. Sieswerda cites an incident with a "harmless" nurse shark as the cause of 22 stitches in his hand—the result of aquarium handling.

Experience tells us that most sharks are timid animals. Fewer than 100 serious assaults by sharks are reported worldwide each year with the average being closer to 50. Less than 35% of these are fatal. More people are killed by pigs. A majority of those few fatal attacks on man are not cases of the infamous great white shark biting the swimmer in two; they involve four- or five-foot sharks causing a major laceration in an arm or leg. Loss of blood due to lack of immediate medical attention is usually the cause of death.

Overplaying the danger is equally unrealistic. Encounters with dangerous sharks by snorkelers on shallow reefs or shipwrecks are rare. When a shark encounters man, it tends to leave the area as suddenly as it appeared.

Bull Shark

Sharks are largely pelagic animals found out in deep open water. Dangerous sharks are seldom found on shallow, clear water, snorkeling reefs. Most dive guides agree. They would change their line of work if they thought a huge set of jaws were awaiting them on each day's dive.

So use common sense. Avoid diving in areas known as shark breeding grounds. Don't join shark dives intended for scuba-equipped divers. Avoid spearfishing and carrying the bloody catch around on the end of the pole. If you do see a shark, leave the water. Above all do not corner or provoke the shark in any manner.

One crowd of fearful bathers in Miami clubbed a baby whale to death in the surf, thinking it was a shark. But, our favorite shark danger story comes from Florida divemaster, Bill Crawford. A young scuba diver begged to see a shark in the water. Finding one presented quite a problem. The area is largely shallow reefs and shark sightings are rare. Thinking hard, the divemaster remembered a big old nurse shark who could be found sleeping under a ledge on one of the outer reefs. She had been there for years totally ignoring the daily stampede of divers and snorkelers. So he took the young man to that spot and, as luck would have it, there was the shark. Upon seeing it sleeping under the ledge, the young diver became frozen with fear. In a wild panic he backed into a wall of coral, putting his hand deep into a hole where a big green moray eel lived. The nurse shark, true to its calm reputation, just kept sleeping. But the moray, incensed at the intrusion, defended its home by sinking its sharp teeth deep into the diver's hand.

Our favorite shark encounter, and one we highly recommend, is the "Jaws" exhibit at Universal Studios in Orlando, Florida, where people wait in long lines for the opportunity to be drenched, buffeted and threatened by a huge, relentless great white shark.

"Jaws" at Universal Studios, Orlando, FL

First Aid for Sea Stings and Coral Cuts

Snorkelers and swimmers exploring coral reefs or coral-encrusted shipwrecks risk Mother Nature's own version of chemical warfare—stinging organisms, urchins and venomous fish.

Most stings caused by marine organisms such as fire corals, fire sponges, and jellyfish are not serious, but can become infected if not cared for immediately. Allergic reactions are also common.

On the other hand, some stings can bring excruciating pain and death within minutes. Extremely dangerous forms of venomous sea life are the Portuguese man-of-war, Pacific sea wasp (a jellyfish), stonefish, cone snail, which harpoons its prey by shooting out deadly teeth, and some species of pufferfish in the Pacific.

It is unlikely you will run into any lethal stinging sea animals while exploring, but it is a good idea to have a first-aid kit on hand for the ordinary varieties. Some household products that may help are meat tenderizer, ammonia, rubbing alcohol, antibiotic salve, and vinegar.

Coral Cuts

Coral leaves behind a hard skeleton, frequently razor sharp and capable of inflicting deep, painful wounds. Some living corals have stinging cells that make tiny punctures that rapidly disappear, but may leave itchy welts and reddening.

Fire corals, the most delicate in appearance, are often the most dangerous. All coral cuts, although usually superficial, can take a long time to heal.

The best strategy is to look, don't touch. Avoid exploring reefs or wrecks subject to heavy surges, wave action, or currents. It is easy for the unprepared diver or snorkeler to be swept or tumbled across a reef. And besides the chance of injury, you risk being fined. Many marine parks have out-lawed wearing gloves and touching coral.

If you do get cut, a tetanus shot is recommended, because live coral is covered with bacteria. Wash with a baking soda or weak ammonia solution, followed by soap and fresh water. When available, apply cortisone ointment or antihistamine cream. An application of meat tenderizer may speed the healing process, because the venom from stinging sea creatures is a protein, which the tenderizer destroys. Mix with water to make a paste and apply. The wound should be covered with a sterile dressing to prevent infection.

A commercial sea-sting kit is useful for minor coral scrapes. Follow up by seeing a doctor.

Jellyfish Stings

Jellyfish have thousands of minute stinging organs in their tentacles. Yet the stinging results only in painful skin irritation. The Portuguese man-of-war and Pacific sea wasp are exceptions: Their stings have, in rare cases, resulted in death.

Do not handle jellyfish. Even beached or apparently dead specimens may sting. Tentacles of some species may dangle as far as 165 feet. Avoid waters where jellyfish are abundant.

If you're stung, remove any tentacles and try to prevent untriggered nematocysts from discharging additional toxins by applying vinegar, sodium bicarbonate, boric acid, or xylocaine spray. Vinegar is the most effective in reducing additional nematocyst discharge.

Do not use fresh water or rub sand on the area—you may cause additional nematocyst discharge.

Antihistamines or analgesics are useful in relieving itching and redness. Meat tenderizer may help the pain. Sea sting kits also are recommended.

Sea Urchin Punctures

Sea urchins are radials with long spines. They are widespread in the Western Hemisphere. Penetration by the sea urchin spine can cause intense pain. The spines can go through wet suits, booties, or tennis shoes.

Large spine fragments can be removed, but be careful not to break them into smaller fragments that might remain in the wound. Alternately soaking the injured body part in hot, then cold water may help dissolve small fragments. Get medical attention for severe or deep punctures.

Clean the wound. Spines that have broken off flush with the skin are nearly impossible to remove, and probing with a needle will only break the spines into little pieces. Some spines have small, venomous pincers that should be removed, and the wound then should be treated as a poisonous sting. Small fragments may reabsorb. Drawing salve may be helpful.

Fish Stings

Venomous fish—such as stonefish, zebra fish, and scorpion fish—are often found in holes or crevices or lying camouflaged on rocky bottoms. Snorkelers should be alert for their presence and should take care to avoid them at all times. If you do get stung, get immediate medical assistance.

Index

Additional Reading

Best Dives of the Caribbean
by Joyce & Jon Huber
ISBN 1-55650-798-4

A scuba and snorkeling travel guide that includes reefs, wrecks and marine parks in Anguilla, Antigua and Barbuda, Aruba, Barbados, Belize, Bonaire, British Virgin Islands, Cayman Islands, Cozumal and Akumal, Curacao, Dominica, Dominican Republic, Grenada, Guadeloupe, the Bay Islands, (Honduras), Jamaica, Puerto Rico, Saba, St. Eustatius, St. Kitts and Nevis, St. Lucia, St. Maarten/St. Martin, St. Vincent and the Grenadines, Tobago and the United States Virgin Islands. It also details hundreds of dive- and diver-friendly resorts, topside attractions and activities.

Adventure Guide to the Florida Keys and Everglades National Park
by Joyce & Jon Huber
ISBN 1-55650-745-3

Includes accommodations for all budgets, aerial tours, boat tours, canoe and kayak tours, cycling trails, nature hikes and walks, Key West's historic Pelican Path, parasailing, scuba diving and snorkeling in the Florida Keys National Marine Sanctuary, dolphin swims, sightseeing and fishing.

Available from better bookstores or internet shops.